D0720135

the LITERACY
GAPS

WITHDRAWN
UTSA LIBRARIES

To our mothers, Blanca Estela Soto and Beverly June Plaugher, who taught us all of the important lessons that books could not.

A nuestras madres, Blanca Estela Soto y Beverly June Plaugher, quien nos enseñarón todas las cosas importantes que los libros no pueden enseñar.

the LITERACY GAPS

Bridge-Building Strategies for English Language Learners and Standard English Learners

Ivannia Soto-Hinman ■ June Hetzel

CORWIN
A SAGE Company

Copyright © 2009 by Ivannia Soto-Hinman and June Hetzel

All rights reserved. When forms and sample documents are included, their use is authorized only by educators, local school sites, and/or noncommercial or nonprofit entities that have purchased the book. Except for that usage, no part of this book may be reproduced or utilized in any form or by any means, electronic or mechanical, including photocopying, recording, or by any information storage and retrieval system, without permission in writing from the publisher.

For information:

Corwin
A SAGE Company
2455 Teller Road
Thousand Oaks, California 91320
www.corwinpress.com

SAGE Ltd.
1 Oliver's Yard
55 City Road
London EC1Y 1SP
United Kingdom

SAGE India Pvt. Ltd.
B 1/I 1 Mohan Cooperative
Industrial Area
Mathura Road, New Delhi 110 044
India

SAGE Asia-Pacific Pte. Ltd.
33 Pekin Street #02-01
Far East Square
Singapore 048763

Printed in the United States of America.

Library of Congress Cataloging-in-Publication Data

Soto-Hinman, Ivannia.
The literacy gaps: bridge-building strategies for English language learners and standard English learners/Ivannia Soto-Hinman, June Hetzel.
    p. cm.
Includes bibliographical references and index.
ISBN 978-1-4129-7520-9 (cloth)
ISBN 978-1-4129-7521-6 (pbk.)
    1. English language—Study and teaching—Foreign speakers. 2. Literacy programs. I. Hetzel, June. II. Title.

PE1128.A2.S595 2009
418.0071—dc22   2009020545

This book is printed on acid-free paper.

09 10 11 12 13 10 9 8 7 6 5 4 3 2 1

Acquisitions Editor:	Dan Alpert
Associate Editor:	Megan Bedell
Production Editor:	Libby Larson
Copy Editor:	Teresa Herlinger
Typesetter:	C&M Digitals (P) Ltd.
Proofreader:	Theresa Kay
Indexer:	Kathy Paparchontis
Cover Designer:	Scott Van Atta

Library
University of Texas
at San Antonio

Contents

Acknowledgments

The authors would like to thank our husbands, Scott and Geoff; families; friends; and colleagues who sacrificed their time with us and cheered us on, supporting us in practical ways, providing much-needed comedic relief, and dragging us away from our work when we needed it.

Thanks also to our editor, Dan Alpert, who provided wisdom, guidance, patience, and kindness. You were a joy to work with, always readily available for questions and answers, and always believing in us. We also want to thank Megan Bedell, associate editor; Libby Larson, production editor; and Teresa Herlinger, wordsmith extraordinaire.

Thanks to our reviewers, who carefully read every word and gave of their time, support, and constructive criticism.

Special thanks to Dr. Linda Carstens of Stanford University, who for 7 years has been a faithful mentor, colleague, and friend along the way for Dr. Soto-Hinman.

Special thanks to Dr. Hetzel's friends and teaching partners—Deborah McIntire; Juanita Lee; Brenda Wyma; the Dixons; and Ana Castillo, one of the finest ELL teachers she has ever known.

We are grateful to our home institution—Biola University—which provided our teaching assistant, Joanna Fuller, who helped us with our source references, permissions, glossary development, and editing.

Thank you especially to our K–12 and university students who made this all possible—to whom we dedicate our careers, because we believe that when teachers are trained to believe that all kids can learn, in fact, they will!

Corwin gratefully acknowledges the contributions of the following reviewers:

Kristina Anstrom, Senior Research Scientist
The George Washington University Center for Equity and Excellence in Education
Washington, D.C.

Linda Carstens, Director of Professional Learning, SRN
School of Education, Stanford University, CA

Ron Klemp, Secondary Literacy Coordinator
Los Angeles Unified School District, CA

Guadalupe Valdés, Bonnie Katz Tenenbaum Professor
School of Education, Stanford University, CA

Yee Wan, Coordinator, English Language Learners Program
Santa Clara County Office of Education, San Jose, CA

About the Authors

Ivannia Soto-Hinman, PhD, Associate Professor of Education at Biola University, specializes in language acquisition, secondary literacy, and urban education. She has presented on literacy and language topics at various conferences, including the National Association for Bilingual Education (NABE) and the American Educational Research Association (AERA).

Soto-Hinman, whose family emigrated to the United States from Costa Rica, began school in kindergarten as an English Language Learner (ELL). Dr. Soto-Hinman's firsthand experience as an ELL has shaped her entire career working with immigrants. Ivannia began her career in the Los Angeles Unified School District (LAUSD), where she taught English and English Language Development (ELD) at the second-largest middle school in the country, Chester W. Nimitz Middle School. While in the LAUSD, Ivannia also served as a literacy coach, and later a literacy specialist, in LAUSD's Local District 6. Dr. Soto-Hinman was a program administrator on a secondary reading grant at the Los Angeles County Office of Education (LACOE) before becoming a full-time faculty member in the School of Education at Biola University.

Soto-Hinman has also served as a consultant to WestEd on behalf of the California Department of Education (CDE), and a variety of school districts in California, providing technical assistance for systemic reform of ELLs and Title III. For the past 3 years, she has worked as a consultant at Stanford University's School Redesign Network (SRN) on systemic school and district redesign. Soto-Hinman is also a contributing author on Houghton Mifflin's reading intervention program for ELLs called *Portals*, recently adopted by the state of California.

June Hetzel, PhD, Professor and Dean of the School of Education at Biola University, earned her MS in Reading Education from Cal State Fullerton and her PhD from Claremont Graduate University. June grew up in the culturally and linguistically diverse basin of the San Francisco Bay Area in the Franklin McKinley School District in south San Jose. Her childhood background shaped her passion for access for all learners. Her teaching experiences with ELLs and SELs in Los Angeles and Orange Counties, and her work in Africa and Thailand, have provided her insight into working with elementary, secondary, and adult students in multilingual, multicultural settings. In addition, she has enjoyed travel through Europe and, on a trip to Oxford University, presented "The Three Literacy Gaps and Title III of NCLB," coauthored with Dr. Soto-Hinman, at the Oxford Round Table at Harris Manchester College, upon which this book is based. Dr. Hetzel conceptualized the three learning gaps in 1996 while doing doctoral studies at Claremont Graduate University, and in partnership with Soto-Hinman, the model has been refined for ELLs and SELs, developing into its current form.

With 30 years in education, Dr. Hetzel remains passionate about literacy. She facilitates local volunteer tutoring partnerships and she and her husband, Geoff, enjoy leading teams of literacy teachers overseas to work with English Language Learners. A long-time member of the Cal State Fullerton's Reading Educators' Guild, the International Reading Association, and the Delta Kappa Gamma Society International, June has authored many literacy resource books and currently freelances for Purposeful Design Publications, serving as a content editor for two textbook series, including the *English as a Foreign Language* series.

1

Introduction to the Achievement Gap and the Literacy Gaps Model

We have a state of emergency in the educational system of the United States. This state of emergency relates to the underachievement of English Language Learners (ELLs) and Standard English Learners (SELs) and the growing gap between ELLs/SELs and their native English-speaking peers. In a country that purports to stand for freedom, education for all, and social justice, this state of emergency educationally and morally mandates that teacher training institutions, teachers, schools, districts, parents, and communities come together to solve this crisis. This book, *The Literacy Gaps: Bridge-Building Strategies for English Language Learners and Standard English Learners*, attempts to do just that. By presenting data regarding the historic and present crisis, we will provide the research-based rationale for a new teaching model that will assist teachers in bridging the gap between ELLs/SELs and the text (readability issues), ELLs/SELs and their teachers (perceptions and expectations), and

English Language Learners (ELLs) are "students whose primary language is not English and whose English language skills are not sufficient to allow them to function fully in academic English" (U.S. Department of Education, 2000).

ELLs/SELs and their peers (differentiation strategies). The Literacy Gaps Model will also have the ability to integrate familiar research-based teaching practices into a coherent, holistic model that can strengthen the framework around which teachers conceptualize effective practices that enable ELLs/SELs to access academic language, literacy, and ultimately success within the American educational system, thereby providing a springboard from which students may enter into mainstream society as educated, productive citizens who will lead the next generation.

This introductory chapter verifies the achievement gap between mainstream and nonmainstream students in the United States, including immigration patterns and specific linguistic and cultural data, detailing recent and historic research. First, we introduce (1) demographic patterns, (2) languages spoken and socioeconomic factors, (3) ELL achievement, and (4) findings from the National Literacy Panel. Second, we will introduce the concept of the Standard English Learner and an emerging body of research that demonstrates specialized linguistic needs. Finally, we will introduce the Literacy Gaps Model around which the book is written, presenting a model that will assist teachers across the United States in bridging the achievement gap of their English Language Learners and Standard English Learners.

Standard English Learners (SELs) are students who grew up speaking variations of Standard English, such as African American Vernacular English (AAVE), Chicano English, or Hawaiian English.

DEMOGRAPHIC PATTERNS

In this section, the analysis of data by Goldenberg (2008) presents a strong foundation for the urgency of meeting the needs of ELLs in today's classrooms. In the past 15 years, the number of students who do not speak English fluently has grown dramatically. Whereas in 1990, an estimated 1 in 20 public school students in grades K–12 was an English Language Learner, today the figure is 1 in 9, virtually a 50% increase. Similarly, the estimate is that in 20 years the figure will be 1 in 4, which will represent yet another 50% increase.

Figure 1.1 represents the dramatic ELL growth over the past 18 years, as well as the continued demographic forecast for this subgroup. It further demonstrates that the issue of closing the literacy and achievement gap is not a temporary need, and that the number of ELLs in U.S. schools will only continue to grow in the next 20 years (Goldenberg, 2008).

In addition, whereas the overall population increased by 20% since 1990, the ELL population grew from 2 million to 5 million in the same time period, representing a 40% increase (Goldenberg, 2008; National Clearinghouse for English Language Acquisition [NCELA], 2006, 2008).

Figure 1.1 K–12 ELL Growth

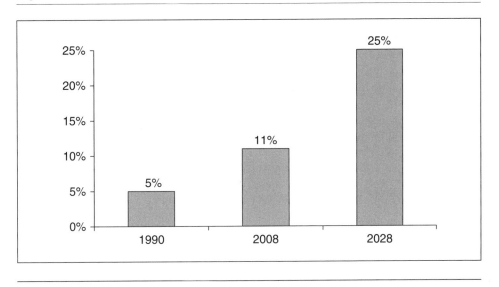

SOURCE: Goldenberg, 2008.

Figure 1.2 represents the 20% increase in overall population in contrast to the 40% increase in ELLs during the same time period. The dramatic increase of this subgroup compared to the general population has created instructional gaps in meeting the specific needs of these learners. Even states that typically have not had to contend with the needs of ELLs, such as Indiana, South Carolina, and Tennessee, all saw an increase of approximately 300% in their ELL population from 1994–1995 and 2004–2005 (Goldenberg, 2008; NCELA, 2008).

Figure 1.2 Percentage of ELL and Overall Population Growth

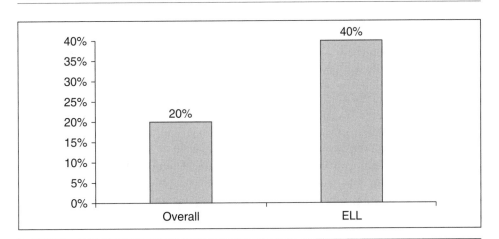

SOURCE: Goldenberg, 2008; NCELA, 2006, 2008.

LANGUAGE SPOKEN AND SOCIOECONOMIC FACTORS

In addition, 80% of ELLs in the United States come from Spanish-speaking homes and the majority of ELLs are Spanish speakers. This group generally comes from lower socioeconomic and educational backgrounds as compared to the general population or other immigrant groups. Whereas 24% of immigrants from Mexico and Central America are below the poverty level (see Figure 1.3), only 9–14% of immigrants from other regions of the world are below the poverty level (Goldenberg, 2008; Larsen, 2004).

Figure 1.3   Poverty Level Percentages

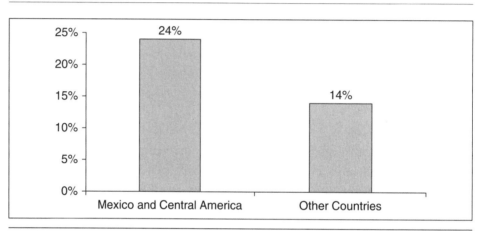

SOURCE: Goldenberg, 2008; Larsen, 2004.

Whereas fewer than 40% of immigrants from Mexico and Central America came to the United States with the equivalent of high school diplomas, 80–90% of immigrants from other countries came with at least a high school diploma (Goldenberg, 2008). Such statistics suggest that ELLs from Mexico and Central America often come to school with less English and more socioeconomic barriers, facing more challenge and adjustments than other immigrants. For example, socioeconomic gaps can create misunderstandings between educators and parents when immigrant parents are not as visible in school because they work multiple jobs in order to provide for their families. Educators can misinterpret parental absence as apathy. Instead, educators must find additional ways to meet the needs of students and families who are merely trying to economically survive in the United States, creating bridges, rather than barriers, in the educational process.

Figure 1.4 represents the fact that immigrants from other countries are more than twice as likely to have graduated from high school as those from Mexico and Central America. Both poverty and education levels become important as they present potential risk factors for students in school. In essence, ELLs from Mexico and Central America have to overcome additional challenges that can interrupt education or present additional challenges in school. As classroom teachers, it is imperative that we understand the distinctive needs that each group of ELLs comes to school with so that we can target instruction and meet needs appropriately.

Figure 1.4 Percentage of High School Diplomas

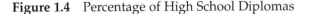
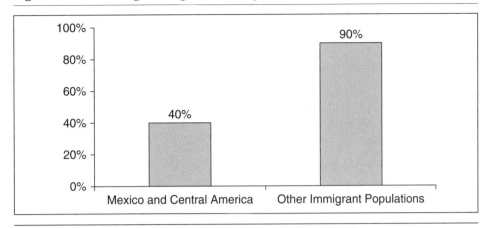

SOURCE: Goldenberg, 2008; Larsen, 2004.

The second-largest group of ELLs in the United States—about 8% of all ELLs—is speakers of Asian languages, including Vietnamese, Hmong, Chinese, Korean, Khmer, Laotian, Hindi, and Tagalog (Goldenberg, 2008; Larsen, 2004). As a subgroup, these students tend to come from higher socioeconomic and educational backgrounds than do other immigrant populations. Socioeconomically, Asian immigrants represent the second-lowest poverty rate, 11.1%, with over 87% having the equivalent of a high school diploma (Goldenberg, 2008; U.S. Census Bureau, 2008). There is, of course, variation among speakers of Asian countries. (See Figure 1.5.) Compared to 87% of Asian immigrants overall who have the equivalent of a high school diploma, only 50% or fewer Cambodian, Laotian, and Hmong adults in the United States have completed high school. In addition, Filipinos, East Indians, and Japanese in the United States have high school completion rates around 90%, while over 60% of Taiwanese and East Indian immigrants have college degrees (Goldenberg, 2008; U.S. Census Bureau, 2008).

Figure 1.5 High School Graduation Rates for Asian Immigrants

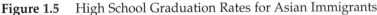
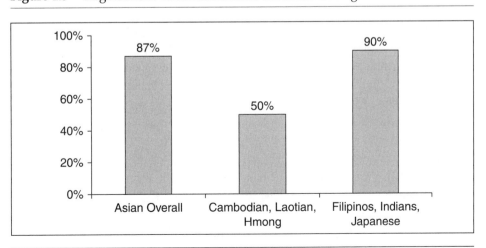

SOURCE: Goldenberg, 2008; U.S. Census Bureau, 2008.

Data suggest that we must not assume that all Asian immigrants come to the United States with the same set of skills and socioeconomic background. In other words, this is not a monolithic group. Group tendencies as well as individual differences must be considered. Schools with large groups of ELLs from Southeast Asia may have some of the same educational gaps as schools with ELLs from Mexico or Central America, and may benefit from some of the same instructional accommodations. However, when an ELL comes from a home where parents are educated and literate, there can be instructional acceleration of social language in order to more quickly address academic language needs.

ELL ACHIEVEMENT

Achievement data suggest that ELLs lag far behind their native English-speaking peers. Nationwide, only 7% of ELLs scored "at or above proficient" in reading on the 2003 fourth-grade National Assessment of Educational Progress (NAEP), as compared to about 30% of students overall. Results on the 2007 NAEP were similar, with only 7.5% of fourth-grade ELLs scoring at least "proficient," while 35.5% of native English speakers scored proficient (Goldenberg, 2008).

Figure 1.6 illustrates not only the gap between ELLs and their native English-speaking peers, but also the fact that ELL achievement has only progressed slightly—less than half a percentage point—while native English learners have progressed by 5.5% over the 4-year period (Goldenberg, 2008). Certainly for an ELL, any assessment becomes an English proficiency assessment of language when these students are in the process of learning language; therefore, educators and educational leaders and systems must become knowledgeable in meeting the needs of this growing ELL population so as to close the gap, not increase it, over time.

The achievement gap between ELLs and native English learners is not just an individual teacher or school issue but is also a systemic issue—one that most states and the nation as a whole must address with fervor. With Title III of the No Child Left Behind (NCLB) Act, districts are held accountable for ELLs' progress in English Language Development (ELD), as well as academic progress and achievement in academic subject areas. Annual measureable achievement objective (AMAO) targets must be reported separately for ELLs by states, districts, and schools. According to Kathleen Leos (U.S. Department of Education, 2005), former director of the Education Department's office of English-language acquisition, "The failure of most states to make [progress] for ELLs means that the language-proficiency standards developed in most states are not developed to a high enough level where they can provide access to academic content achievement" (p. 12). Data from California, where both standards and assessments have been developed for ELLs, suggest that although students become fluent in English by reclassifying into ELD, the rigor of the ELD standards and California English Language Development Test (CELDT) are not enough to provide access to grade-level content. It is then often the

Figure 1.6 NAEP Reading Results: ELL vs. Overall

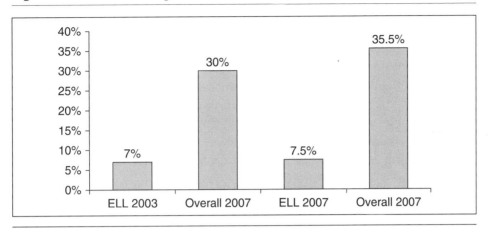

SOURCE: Goldenberg, 2008.

job of the classroom teacher and school system to reconcile ELD and content area standards.

STANDARD ENGLISH LEARNERS

Standard English Learners (SELs) are students who grew up speaking variations of standard English, such as African American Vernacular English (AAVE); wide variations of Chicano English; Hawaiian Pidgin English; or other English variations of indigenous peoples, such as Native American tribes, that may have established vocabulary, syntax, grammar, and register patterns that differ from Standard English. Standard English Learners can also be students who live in isolated rural settings where they rarely hear Standard English spoken in their home or community. These students, then, naturally arrive at school with a uniquely rich linguistic heritage, yet one that differs from the Standard Academic English experienced in the American classroom. These unique and rule-consistent English variations ought to be considered a linguistic and cultural asset (Hollie, 2001b)—that SELs have internalized an English structure that is combined with an indigenous structure, creating a new language structure—yet educator attitudes often create a barrier for these students in school (LeMoine, 2006).

According to LeMoine (2006), Standard English Learners often have some of the lowest achievement scores, yet we do not have a process in place in the United States that systematically disaggregates test data across schools, districts, states, and regions, identifying and supporting Standard English Learners. For example, we collect Home Language Surveys to determine whether another language is spoken in the home—and if another language is spoken, we provide additional language assessment. However, we do not systematically conduct nationwide data collection on variations of Standard English spoken in the home. We do disaggregate data from the perspective of ethnicity, but this lumps everyone into the same category, inviting false assumptions. For example, every Latino child is *not* an English Language Learner, a Standard English Learner, or an immigrant. Many Latino children are born in America, grow up in America, are children of educated parents, and hear Standard English modeled in their homes every day. However, there is also a large group of Latino children who speak English, but it is a variation of Standard English. These students, when coming to the text—just like an ELL—experience a mismatch between their home language and the language of the classroom, and therefore have an additional academic challenge as compared to their Standard English–speaking peers, yet they often go without specialized linguistic mentorship.

In the same way, we can look at test scores for African American children, but not every African American child is a Standard English Learner. Many African American children grow up in affluent, well-educated homes where they hear Standard English spoken every day. These African American children speak Standard English and excel in school; however, there is another group of African American children who speak African American Vernacular English or both AAVE and Standard English. For those children who only speak AAVE, and not Standard English, a mismatch between their home language and the language of their school exists. Consequently, these students experience unique linguistic challenges in the educational process.

We can also look at the scores for Caucasian children and lump them all together, but then we miss the linguistic variations and challenges of the Appalachian child raised in an impoverished environment with non-Standard English spoken at home, or the Caucasian student who is the first in his family to complete high school or go to college. We say all this only to underscore that there are subgroups of English-speaking children whose linguistic needs systematically go undetected, leading to larger literacy gaps over time—children who grow up in English-speaking homes where non-Standard English is spoken, yet are not identified in a systematic way for specific linguistic assistance. SELs are not ELLs, but their academic performance, or lack thereof, cries out for linguistic mentorship in a similar way. Therefore, as we have conceptualized this book, we want to expand the reader's thinking with regard to the literacy gaps and the Literacy Gaps Model that we will propose. We want you to consider the literacy gaps in light of any students who are still acquiring Standard English skills and offer them every advantage of linguistic mentorship that you would offer the ELL, so as to minimize the fossilization of non-Standard English to the exclusion of acquiring Standard English, and instead treating their non-Standard English as an L1 (first language: non-Standard English) that can be contrasted with their L2 (second language: Standard English).

> SELs are not ELLs, but their academic performance, or lack thereof, cries out for linguistic mentorship.

> L1 refers to a student's first language. L2 refers to a student's second language.

Educators and linguists have documented that Standard English Learners can benefit, both culturally and linguistically, from many of the same practices utilized in English Language Learner methodology (Hollie, 2001a). Affirming one's home language, explicitly contrasting that home language with Standard English, and expanding students' linguistic "repertoire" to include both their non-standard language as well as academic English, empower students to succeed and enter mainstream society (Hollie, 2001a).

Our shared goal is academic English competence for all children so that all students have access to college and the workplace. The Literacy Gaps Model applies to both ELLs and SELs, and where there are specific skills and approaches for each group, they will also be addressed for further differentiation. We address the common needs of ELLs and SELs in order to make instruction manageable for teachers in a classroom, but differentiation needs to also occur, especially with ELLs at the beginning stage. The needs of SELs and ELLs become more similar at the Early Advanced and Advanced stages of English Language Development. Although we do not currently have a body of research to cite for achievement scores for differentiated SELs, we do see emerging evidence (California State Department of Education, 2007, p. 301) of acknowledgment of SEL groups, such as the acknowledgment of AAVE by the California Department of Education's Reading/Language Arts Framework. In addition, we see research, such as Labov (1998), that uniquely identify the coexistent systems within AAVE. Labov's work, and others', helps us understand that variations of English have unique linguistic systems that demonstrate grammar consistency, yet differ from Standard English, and the speakers of these variations require unique linguistic support. This book primarily focuses on the needs of ELLs, but as commonalities emerge, the needs of SELs will also be addressed.

> Our shared goal is academic English competence for all children so that all students have access to college and the workplace.

THE NATIONAL LITERACY PANEL

Emerging research by the National Literacy Panel (Center for Applied Linguistics [CAL], 2006) has provided guidance in the best instructional practices to bridge grade-level content achievement gaps for ELLs. The authors of this book believe that these findings can benefit ELLs, SELs, and all children. In 2001, the U.S. Department of Education and the Institute of Education Sciences convened a National Literacy Panel (NLP) of expert researchers from the fields of reading, language, bilingualism, research methods, and education. According to the Center for Applied Linguistics Web site,

> The charge of the panel was to conduct a comprehensive, evidence-based review of the research literature on the development of literacy among language minority children and youth. The panel was to produce a report evaluating and synthesizing this research literature to guide educational practice and inform educational policy. (p. 1)

In 2000, the National Reading Panel conducted a similar study synthesizing findings on experimental studies of reading instruction in phonological awareness, phonics, and vocabulary; reading fluency; and reading comprehension, although it excluded studies of ELLs. In contrast, the NLP looked specifically at experimental studies of instructional procedures with ELLs. The findings of both the NLP (CAL, 2006) and the Center for Research on Education, Diversity, and Excellence (CREDE; Genesee, Lindholm-Leary, Saunders, & Christian, 2006) produced three common conclusions as shown in Figure 1.7.

Figure 1.7   Findings of NLP and CREDE, 2006

- Instruction in the primary language aids achievement;
- Good instruction for ELLs is similar to good instruction for other, English-speaking students; but
- ELLs require instructional accommodations.

SOURCE: Center for Applied Linguistics, 2006; Genesee, Lindholm-Leary, Saunders, & Christian, 2006.

Since the publication of findings of the NLP, as well as CREDE, in 2006, we have current, research-based insight on closing the achievement gap with ELLs, and therefore their research serves as the underpinning of this book. The following is a summary of the NLP findings and how they have impacted the book:

• **Instruction in the primary language aids achievement**—There are two main methods of educating ELLs (although there are also variations within these two), which include English immersion and bilingual education. English immersion provides instruction in English with sheltered or scaffolded support, while bilingual education teaches ELLs subjects both in English and their primary language. Meta-analysis by the NLP (CAL, 2006) with 17 studies comparing English immersion and bilingual education concluded that teaching ELLs to read in their primary language and then in their second language, or in both languages simultaneously at different times of the day, compared to only in English, increases reading achievement in English. The reason for this seems to be what educational psychologists and cognitive scientists call *transfer*. That is, when you learn something in your first language (L1), you are able to transfer those concepts and skills into the second language (L2) more rapidly. Specific strategies for transferring knowledge and skills between two languages, such as cognate word walls, will be addressed in the practical strategies infused throughout this book.

• **Good instruction for ELLs is similar to good instruction for other English-speaking students**—As with English-speaking students, ELLs benefit from clear goals and objectives, well-designed instructional routines, active engagement and participation, informative feedback, opportunities to practice and apply new learning and transfer it to new situations, periodic review and practice, opportunities to interact with other students, and frequent assessments, with reteaching as needed. It is important to note, however, that although these elements are considered good instruction for English-speaking students, these elements are *essential* and *imperative* for ELLs who are engaged in the complex task of learning content and English at the same time. These two simultaneous processes—acquiring subject matter content and learning English—are critical to the "good instruction" that is typically taken for granted even in classrooms of native English-speaking students. In addition, findings by the NLP (CAL, 2006) were similar to those of the National Reading Panel (2000) in the area of reading instruction indicate that phonemic awareness (manipulation of sounds); phonics (decoding words); as well as focused instruction in vocabulary, reading fluency, and comprehension were also effective for ELLs. It was found that with systematic, explicit instruction, ELLs can make similar progress to native English speakers in the early stages of reading. Progress in vocabulary and in the content areas, however, begins to slow around the third grade when academic expectations begin to accelerate. Specific needs of ELLs in decoding and comprehension will be addressed in Chapters 2 through 5.

• **ELLs require instructional accommodations**—Although there are several common instructional needs between ELLs and their native English-speaking peers, there are also differences that must be specifically addressed. The NLP (CAL, 2006) found that ELLs especially benefit from opportunities to practice and extend oral English skills, as well as lessons that target both language and content objectives. These components will be addressed throughout the book. The following scaffolding techniques create academic bridges that prove beneficial for ELLs:

- Strategic use of primary language (e.g., cognate walls)
- Predictable, clear, and consistent instructions, expectations, and routines
- Extended explanations and additional opportunities for practice
- Redundant information that strengthens context-embedded access to information, such as visual cues and physical gestures
- Focus on the similarities/differences between English and the native language (e.g., contrastive grammar analysis)
- Building upon students' knowledge and skills in their native languages
- Identifying and clarifying difficult words and passages
- Consolidating text knowledge through summarization
- Providing extra practice in reading words, sentences, and stories
- Targeting vocabulary and frequent comprehension checks
- Teacher paraphrasing of students' remarks and encouraging expansion (e.g., use of English language stems)

These instructional accommodations assist in closing gaps for ELLs, both in English Language Development and across the content areas, as well as support Standard English development for SELs, and will be addressed at length throughout this book.

THE LITERACY GAPS MODEL

In order to close the literacy gaps, educators must examine every possible venue for increased quality of learning in the United States school system by increasing the quality of preservice and inservice teacher training, instructional practice, and measurement of learning outcomes. This book focuses on the needs of ELLs and SELs, presenting a theoretical teacher training model, the Literacy Gaps Model (Hetzel & Soto-Hinman, 2007), which illustrates the complex barriers that inhibit student learning in the classroom (the gap between the students and the text, the student and the teacher, and the student and his or her peers) and offers bridge-building strategies that close these gaps, specifically for English Language Learners, including Standard English Learners, who are so often "left behind."

To help the goal of closing the literacy gaps to become reality for all students, preservice teacher training models and inservice professional development opportunities must be modified to include a deeper under-standing of individual differences and how these play out in classroom dynamics, particularly in the area of reading comprehension and literacy in general (Infante, 1996; Peterson, 2006; Turbill, 2006). The following three literacy gaps hinder student learning and must be understood by every teacher:

(1) The gap between the student and the text, including readability issues such as decoding and comprehension, which are greatly affected by background knowledge and experience; the student's L1 (first language); and the student's level of English Language Development; (see Figure 1.8)

(2) The gap between the teacher and the student, including teacher perceptions and expectations, cultural differences between the teacher and the student, and socioeconomic differences (see Figure 1.9)

(3) The gap between the student and his of her fluent English-speaking peers, including primary language(s) and English-language proficiency levels. These can be addressed by creating micro structures within the class-room, such as homogeneous and heterogeneous groupings, coupled with open-ended, flexible, tiered assignments and broadspan teaching, as well as macro structures, such as grouping across grade levels and schoolwide pro-grams that support global citizenry through language study, immersion programs, and heterogeneous and homogenous groupings. (see Figure 1.10).

The Literacy Gaps: Bridge-Building Strategies for English Language Learners and Standard English Learners provides a model around which teachers can rally, organizing their literacy strategies and strengthening their classroom

Figure 1.8   The Gap Between the ELL Student and the Text

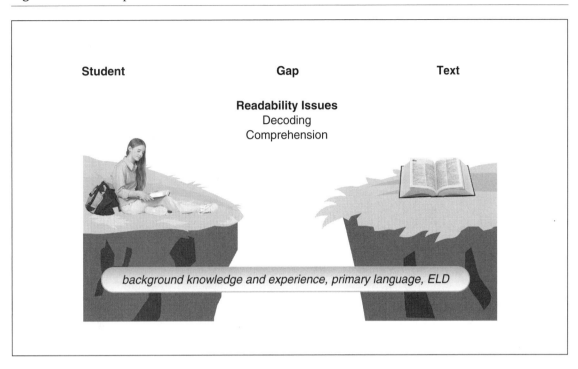

Figure 1.9   The Gap Between the ELL Student and the Teacher

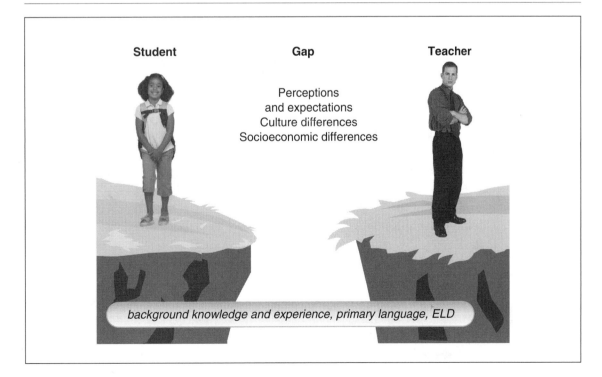

Figure 1.10 The Gap Between the Student and His or Her Peers

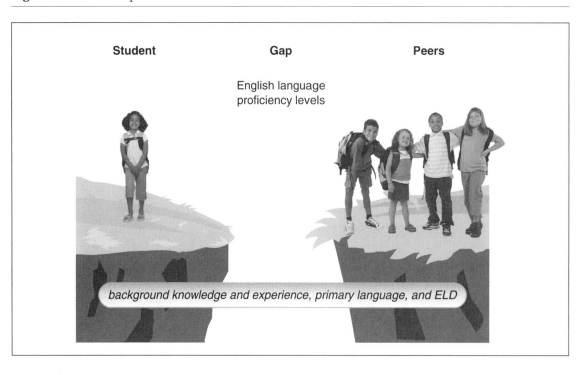

practices. This book, based upon an article by the authors (Hetzel & Soto-Hinman, 2007) that was presented at the 2006 Oxford University Round Table and published in the *Journal on Public Policy,* offers a model for reorganizing instructional practice for a variety of educational audiences, including teacher education, teacher induction, and professional development. The model of the three literacy gaps—the gap between the student and written text, the student and the teacher, and the student and his or her peers—provides a framework around which educators can organize current, research-based instructional practices so as to close the gaps and increase English Language Learners' and Standard English Learners' academic achievement.

The Literacy Gaps: Bridge-Building Strategies for English Language Learners and Standard English Learners begins with the research-based rationale for this book and the urgency for educators to immediately attend to the needs of our ELLs and SELs across the nation. Then, as we have only briefly introduced the Literacy Gaps Model, we will unpack the model in detail throughout the remainder of the book. The middle section of the book provides detailed treatment of each of the literacy gaps. Each gap corresponds to subcomponents that are carefully crafted and unpacked within the context of research-based theory and practical experience. Practical strategies are introduced and supported with examples that can immediately be used in a classroom context. The text's language is intended to be user-friendly for classroom teachers, yet with enough research included to be a support in the university classroom. We hope that you as the reader, and ultimately your students, will greatly benefit by having spent some time in studying this book.

The text is applicable for classroom practice in that it provides contextualized experiences and classroom conversations that demonstrate how to apply the principles in a classroom context. Readers should find focused and detailed suggestions for incrementally altering instructional practice. The scenarios outlined will assist you in visualizing yourself in the classroom, and hopefully, after you have read this book, you will implement change that will fundamentally impact ELL and SEL student achievement.

OVERVIEW OF BOOK CHAPTERS

A brief summary of the remainder of the book follows.

Chapters 2 through 5 relate to the first gap, the gap between the student and the text (see Figure 1.11).

Literacy Gap #1: The Gap Between the Student and the Text

Chapter 2, "Decoding," examines concepts of print, phonemic awareness, phonics, sight words, and automaticity in the context of developing word recognition and reading fluency for ELLs and SELs. Chapter 3, "Background Knowledge and Experience," helps teachers understand the role of background knowledge and experience, or schema, as the critical foundation for understanding text. In Chapter 4, "Comprehension," the reader studies meaning-making strategies, considering how academic language, including vocabulary, syntax, and text structure, affects comprehensibility of text for ELLs and SELs. In addition, strategies are presented to support comprehension monitoring as well as (re)organization of text, including appropriate questioning.

Chapter 5, "English Language Development and Academic English," guides the teacher, step-by-step, through the process of sensitive language mentorship for English Language Learners, including Standard English Learners whose language might be associated with African American vernacular, variations of Chicano English, or Hawaiian Pidgin.

Literacy Gap #2: The Gap Between the Student and the Teacher

Chapters 6, 7, and 8 address the second gap, that between the student and the teacher. (See Figure 1.12.) This section unveils three important barriers between the student and the teacher that affect learning—perceptions and expectations, cultural differences, and socioeconomic differences. Chapter 6, "Perceptions and Expectations," refers to mental models and belief systems educators hold about ELLs and SELs and their ability levels. These perceptions are unpacked and practical strategies are provided to

Figure 1.11   Gap #1: The Gap Between the ELL Student and the Text

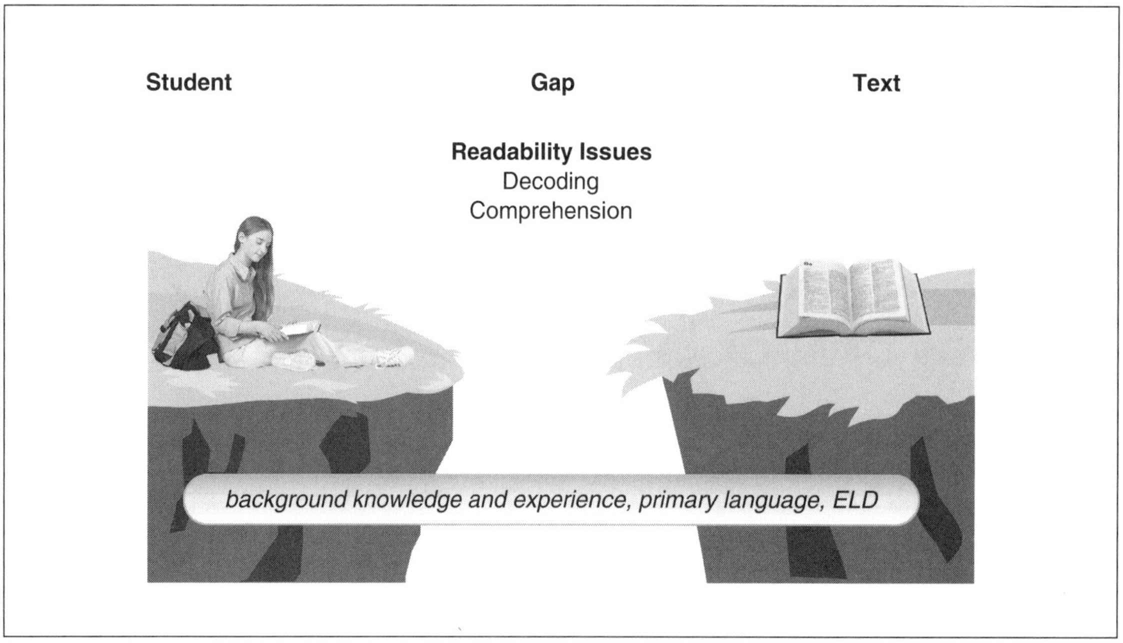

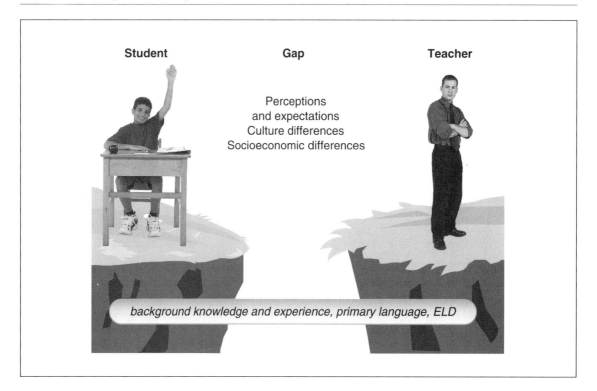

Figure 1.12   Gap #2: The Gap Between the ELL Student and the Teacher

assist teachers in bridging this gap. Establishing and holding high expectations for all students is an essential component to successfully meeting individual needs (August & Hakuta, 1997; August & Pease-Alvarez, 1996; Brisk, 1998; Education Trust, 2003). Moreover, teachers' expectations of students are inextricably linked to their perceptions about students' abilities, their own pedagogical skills, and their content knowledge (Ferguson, 1998; Howard, 1995; Wenglinsky, 2001). When educators are not well-informed regarding the population and needs of the students they instruct, they can unknowingly hinder rather than further educational progress. This chapter steps into the gap and bridges this divide.

Chapter 7, "Cultural Differences," examines mismatches between the teacher and his or her students that can create gaps of misunderstanding. Caring teachers must know their students and build bridges to their students' home cultures. For example, Valdés (1996) suggests that assistance to Mexican-origin families must be based on "an understanding and an appreciation and respect for the internal dynamics of these families" (p. 203). Chapter 7 prepares educators to explore these cultural differences as assets to school life both inside *and* outside the classroom. Teachers reframe their thinking, discovering that cultural differences can inform them in how to do their work better, as opposed to viewing cultural differences as potential deterrents to educational progress.

Chapter 8, "Socioeconomic Differences," examines another major gap between the teacher and so many, though not all, of his or her ELLs or SELs. Parents in the lower socioeconomic class, like the parents of middle- and upper-class children, want their children equipped with academic language skills for college and beyond. And, since children from impoverished homes may not already be equipped with implicit linguistic academic codes, it is the responsibility of teachers to make those codes explicit for them. In Chapter 8, teachers learn how to provide explicit literacy instruction for varied language registers, involving the teaching of conventions of reading and writing in a reflective manner, with real-life, culturally appropriate examples. Teachers learn strategies to bridge socioeconomic differences so that students are able to use academic language for a range of purposes in a contextually embedded, accessible learning environment. In this way, teachers build bridges to fill in gaps between students' home language registers that might reflect a lower socioeconomic status to that of the language registers of the dominant culture, by explicitly understanding and teaching the idiosyncrasies of the dominant language, all the while respecting the home language and any derivations of Standard English the student might be speaking.

Literacy Gap #3: The Gap Between the Student and His or Her Peers

Chapter 9, "Language Proficiency Levels," unveils the mystery behind assessments and formally identified English Language Development levels. Language proficiency levels are often used much too rigidly to

Figure 1.13 Gap #3: The Gap Between the Student and His or Her Peers

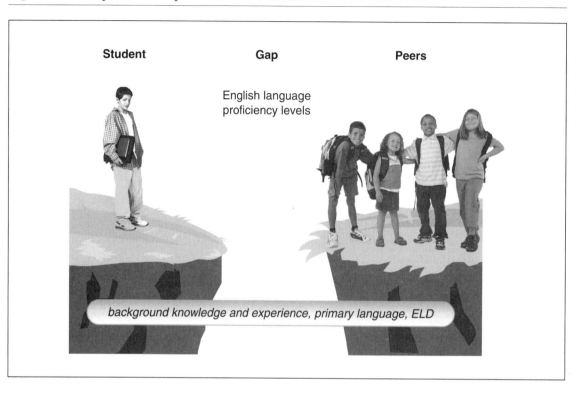

depict what students *cannot* do, instead of the intended usage, as a means of giving a range of what they *can* do. For example, if a student has been identified at a beginning level, he or she might be expected to write simple words. Some educators might keep to this descriptor much too rigidly and not expect students to write both simple words and phrases. Some educators might also assume that all ELLs are the same, despite first-language ability. In Chapter 9, the authors expand the reader's understanding of language proficiency levels and assessments, and then provide practical techniques to maximize language acquisition, using the first language to assist the second language acquisition process. (See Figure 1.13.)

Chapter 10, "Grouping Strategies," puts the puzzle pieces together, providing practical insight on grouping strategies based upon proficiency levels. The gap between the student and his or her peers with regard to language acquisition, the art of differentiation, can be bridged by creating micro structures within the classroom, such as homogeneous and heterogeneous groupings, coupled with open-ended, flexible, tiered assignments, and broadspan teaching. Chapter 10 then addresses grade level and schoolwide programs.

Chapter 11, "Beyond the Gap," explores potentials for moving students beyond the achievement gap, nurturing lifelong learning, and preparing them for successful futures. Chapter 11 invites educators to create sociocultural environments in which ELLs and SELs thrive, gain confidence through their academic achievements, capitalize on the rich funds of knowledge that they bring to society, experience equitable access to all that society offers, and ultimately gain the skills to be the leaders of tomorrow.

As educators, we must reenvision a future with success for all students, including ELLs and SELs. We cannot lose hope. We must embrace the reality that standardized test scores show that we, as educators, are failing many of our students, demanding that we change educational and literacy practices. Naturally, demographic transformation requires renovations in instructional practice so as to meet the needs of all students. Chapter 11 highlights the redesign of teacher preparation and instructional practice for ELLs through the introduction of the Literacy Gaps Model, one that can encompass familiar as well as new research-based instructional practices, assisting and enabling teachers nationwide to indeed have "no child left behind."

SUMMARY

Chapter 1 establishes the historical evidence of the literacy gaps provided by Goldenberg (2008) and the National Literacy Panel (2006), paving the way for research-based methodology to close the literacy gaps for ELLs and SELs. The Literacy Gaps Model (Hetzel & Soto-Hinman, 2007) provides a conceptual structure around which conversations can occur in professional communities, observations can be made, gaps can be identified, and bridges can be built, especially for the English Language Learner and the Standard English Learner, in order to help every child succeed. Now, journey with us as we step into Literacy Gap #1, the gap between the student and the text.

REFERENCES

August, D., & Hakuta, K. (Eds.). (1997). *Improving schooling for language-minority children: A research agenda.* Washington, DC: National Academies Press.

August, D., & Pease-Alvarez, L. (1996). *Attributes of effective programs in classrooms serving English language learners.* Santa Cruz, CA: National Center for Research on Cultural Diversity and Second Language Learning.

Brisk, M. E. (2005). *Bilingual education: From compensatory to quality schooling* (2nd ed.). Mahwah, NJ: Lawrence Erlbaum.

California State Department of Education. (2007). *Reading/language arts framework: Kindergarten through Grade Twelve.* Sacramento, CA: Author.

Center for Applied Linguistics. (2006). *Project archive: National Literacy Panel on Language Minority Children and Youth.* Retrieved March 25, 2009, from http://www.cal.org.

Education Trust. (2003). A new core curriculum for all: Aiming high for other people's children. *Thinking K–16, 7*(1), 1–33.

Ferguson, R. (1998). Teachers' perceptions and expectations and the black–white test score gap. In C. Jencks & M. Phillips (Eds.), *The black–white test score gap.* Washington, DC: Brookings Institution.

Genesee, F., Lindholm-Leary, K., Saunders, W., & Christian, D. (2006). *Language learning and academic achievement.* Berkeley, CA: CREDE Publications.

Goldenberg, C. (2008, Summer). Teaching English language learners: What the research does—and does not—say. *American Educator.*

Hetzel, J., & Soto-Hinman, I. (2007, Winter). The three literacy gaps and Title III of NCLB. Oxford Round Table 2006. *Journal on Public Policy.* Available online at http://www.forumonpublicpolicy.com/papersw07.html#students.

Hollie, S. (2001a, September). Acknowledgement, affirmation, and accommodation: The non-standard language approach. (Language Teaching & Learning). *Academic Exchange Quarterly,* 1096–1453. Retrieved September 22, 2008, from http://www.thefreelibrary.com//print/PrintArticle.aspx?id=80679270.

Hollie, S. (2001b, March). Acknowledging the language of African American students: Instructional strategies. *English Journal, 90*(4), 54–59. Retrieved September 22, 2008, from http://www.jstor.org/stable/821903?seq=1.

Howard, J. (1995). You can't get there from here: The need for a new logic in education reform. *Daedalus Journal of the American Academy of Arts and Sciences, 123*(2), 47–64.

Infante, M. (1996). International reports in literacy research: Chile. *Reading Research Quarterly, 41*(1), 134.

Labov, W. (1998). Coexistent systems in African-American English. In S. Mufwene, J. Rickford, J. Baugh, & G. Bailey (Eds.), *The structure of African-American English* (pp. 110–153). London: Routledge.

Larsen, L. J. (2004, August). The foreign-born population in the United States: 2003. *Current Population Reports.* Washington, DC: U.S. Census Bureau.

LeMoine, N. (2006). Language variation and literacy acquisition in African American students. In J. Harris, A. Kamhi, & K. Pollock (Eds.), *Literacy in African American communities* (pp. 169–194). Mahwah, NJ: Lawrence Erlbaum.

National Clearinghouse for English Language Acquisition. (2006). *How has the English language learner population changed in recent years?* Washington, DC: Author. Retrieved April 1, 2008, from http://www.ncela.gwu.edu/expert/faq/081eps.html.

National Clearinghouse for English Language Acquisition. (2008, April). *ELL demographics by state.* Washington, DC: Author. Retrieved April 1, 2008, from http://www.ncela.gwu.edu/stats/3_bystate.htm.

National Reading Panel. (2000). *National Reading Panel report.* Washington, DC: U.S. Government Printing Office. Available online at http://www.national readingpanel.org.

Peterson, S. (2006). International reports in literacy research: Canada. *Reading Research Quarterly, 41*(1), 133–134.

Turbill, J. (2006). International reports in literacy: Australia and New Zealand. *Research Reading Research Quarterly, 41*(1), 133.

U.S. Census Bureau. (2008). *Fact sheet: Race, ethnic, or ancestry group.* Washington, DC: Author. Retrieved April 1, 2008, from http://factfinder.census.gov/servlet/SAFFFactsCharIteration?_submenuId=factsheet_2&_sse=on.

U.S. Department of Education. (2000). *R30 Language Census.* Washington, DC: Author.

U.S. Department of Education. (2005). *Press Release: Kathleen Leos to head Office of English Language Acquisition.* Retrieved March 24, 2009, from http://www.ed.gov/news/pressreleases/2005/09/09072005.html.

Valdés, G. (1996). *Con respeto: Bridging the distances between culturally diverse families and schools.* New York: Teachers College Press.

Wenglinsky, H. (2001). *Teacher classroom practices in student performance: How schools can make a difference.* Princeton, NJ: Educational Testing Service.

2

Decoding

Word Recognition Strategies and Fluency

For some students, literacy learning comes easy. However, for the immigrant child, the English Language Learner (ELL), or the child who speaks non-Standard English (an SEL—Standard English Learner), literacy acquisition can be extremely difficult. These students have specialized literacy gaps that emerge from the incongruity between their home and school worlds. The first gap that emerges is the gap between the student and the text itself. This literacy gap encompasses the many issues that create barriers between the child and the comprehension of the text. This chapter will discuss best practices for students to decipher print, including word recognition strategies and fluency, such as concepts of print, phonemic awareness, phonics, sight words, and automaticity—all with the backdrop of language transfer as it relates to the ELL and SEL reader. As we discuss aspects of the decoding branch of reading, we will emphasize instructional practices and accommodations that assist ELLs and SELs in literacy success as identified by the National Reading Panel (2000) and by the National Literacy Panel (Center for Applied Linguistics [CAL], 2006), highlighted in Chapter 1. Chapter 3 will discuss background knowledge and the critical foundation of a child's first language and experience as it relates to his or her literacy development. Chapter 4 includes discussion of the comprehension branch of reading, including academic language considerations and accommodations that support ELLs in vocabulary, syntax, text structure, comprehension monitoring, and (re)organizing text. We will then move on to English Language Development (ELD) and Academic English (AE) and examine the types of ELLs that we generally have in the United States who can fall through the gaps. Chapters 2 through 5 encompass the major components related to the gap between the ELL student and the text, though there are an infinite number of potential barriers or "gaps" that might create a mismatch between student and text.

THE GAP BETWEEN THE STUDENT AND THE TEXT

Figure 2.1 illustrates the gap between the ELL student and the text he or she is to read. Potentially included in that gap are components of readability, the specialized needs of the ELL and the SEL, and any issue that might create a barrier. An infinite number of possibilities could be placed in the gap, as each ELL and SEL has numerous barriers that might prevent comprehension of text. It is the astute practitioner's great privilege to consider each student's gaps and to consider bridge-building strategies to help him or her overcome those gaps, enabling the student to ultimately become a proficient, lifelong reader of English who enjoys reading and writing and meaningfully interacts with text at home, school, and work.

DECODING AND READABILITY OF TEXT

Multiple factors affect readability of text. Readability, in the strictest sense, is a formula for calculating a grade-level equivalent for a particular passage, usually involving sentence length and numbers of words or syllables. It allows the teacher to identify a particular book as written at a particular grade level (e.g., the fourth-grade readability level, 4.0). She would then match a fourth-grade reader (4.0) with a fourth-grade book (4.0). This pairing between the text's readability level and the student's reading level would be considered an appropriate student-text match. The assumption would be that the text would be at the student's *instructional* level, because there was a match between the book's readability level and the student's identified reading level. The assumption is also that appropriate instructional progress can be made when a teacher matches the student's reading level to the text's readability level; however, this is not always the case. Figure 2.2 illustrates an appropriate student-to-text match—the student contentedly reads along at a comfortable pace with just enough challenge; however, many students experience mismatches on a regular basis for a variety of reasons.

One should keep in mind that there are three student-text matches when it comes to readability: the *independent* reading level, the *instructional* reading level, and the *frustrational* reading level.

If an ELL or SEL student can read a text on his or her own with about 95% degree of accuracy in decoding and 90%-plus comprehension, we generally say that the book is at the student's *independent* reading level. When the book contains significant challenges in decoding or comprehension, but

Figure 2.1 Gap #1: The Gap Between the Student and the Text

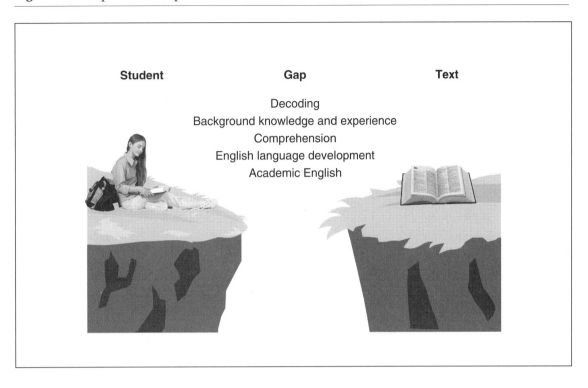

Figure 2.2 Student and Text Match

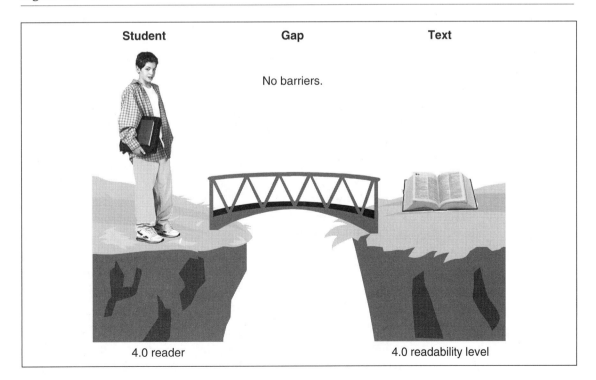

the book is accessible with teacher support in guided reading, then we identify that book as being at the child's *instructional* level. But when the book is so challenging to read that the child may become frustrated (e.g., less than 90% accuracy in decoding or less than 70% comprehension), then we generally say this text is at the child's *frustrational* level. However, the more challenging text might be perfect for an instructional read-aloud (IRA), as the teacher does the decoding while the student listens and follows along, with the teacher explaining difficult concepts or words along the way (see Figure 2.3). The IRA allows a student to focus on comprehension, rather than decoding a text that may be above his or her independent reading level. By using the IRA, a teacher can also model for students important metacognitive techniques that occur during reading. For example, a teacher can use a think-aloud, whereby he orally describes for students how he makes meaning around a text. The teacher may choose to focus on the comprehension strategy of schema while reading a text aloud, and describe for students the text-to-text, text-to-world, or text-to-life connections that he is making while he reads. He can then gradually release responsibility to the students around making those connections with texts at their independent reading level.

Figure 2.3   Reading Levels With Varied Purposes

Levels	Purposes
Independent Reading Level	Recreational reading; fluency development; reinforcement; child reads alone.
Instructional Reading Level	Teaching level; instructor provides support for *appropriately* challenging text.
Frustrational Reading Level	Instructional Read Aloud (IRA); provides opportunity for student to hear teacher read text above his current ability; teacher helps build and model new understanding of concepts and vocabulary.

Making an appropriate student-to-text match is an extremely complex process because of the multifaceted nature of reading instruction and acquisition, particularly in the context of ELLs and SELs. Shefelbine (1998), as shown in California State Department of Education (2007), developed a descriptive chart to exemplify the key components of effective language arts instruction as shown in Figure 2.4.

Figure 2.4 describes the organization of reading skills that affect a student's decoding and comprehension of written text, which results in the student's ability to decode and comprehend a particular text with a designated readability (e.g., fourth-grade readability). Though the most essential concepts for reading are captured in the diagram, we would prefer to organize the chart a bit differently, particularly for the English Language Learner and the Standard English Learner. We will place background knowledge and experience as the foundational base for all the literacy skills (Gutiérrez, 2000; Moll & Gonzalez, 2004; National Literacy Panel, 2006), delving deeply into both throughout the text, because background knowledge and experience inform a child's decoding skills, such as concepts

Figure 2.4 Key Components of Effective Language Arts Instruction

Decoding					Comprehension				
Word Recognition Strategies			**Fluency**		**Academic Language**		**Comprehension Strategies**		
Concepts about print	Phonemic awareness	Phonics	Sight words	Auto-maticity	Background knowledge	Vocabulary	Syntax -------- Text structure	Compre-hension monitoring	(Re) organizing text

SOURCE: California State Board of Education, 2007. Reprinted by permission from the California Department of Education, CDE Press, 1430 N Street, Suite 3207, Sacramento, CA 95814.

of print (e.g., read from front to back, left to right), as well as his or her academic language (vocabulary, syntax) and comprehension (see Figure 2.5). In addition, primary language proficiency is included in background knowledge and accelerates the reading process (National Literacy Panel, 2006). According to Goldenberg's analysis (2006) of the National Literacy Panel findings, "teaching reading skills in the first language is more effective in terms of second language achievement." However, the caveat, according to Goldenberg (2006), is that "Primary-language instruction is no panacea, just as phonics instruction is no panacea. But, in general, it makes meaningful contributions to cognitive and academic growth" (p. 3).

Some educators might wonder why we chose to move background knowledge and experience and place it across the foundation of the entire "Literacy Framework Describing Key Components of Effective Language Arts Instruction" in Figure 2.5, stretching across both the decoding and comprehension branches. Of course, background knowledge and experience most affect the comprehension branch. However, they do not just affect vocabulary acquisition; they also affect passage comprehension as a reader brings knowledge of, for example, *story*, from his L1 (say, Spanish), which then informs his ability to comprehend story in his L2 (English).

Somewhat controversial is this idea that background knowledge and experience also affect the decoding branch. Let the reader consider this example: Author Hetzel, while teaching in Africa, came across this hurriedly handwritten sign in French, posted on the school building one morning as she arrived early to teach: *S'il Vous Plaîs Utilisez L'Entréde de L'Administration*. While Hetzel has never studied French, she does have decoding and comprehension background knowledge and experience in her L1 (English) and limited studies in Spanish and German. She took one look at the sign, and using her decoding skills and her knowledge of cognates, understood immediately that she was to use the administrative entrance. Though she may not have thought of the correct pronunciation in French as she viewed the French words, her decoding skills led her to surmise that *"S'il Vous Plaîs"* meant "please" (leaning upon a commonly used oral phrase she had heard in conversation and making a connection with the written representation). *"Utilisez"* looked very much like *use* or *utility*. *L'Entrée de L'Administration,* again using her decoding skills, looked like "entrance of the administration." While Hetzel's pronunciation and interpretation of the sign may be approximate, and while she took advantage of context to add meaning to her interpretation of the French sign, the illustration demonstrates how naturally and seamlessly one utilizes knowledge and experience in one's L1 (and other languages of which the reader has some knowledge) to inform decoding *and* comprehension of one's L2.

We would also place another foundational base at the bottom of the literacy framework: English Language Development (ELD), which is to include the four literacy processes of reading, writing, listening, and speaking. The reason that we would also place ELD across the foundation of the entire framework is that the literacy classroom for the ELL or SEL student—or any student, for that matter—is ELD all the way (oral and written). Hence, an adapted version of the chart for ELLs would look like Figure 2.5.

Figure 2.5   ELL Literacy Framework Describing Key Components of Effective Language Arts Instruction

Decoding					Comprehension			
Word Recognition Strategies			**Fluency**		**Academic Language**		**Comprehension Strategies**	
Concepts about print	Phonemic awareness	Phonics	Sight words	Auto-maticity	Vocabulary	Syntax -------- Text structure	Compre-hension monitoring	(Re)organizing text
English Language Development								
Background knowledge								

SOURCE: Adapted from California State Board of Education, 2007.

Teachers and parents must understand that all of the literacy skills must come together at once in order for an ELL or an SEL to comprehend text and that background knowledge and English Language Development form the foundation for the ELL's and the SEL's success in the literacy classroom. Building on the foundation of background knowledge and English Language Development, classroom teachers of ELL and SEL students must systematically build decoding and comprehension skills. In addition, distinctions must be made between reading processes and language acquisition. Although there are overlaps and similarities, ELD is the acquisition of a second language. This encompasses learning to read in a second language, but also includes the additional processes of learning to listen, speak, and write in another language. Depending on the level of primary language proficiency, the ELL may rely more heavily on primary language support and indeed benefit from it (CAL, 2006).

In this chapter, we will consider the left branch of the ELL Literacy Framework: decoding. In Chapter 4, we will consider the right branch of the framework: comprehension. During both discussions, we will continue to visit the concepts of English Language Development and the importance of background knowledge and experience, which form the foundational concepts for ELLs' and SELs' literacy development. Background knowledge will be unpacked in depth in Chapter 3, comprehension covered in Chapter 4, and English Language Development and Academic English discussed in Chapter 5 as well as infused throughout the book. Let us now discuss each section of the framework, beginning with decoding.

DECODING

The *decoding* branch of reading instruction includes word recognition strategies, such as concepts about *print* (e.g., left to right sequence), *phonemic awareness* (understanding that words can be segmented into individual sound units), *phonics* (the study of phoneme–grapheme relationships), and *sight words* (often called high-frequency words). The *fluency* side of decoding also involves student knowledge of sight words that may not have consistent phoneme–grapheme relationships. Fluency generally includes *prosody* (expression) and speed; whereas the term *automaticity* is commonly defined as the ability to fluidly and naturally decode, in a programmed sort of way, where everything comes together all at once in a seemingly effortless fashion. Automaticity needs to be present in the context of word-attack skills to create neurological space for comprehension. In other words, if a student expends incredible effort to sound out a word, she will lose the gist of the passage by the time she gets to the end of the sentence, because the student would have maxed out her short-term memory. Automaticity facilitates comprehension by having decoding skills so streamlined, or automatic, that the focus of the reader is not decoding, but instead, comprehension.

Secondary ELLs/SELs and Decoding

It is important to note that many secondary ELL and SEL students will not need extended instructional time with decoding skills, unless they have had little schooling or interrupted schooling. It is essential that teachers of secondary ELLs and SELs determine specific decoding needs, target and sensitively teach only those skills that are needed, and move on when those skills have been acquired. It is also vital that cognitively respectful curricular materials be utilized, and that the social dimensions of learning are addressed as basic decoding skills are filled in. The Strategic Literacy Initiative at WestEd (see www.wested.org) provides guidance in this area through their professional development series called Reading Apprenticeship (RA). In the supplementary RA text, *Reading for Understanding: A Guide to Improving Reading in Middle and High School Classrooms*, authors Schoenbach, Greenleaf, Cziko, and Hurwitz (1999) suggest that there are four dimensions to the secondary reader, which must be addressed and accessed in order for secondary readers to thrive and succeed. These four dimensions are as follows:

1. Social Dimension—creating safety, relationships, reading processes

2. Personal Dimension—reader identity, metacognition

3. Cognitive Dimension—problem-solving, monitoring comprehension

4. Knowledge Building Dimension—schemata regarding topic, text structures, discipline

The cognitive and knowledge building dimensions will be addressed further in Chapter 4, and will not be discussed specifically here. Unfortunately, many secondary ELLs are relegated to rote and meaningless, cognitively disrespectful materials and lessons, when in fact they are ready for so much more rigor related to the reading comprehension processes. The intersection between cognitively respectful reading materials and strategies, along with the social dimension in particular, will be addressed further here. The social dimension includes the relationships—between teacher and student, and student and student—as well as the safety in a classroom that must go along with building reading processes. Teachers can accomplish both of these things, and need to do both of these, with struggling readers and decoders who will often wear masks to hide their literacy gaps.

Klemp, Hon, and Shorr (1992) combine the psychosocial issues that adolescents bring to school with the literacy gaps that may exist in a classroom, with an approach called Cooperative Literacy. This approach, similar to Reading Apprenticeship, honors the adolescent readers' needs by surmising that, "while all teachers are teachers of literacy, students are also responsible for promoting each other's literacy in a community of learning" (p. 2). Central to Cooperative Literacy is the use of pods, where students are organized into interdependent learning teams of four or five students. The number of students in each pod is by design, so that there is maximum performance—pods beyond four or five make it possible for students to "hide out" and not participate in the group. In these pods, students practice new literacy strategies and skills with each other. For example, when teaching students reciprocal teaching roles of summarizer, questioner, predictor, and connector, a teacher will already have students grouped in pods so that each student can take on one of the roles as an expert. Students can then also have a discussion about a text, knowing that their pod is relying upon them for success with the topic, when that role is completed and discussed. Cole (1998) suggests, "Cooperation leads to ownership, involvement, and great opportunities for self-discipline, but first must come trust. Students learn to trust through opportunities to take ownership and take responsibility for their own actions and those of others" (p. 8). This sense of interdependence and learning via trust becomes essential to closing literacy gaps, especially when adolescent

ELLs and SELs are behind in reading development. Educators must be sure to make use of classroom structures, such as pods, as well as areas of expertise of the individual students themselves, as assets to filling in literacy gaps quickly and respectfully.

The following sections will briefly explain each area of the decoding branch of instruction and provide helpful, bridge-building instructional strategies to help students overcome these decoding gap barriers (see Figure 2.6).

Figure 2.6   Decoding Gap

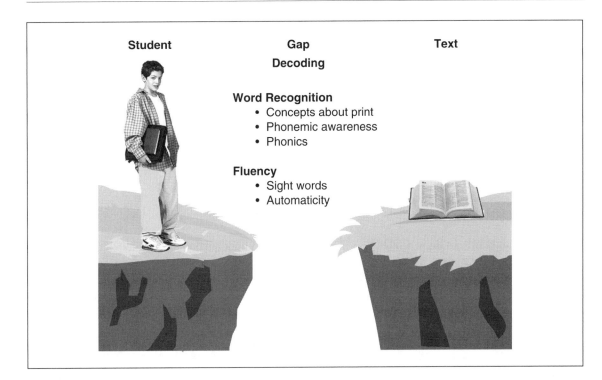

Word Recognition

Regardless of the student's first language(s), as he learns Standard English he must acquire word recognition skills, including an understanding of English concepts of print, a basic grasp of phonemic awareness, a deep understanding of phoneme–grapheme relationships, and a memory bank of sight words so that all these skills can come together simultaneously, demonstrating fluency and automaticity in the processing of English text. When two languages are similar phonetically, or if the student demonstrates proficiency in the primary language, this process can be accelerated. Word recognition encompasses all of these areas: concepts about print, phonemic awareness, and phonics.

Concepts About Print

When a newcomer enters your room, it is important to know what concepts of print the student brings with him or her. Students do not come to us as empty vessels, and we must build upon the knowledge and skills with which they come to school. In determining the assets and skills that students bring with them, it is important to administer a pre-assessment. A pre-assessment that a classroom teacher might use regarding concepts of print includes the following. How would the student answer these questions as they relate to his or her home language?

1. Do we read left to right, right to left, top to bottom, or bottom to top?

2. Does the book open from the left or the right?

3. Where is the text located? Where are the illustrations located?

4. Where is the front of the book? The back of the book? The spine of the book?

5. Where do we begin reading on the page?

6. Point to the words as I read them. (Teacher notes one-to-one correspondence and sweep to next line.)

Then, consider how these concepts of print questions would be answered in the context of English. Any differences in those answers represent gaps between the English Language Learner and the text he or she is to read. For example, since Arabic reads from right to left, an Arabic

Figure 2.7   Concepts About Print

Decoding					Comprehension			
Word Recognition Strategies			**Fluency**		**Academic Language**		**Comprehension Strategies**	
Concepts about print	Phonemic awareness	Phonics	Sight words	Auto-maticity	Vocabulary	Syntax -------- Text structure	Compre-hension monitoring	(Re)organizing text
English Language Development								
Background Knowledge								

SOURCE: Adapted from California State Board of Education, 2007.

reader is used to reading from what English readers regard as "the back of the book to the front," just the opposite of an English reader. However, a Japanese reader is used to reading from top to bottom. Both of these students will have a larger adjustment than a Spanish reader, who reads horizontally from left to right, related to concepts about print when learning to read English. Similarly, both the Arabic and Japanese readers will need to adjust to a new symbol system, whereas the Spanish reader will enjoy a similar symbol system and therefore be able to readily transfer alphabetic concepts, though many of the phonetic and grammatical concepts will differ.

Contrastive analysis related to basic concepts about print can clarify issues in the first day or two of literacy instruction for the older student; however, a young child may take weeks or months to make the adjustment. Directionality (left–right, top–bottom) can be a particularly challenging concept for a young child. Careful and patient instruction is required as young ELLs learn new concepts of print. For example, the teacher could say, "Watch how I hold my book. Now, you do the same. Carefully open your book and place it in front of you so that it looks like this." (The teacher waits for each student to accomplish the task correctly, assisting as needed.) Understanding particularities for each ELL in your classroom will assist you in helping them make adjustments related to concepts of print.

Phonemic Awareness

Mastering phonemic awareness in the early years is critical for later success. *Phonemic awareness* means that the students understand that individual sounds, or phonemes, make up spoken words. There are 44 phonemes in the English language. For example, *bat* has three phonemes (/b/ /a/ /t/), and *shut* also has three phonemes or distinct sounds (/sh/ /u/ /t/). (/Sh/ is a digraph and makes one sound that cannot be divided.) Studies indicate that you can predict children's later reading

Figure 2.8 Phonemic Awareness

Decoding					Comprehension			
Word Recognition Strategies			Fluency		Academic Language		Comprehension Strategies	
Concepts about print	Phonemic awareness	Phonics	Sight words	Auto-maticity	Vocabulary	Syntax -------- Text structure	Compre-hension monitoring	(Re)organizing text
English Language Development								
Background Knowledge								

SOURCE: Adapted from California State Board of Education, 2007.

achievement by examining their first-grade phonemic awareness scores (Yopp, 1992), and that "eighty-eight percent of poor readers in first grade have the probability of being poor readers in fourth grade" (Michigan Department of Education, 2007, n.p.). Similarly, both the National Reading Panel (2000) and the National Literacy Panel (CAL, 2006) found that ELLs benefit from instruction in discriminating and manipulating sounds of the language. Phonemic awareness has a variety of components, and mastery of these lays the foundation for successful study of phonics, the study of sound and its relationship to print (i.e., phoneme–grapheme relationship).

Components of phonemic awareness (PA) include word awareness, rhyme recognition, rhyme production, sound matching, sound matching production, sound isolation, phoneme blending, sound addition or substitution, sound segmentation, and phoneme manipulation. Teachers can assist children in the development of phonemic awareness skills by reading aloud books that promote language play, such as poetry and Dr. Seuss books, as well as playing games that promote phonemic awareness. For example, a teacher or parent might say, "I'm thinking of a mystery word, /p/ /u/ /p/ /ee/. What word is it?" The child verbally blends the phonemes (sounds) to identify the word *puppy*. This type of oral language play helps support skills later needed for phonics in the context of decoding printed text.

Success with phonemic word play demonstrates understanding of the underlying phonemic content of individual words. As the students strengthen phonemic awareness skills in the early years, foundational concepts are built for the mastery of the study of phonics. Once phonics skills are gained, students can more accurately decode words, having a better chance of understanding the words if they are already familiar with the vocabulary and concepts.

For the Standard English speaker, the phonemic awareness exercises described in Figure 2.9 on page 34 can appear simple and straightforward; however, these exercises can be fraught with landmines for the English Language Learner and the Standard English Learner. Challenges for ELLs in the context of phonemic awareness activities include but are not limited to the following:

1. Focusing on Meaning Rather Than Sound: As English Language Learners hear their teachers ask them to repeat words and phrases, they may have had limited exposure to them. Cognitively, the words hold little to no meaning; therefore, ELLs, in their struggle to seek meaning, may be distracted by the actual phonemic awareness task of word play, which often focuses exclusively on manipulating sound, rather than seeking meaning. ELLs can "acquire skills [such as those in Figure 2.9] and are able to pass benchmark tests. Yet, the words lack meaning. They read in a colorless way—disconnected from the joy of a good story—much like one who feasts on excellent food without being able to taste" (Juanita Lee, personal communication, June 2008). Bridge the gap by first directing the student to simply play with sound, virtually ignoring meaning, while manipulating the sounds of the language. Second, scaffold phonemic awareness exercises by systematically modeling sounds and utilizing the posted alphabet to reinforce phonemes as needed to establish the phoneme–grapheme relationship (i.e., the sound–symbol relationship).

2. Lack of Exposure to Some English Sound(s): The brain assigns clusters of neurons to each phoneme or sound of a child's first language. The languages a child hears in his environment during his infancy and early years form a foundation for language acquisition. If a child has not heard certain English phonemes in his early years (because these phonemes were not common to his first language), he may be challenged to hear and repeat those phonemes correctly in later years in the context of learning English. Bridge the gap with the *My Fair Lady* technique. (Remember the scene in this classic movie where the professor attempts to help Eliza pronounce words correctly by playing words s-l-o-w-l-y on an old phonograph?) Provide foundational phonemic awareness exercises by s-t-r-e-t-ch-i-n-g out each word, emphasizing each phoneme separately. Promote practice with words that have unfamiliar phonemes for your English Language Learners, or phonemes that traditionally are dropped. For example, many speakers of Cantonese and Mandarin often leave off the ending /s/ phoneme in English, indicating the plural, because they are not used to providing a suffix to indicate the plural in their home language. Another example is that the final /d/ and /t/ phonemes are often left off in English by speakers of many languages, such as Thai or Spanish. Recognizing the linguistic commonalities and differences between your students' first language(s) and Standard English assists you in focusing in and adapting pronunciation and phonemic awareness exercises.

3. Pronunciation Issues: Some ELLs may struggle with pronunciation in English. Pronunciation issues are foundational to oral language and should precede and accompany phonemic awareness exercises. These pronunciation exercises should not take over the literacy process but should gently and subtly infuse the literacy process at all levels as needed.

The following Phonemic Awareness Chart (Figure 2.9) has been adapted to consider the specialized needs of English Language Learners. A careful study of Figure 2.9 will help the reader understand some of the special needs of ELLs in the context of phonemic awareness acquisition.

Phonics

Mastering phonemic awareness and then moving to decoding skills in the context of phonics study is the foundation of being able to decode English (see Figure 2.10 on page 37). Keep in mind, however, that ELLs and SELs can strengthen their phonemic awareness skills in the context of phonics study as well, so do not wait for mastery of PA before moving to phonics—you can introduce many of the concepts simultaneously. Interestingly, many African American Vernacular English (AAVE) SELs will demonstrate a particular strength in rhyme, which lends itself well to

Figure 2.9 Phonemic Awareness Elements Adapted for English Learners

Components of Phonemic Awareness	What the Student Can Do	English Language Learner Considerations
Sound Awareness	The student can hear, identify, and distinguish the 44 sounds of the English language. Teacher: B says /b/. Raise your hand each time you hear /b/. /b/, /v/, /b/, /b/, /s/, /v/, /b/. Student: Raises his hand four times, each time as he hears /b/.	Foundational for ELLs. Provide exercises to ensure familiarity regardless of grade level if in pre-literate stage. (Screen auditory processing problems and physical hearing loss with specialist if student does not rapidly demonstrate this skill.)
Sound Production	The student can accurately produce the 44 sounds of the English language. Teacher: A says /a/. Repeat. Student: /a/. Teacher: B says /b/. Repeat. Student: /b/.	Foundational for ELLs. Provide exercises to ensure familiarity regardless of grade level if in pre-literate stage.
Word Awareness	The student can identify the number of words in a sentence. Q: How many words in this sentence—"I see a puppy." A: Four.	Comprehension of the meaning of the sentence required before an ELL student can identify the number of words in an oral sentence. Keep vocabulary simple, in present tense, and within the oral comprehension level of your ELL students. For example, "I see two girls," rather than "I saw two teenagers."
Rhyme Recognition	The student recognizes two words that rhyme. Q: Do *sat* and *rat* rhyme? A: Yes. Q: Do *sat* and *sit* rhyme? A. No.	Comprehension of meaning of rhyme required. Provide daily modeling and guided practice. Be wary of overusing predictable text (rhyming words) to the detriment of ELLs attending to word features, especially at the early stages of word recognition.
Rhyme Production	The student, when given a word (e.g., *bat*), can produce other words (e.g., *cat*) that rhyme. Q: What rhymes with *bat*? A: *Rat, sat, mat.*	Comprehension of meaning of rhyme required for ELLs and knowledge, bank of English sounds and words must be in long-term memory. Scaffold by using alphabet strip to reference sounds. Utilize Word Walls for word families. Color code rhyming words in poetry.
Sound Matching	The student can identify which words, from a group of words, begin with the same sound. Q: Which words start with the same sound? *sit, sip, pass* A: *Sit* and *sip.*	ELL student must comprehend directions. Provide demonstration and guided practice until student comprehends directions.

Components of Phonemic Awareness	What the Student Can Do	English Language Learner Considerations
Sound Matching Production	The student can produce another word with the same initial sound. Q: Tell me another word that starts with the same sound as tickle. A: *Pickle.* Q: Try again. Pickle rhymes with tickle, but I want you to tell me a word that starts with *t-t-tickle.* A: Okay. T-t-time.	Bank of English words required in long-term memory in order to be successful. Depending on needs, consider providing several oral examples and inviting the ELL student to identify correct answers in an oral, multiple-choice format. Utilize Word Walls and time for "Read-the-Room" activity.
Sound Isolation	The student can identify which sound is heard at the beginning, middle, or end of a word. Q: What sound do you hear at the beginning of *chip*? A: /ch/. Q: What do you hear in the middle of *chip*? A: /i/. Q: What do you hear at the end of *chip*? A: /p/.	The ELL student must be able to comprehend and apply the meaning of the terms beginning, middle, and end. In daily routines, teach these concepts (e.g., ordinal words, "Who is at the beginning of our line? The middle of our line? The end of our line?"). Provide modeling and guided practice as needed.
Phoneme Blending	The student can blend isolated sounds into words. Q: What is the secret word? /ch/ /a/ /t/ A: Chat.	Scaffold meaning by using the target word in a sentence after the child blends a word. For example, "/ch/ /a/ /t/. Chat. To chat is to talk. The boy and his friend had a chat."
Sound Deletion, Addition, or Substitution	The student can add or substitute one sound for another in words, songs, and rhymes. Teacher: *Sam.* If I take away /s/ and make the beginning sound /r/, what is my new word? Student: Ram. Phoneme substitution is exemplified in this oral game played between teacher and student. Notice how the student selects a rhyming word with a different onset (starting sound) for each substituted word. Teacher: Teacher sees a *pickle.* Johnny: Johnny sees a *nickel.* Teacher: Teacher sees a piece of *corn.* Johnny: Johnny sees a shiny *horn.* Teacher: Teacher sees two blue *stars.* Johnny: Johnny sees four red *cars.*	The ELL student requires a bank of English words in long-term memory. Allow for nonsense words so that the teacher assesses the phonemic awareness task and not comprehension.

(Continued)

(Continued)

Components of Phonemic Awareness	What the Student Can Do	English Language Learner Considerations
Sound Segmentation	The student can isolate sounds in a spoken word. Q: What sounds are in *bat*? A: /b/ /a/ /t/.	Utilize the same strategies for native English speakers, ELLs, and SELs.
Phoneme Manipulation	The student can change the order of phonemes or manipulate sounds within or between words. Q: Can you place an /h/ at the beginning of every word in this series of words? *Mary, Mary, Mark, Mark* A: Harry, Harry, Hark! Hark! Q: Can you place an /h/ at the beginning of every word in this series of words? *Trudy, Trudy, Jim, Jim* A: Hoody, Hoody, Him, Him.	Extremely complex task for a non-English speaker. Limit exercises in this area. When introducing this task, ensure that the ELL truly understands the task. Ask for phoneme manipulation on one word at a time and then build up to multiple words or phrases.

SOURCE: Hetzel, 1996.

the mastery of phonics. However, the challenge of varied pronunciations (e.g., /aks/ versus /ask/ for *ask*) for AAVE SELs causes difficulties if not explicitly taught through contrastive analysis of standard English and AAVE pronunciation. In addition, some ELLs demonstrate patterns in grammar (e.g., leaving off plurals) that also require explicit contrastive analysis. The systematic study of phonics involves the study of phoneme–grapheme (sound–letter) relationships, including individual letters (consonants and vowels), blends (e.g., *mp* in *lamp, pl* in *plight, sn* in *snail*), digraphs (e.g., *ch, sh, th, wh, ph, tch*), diphthongs (e.g., *oy, oi, au, aw*), phonograms, plurals, verb endings, compound words, contractions, syllabication, schwas (e.g., *the*), plural and singular possessives, affixes (prefixes and suffixes), word derivations, and so forth. The systematic study of phonics is especially important for ELLs because of the multiple spellings of English phonemes, particularly vowel sounds, which is different from some ELLs' first languages (e.g., Spanish and Polish are phonetic). For example, the long sound of "o" in English can be spelled in a variety of ways (e.g., *boat, vote, bow, though*). Mastering phonics requires systematic, daily study in the early years of English acquisition. Constant drill games, whiteboard activities, and so forth are imperative. Varied, hands-on strategies for reinforcement, such as the use of letter cards, alphabet blocks, magnetic letters, and illustrations, are helpful reinforcements.

When practicing phonics skills with ELLs, it is important not to overuse or emphasize phonetically consistent sentences that are contrived—for

Figure 2.10 Phonics

Decoding					Comprehension			
Word Recognition Strategies			Fluency		Academic Language		Comprehension Strategies	
Concepts about print	Phonemic awareness	Phonics	Sight words	Auto-maticity	Vocabulary	Syntax -------- Text structure	Compre-hension monitoring	(Re)organizing text
English Language Development								
Background Knowledge								

SOURCE: Adapted from California State Board of Education, 2007.

example, the sentence, "The cat sat at the mat." Some phonics programs introduce such sentences and phrases in order to maintain and reinforce phonetic consistency and controlled vocabulary. Such language, however, can be confusing for an ELL who may not be able to make a distinction between the phonetic processes and the manner in which one speaks.

Explicit bridge-building strategies for non-English speakers and non-Standard English speakers can be quite effective, including contrastive analysis in the examination of pronunciation (focus on phonemes) and the study of symbol systems (focus on graphemes); tutorial support through teaching assistants, parent volunteers, and peers; and books on tape, bilingual books, and translation assignments (Figure 2.11).

Contrastive analysis, a method by which linguistic differences, such as pronunciation and symbol systems, can be highlighted between two target languages, is one way in which phonetic differences can be explicitly taught. For example, in pronunciation, Spanish-speaking ELLs often invert the phoneme /b/ for /v/ as in the words *berry* and *very.* When such inversions are made, ask students to repeat the phonemes /b/ and /v/ and ask them to analyze where in the mouth the words are formed. It can then be explained that the phoneme /b/ is a *bilabial* sound, which is formed when the front of one's lips touch. In contrast, the phoneme /v/ is a *labial-dental* sound, which is formed with one's two front teeth touching the front of the bottom lip. Teachers can have the students use a mirror so as to view the formation of such sounds if they cannot feel them. In addition, this kind of pronunciation work should be done sensitively and works best either one-on-one or in small homogenous groups according to student needs. Excessive attention should not be given to students who struggle with sound formation.

Symbol systems vary greatly. Students with backgrounds that include Mandarin and Cantonese are used to character-based rather than phonetic languages, whereas Arabic and Spanish speakers are accustomed to their languages being represented phonetically. Bridge-building strategies for these non-native English speakers involve explicitly pointing out these differences

Figure 2.11 Phonics Bridge-Building Strategies

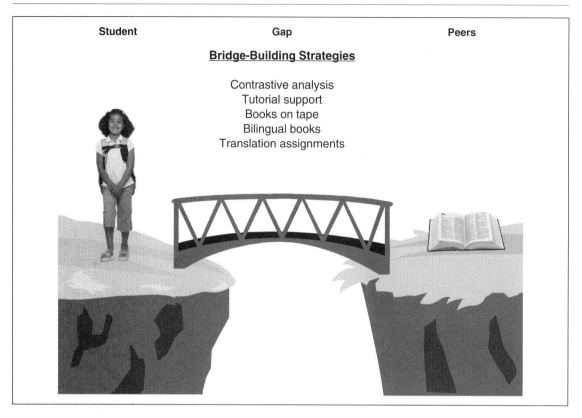

and providing *tutorials* and scaffolding strategies to help fill in the gaps. Utilizing *teaching assistants* and *parent volunteers* who are fluent in the students' native languages can be particularly effective. In addition, you can ask the ELLs themselves to compare their L1 and L2 languages. For example, one Laotian student in a fourth-grade class particularly enjoyed creating a chart that illustrated his L1 alphabet. He proudly shared this chart with his classmates and pointed out differences between his L1 and English, his L2. Classmates were intently interested and asked myriad questions. We also find that ELLs enjoy sharing words and phrases from their L1 in daily conversation. The teacher's interest in students' L1 affirms the value of their primary language as well as providing ELLs a unique fund of knowledge to share with teachers and classmates.

A powerful bridge-building strategy for all learners is to utilize English-only *books on tape* with photographs and illustrations as well as printed *bilingual books* that show both languages. ELLs can use these resources to hear differences in pronunciation and see differences in symbol systems.

For students who are in a bilingual instructional program, bilingual books can be an effective bridge-building strategy. After reading a bilingual text, students can write an assignment in their native language first and then translate the assignment into English. This works well for students who have a strong L1 literacy education. A variation is to have students write a piece in their L1 while inserting English words and phrases along the way (in text, above text, or below text) as needed. The teacher or tutor would then follow up and work with the student to bring clarity to some of the word retrieval challenges. June Hetzel, author, found the *translation assignment* strategy particularly powerful with her Portuguese-speaking and Laotian students who had strong literacy training in their L1. *Peer assistance* and *cross-age tutoring* for Hetzel's Spanish-speaking students in California and Arabic-speaking and French-speaking students in Africa was another powerful bridge-building strategy, particularly for groups of children who have strong social and family networks and enjoy collaborative learning.

Fluency

As ELLs gain decoding skills through the development of their phonics understanding, and as comprehension increases, reading becomes a natural process and students begin to read with expression (prosidy) and appropriate speed (automaticity), thereby increasing fluency. Reading regularly at a comfortable level (an appropriate student-text match) sharply increases students' reading fluency (Anderson, Hiebert, Scott, & Wilkinson, 1985; Armbruster, Lehr, & Osborn, 2001; Perfetti, 1985), automaticity (Anderson et al., 1985; Perfetti, 1985), and enjoyment of the reading process (Anderson et al., 1985; Perfetti, 1985; Wutz & Wedwick, 2005). *Reading fluency* not only involves a reader's fluidity with text but also her understanding of *prosidy,* or her ability to read with appropriate expression and intonation. Plays, short skits, and Reader's Theater are fun bridge-building activities to promote prosidy and fluency. Children particularly enjoy reading and rereading aloud with expression, especially when performing for their classmates. For example, one of the authors, Hetzel, when teaching in Southern California, would often use short Reader's Theater scripts or would have children write scripts for short

Figure 2.12   Fluency

Decoding					Comprehension			
Word Recognition Strategies			Fluency		Academic Language		Comprehension Strategies	
Concepts about print	Phonemic awareness	Phonics	Sight words	Auto-maticity	Vocabulary	Syntax -------- Text structure	Compre-hension monitoring	(Re)organizing text
English Language Development								
Background Knowledge								

SOURCE: Adapted from California State Board of Education, 2007.

chapter books read. These skits and plays were then repeatedly practiced with great exuberance and performed for other classes in their elementary school. Soto-Hinman, author, would do the same at the secondary level with her Spanish-speaking students, utilizing more complex scripts and novels. Flashcards can also assist with instant word recognition and time spent in independent reading is invaluable practice for reading fluency (Reis, Eckert, McCoach, Jacobs, & Coyne, 2008).

Sight Words

While teaching students mastery of decoding skills through their acquisition of phonics skills, it is also critical to assist students in mastering a basic list of high-frequency or sight words. (See Figure 2.13.) Mastery of these words (e.g., Dolch Words, Fry Words) provides the ELL, SEL, or

Figure 2.13   Sight Words Bridge-Building Strategies

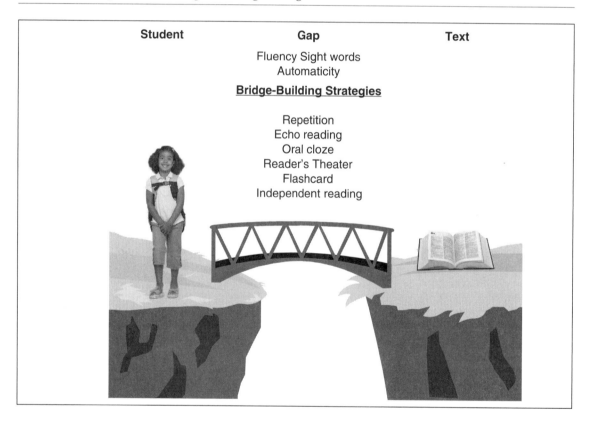

any student with a powerful base of automatically recognized words. For example, Edward Fry (2001) has a 1,000 Instant Word List:

- The 100 most common words make up 50% of all written material.
- The 300 most common Instant Words make up 65% of all written material.
- The 1,000 most common Instant Words make up 90% of all written material. (p. 4)

Figure 2.14 Sight Words

Decoding					Comprehension			
Word Recognition Strategies				Fluency	Academic Language		Comprehension Strategies	
Concepts about print	Phonemic awareness	Phonics	Sight words	Auto-maticity	Vocabulary	Syntax --------- Text structure	Compre-hension monitoring	(Re)organizing text
English Language Development								
Background Knowledge								

SOURCE: Adapted from California State Board of Education, 2007.

Stated simply, if a student has mastered the first 100 sight words on Fry's Instant Word List, he would know half the words in the morning newspaper, his basal reader, or the novel he picks up after school. Fry (2001) calls the instant words "glue words" (p. 5). Because sight words are often "function words" such as *the, when,* and *would,* it can be particularly difficult for the ELL to visualize them (Fry, 2001). Therefore, Fry recommends ELLs also study Picture Nouns, which is a list of 100 easily visualized nouns that provide the ELL with a good starting point in instant vocabulary recognition.

Hetzel remembers working with a seventh grader who had decoding skills at about the third-grade level. Though Miguel had mastered phonics skills, he had never memorized sight words that often have inconsistent grapheme–phoneme relationships. After just a few months of exercises that embedded *repetition* (e.g., flashcards), his reading fluency took a tremendous leap and comprehension followed. Some of the exercises used to reinforce automatic recognition of sight words included echo reading, oral cloze, Reader's Theater, and flashcards. However, the critical focus of Miguel's tutorial was mastery of sight words.

Echo reading is a highly scaffolded activity where the teacher and student read orally in unison with the teacher just ahead of the student. As the student "echoes along," he or she begins to feel what fluent reading is like, and sight words as well as phonetically consistent words are reinforced throughout the exercise. The student also hears and feels the teacher's prosidy, or voice expression, during the reading. The student can then begin imitating the teacher's oral language modeling. For an ELL, this provides immediate language assistance with fluency, automaticity, and pronunciation, which are skills that may be commonly difficult for this group of students.

Oral cloze is another highly scaffolded activity, one in which the teacher reads aloud and the student follows along. When the teacher pauses, the student orally fills in the missing word. The teacher purposely pauses at words with which the student is already familiar. In this quick-moving process, the student "experiences" fluency and continues to have opportunity for multiple exposures of sight words in context as well as opportunity to hear voice expression. This process strengthens an ELL's intonation and automaticity of words. It also assists the teacher in determining to what extent a student is comprehending text.

Reader's Theater is a fun exercise, enjoyed by most students, that involves a script and multiple opportunities to read passages individually or in unison with classmates. In the ELL context, it is highly recommended that unison reading be the primary exercise in the Reader's Theater to provide multiple read-aloud opportunities in context and with the support of classmates. Reader's Theater, with its wonderfully embedded repetition, is an excellent place for ELLs to experience and develop fluency and prosidy.

Without the glitz of Reader's Theater, *flashcards,* at first glance, may appear to be an archaic and boring way to reinforce sight words for your ELL students. However, they are effective in that the flashcards themselves narrow down the scope of the practice to just the words that need to be reinforced. In addition, students can practice flashcards independently, with a partner, or in the context of taped exercises that reinforce correct pronunciation. Students enjoy quizzing each other, can keep track of progress, and can utilize the flashcards in the context of board games. Providing flashcards with illustrations and photos is also a powerful way to reinforce vocabulary.

ELLs need to clearly understand the meaning of the sight words as they study them. Presenting sight words in context helps provide a visual and auditory imprint for the ELL student. For example, ELLs often struggle with prepositions, and prepositions show up on the frequency word lists. Ask each student to pick up his or her pencil. Provide the following instructions orally while demonstrating the actions and have students follow in kind:

"Put your pencil *on* your desk." (Teacher models by placing a pencil on top of her desk.)

"Put your pencil *under* your desk." (Teacher puts her pencil under her desk and allows students to do the same.)

"Put your pencil *on* the book." (Teacher places her pencil on a book, and students do the same.)

"Put your pencil *under* the book." (Teacher places the pencil under a book.)

"Put your pencil *in* your desk."

"Put your book *in* your desk."

As students master a given set of sight words, continue to work with flashcards to increase automaticity.

Anchor sentences with visuals also help imbed the meaning of the sight words in the student's mind. For example, when studying visually similar sight words, such as *through, thorough,* and *threw,* use anchor sentences:

"He walked *through* the entrance."

"She did a *thorough* job on her report."

"She *threw* the baseball."

Students can then illustrate their own anchor sentences for reference, or add to their personalized picture dictionary. Teachers can also post illustrated anchor sentences on their bulletin boards and walls.

Educator and publisher Carolea Williams (2008) offers excellent teacher resources to assist ELLs with what she calls "Sight Word Sentence Frames" (www.teachbright.com/activity.html). Students build sentence frames using sight words and then fill in the frames with vocabulary words that are supported by photos, to work on fluency, vocabulary, and comprehension all at once (see Figure 2.15). Students have to use active

Figure 2.15 Teach Bright Sight Word Sentence Frames Level 1

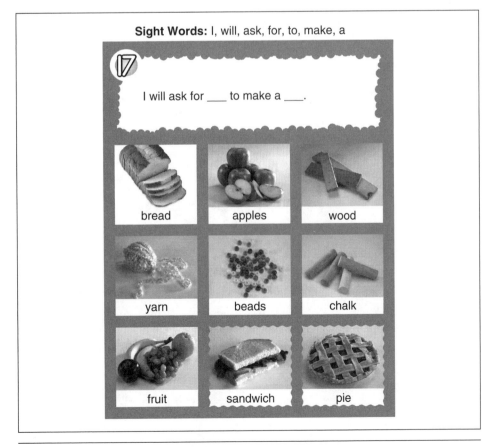

SOURCE: © 2008 Teach Bright. www.teachbright.com. Used with Permission.

comprehension strategies, utilizing sight words in context, to fill the sentence in so that it makes sense. For example, in the worksheet, students use several sight words (e.g., *I, will, for, to, make, a*) to form the sentence frame: I will ask for _____ to make a _____. Then, students select from the word bank of photographed vocabulary words such as *apples* and *pie* to create the sentence, "I will ask for *apples* to make a *pie.*" Students then create additional sentences (e.g., I will ask for *bread* to make a *sandwich*), which provides additional and simultaneous practice with both sight words and vocabulary words. Conceptual and contextual practice around which students can master sight vocabulary provides stimulating and memorable visual reinforcement for long-term retention.

Mastery of sight words can be a critical building block in the ELL's fluency development, and repetition is critical. The average ELL needs 10–15 repetitions to place a particular sight word into long-term memory (Francis, Rivera, Lesaux, Kieffer, & Rivera, 2006).

Important to note is the fact that "fluency is a critical component of skilled reading" (Reis et al., 2008, p. 305). The more time students spend reading independently, the greater the increase in their fluency (p. 301). Therefore, book access is critical for the ELLs and SELs, particularly those from lower socioeconomic backgrounds. As the teacher, ensure that the students and parents have ready access to the free libraries in your community. In addition, assist ELLs and SELs in independently identifying books of interest to them that are at their appropriate reading level so as to make book access a regular part of their lives.

Automaticity

Automaticity refers to the efficient, automatic processing of printed text or the ability to rapidly decode in meaningful chunks. For example, a slow reader will often stop or fixate on every letter, syllable, or word as he reads,

Figure 2.16   Automaticity

Decoding					Comprehension			
Word Recognition Strategies			**Fluency**		**Academic Language**		**Comprehension Strategies**	
Concepts about print	Phonemic awareness	Phonics	Sight words	Auto-maticity	Vocabulary	Syntax -------- Text structure	Compre-hension monitoring	(Re)organizing text
English Language Development								
Background Knowledge								

SOURCE: Adapted from California State Board of Education, 2007.

whereas an average reader may see and comprehend a couple of words at a time. However, a good reader may look at meaningful word groupings in an efficient way, refraining from reading individual words (Wassman & Rinsky, 1993). Note Wassman and Rinsky's visual examples in Figure 2.17, related to readers' eye fixations. Read these examples aloud, allowing the dots to represent conscious eye stops and voice pauses. Notice the change in automaticity as you move from word-by-word reading, to short phrase-by-phrase reading, to long phrase-by-phrase reading. With increased automaticity of decoding skills, the student moves from letter-by-letter and word-by-word reading to reading groups of words. As the student reads phrases, rather than small sound bites, he or she focuses increasingly on meaning and less on the mechanical skills of decoding.

As can be seen from Wassman and Rinsky's (1993) example, when an individual is reading at his or her *independent level* and reading efficiently, the automaticity of the mechanical process takes a backseat and reading for meaning can take a front seat. If an ELL eighth-grade native Spanish speaker has an independent reading level in his or her home language at the sixth-grade level, that means the student can read Spanish materials at ease at the sixth, fifth, fourth, third, second, first, and primer grade levels. Voracious reading of materials at the independent reading level exercises the brain; expands language capacity; and builds grammar, schema, vocabulary, background knowledge, and enjoyment of the reading process as the student reads materials of interest to him. However, the same eighth-grade ELL student who had an independent reading level of Grade 6 in Spanish may only be able to independently read second-grade materials in English. Therefore, this student will need to have a plethora of materials of interest to him, and time to read these materials at the independent reading level in English, in order to "master" the independent reading level with Grade 2 English materials, thereby setting the stage to move rapidly up the hierarchy, reading with automaticity. Luckily for this particular student, he already has strong reading skills in Spanish. Reading skills will readily transfer from the L1 to the L2. As he quickly builds his fluency in English reading, he can readily transfer familiar concepts from Spanish to English. Figure 2.18 on page 47 shows this eighth grader's reading levels as he entered an English-speaking school.

It is essential that ELLs have a plethora of reading materials available at their independent reading level in both their L1 (if in a bilingual program) and L2 in order to support fluency and automaticity in both languages. Decades of past research have suggested that independent, silent reading in school is associated with gains in reading achievement and vocabulary growth (Anderson et al., 1985). In one study, sustained silent reading (SSR) with student agency and including peer interaction groups led to higher reading achievement than additional time spent in basal reading programs or SSR combined with individual teacher–student interaction (Reis et al., 2008). The relationship between independent reading and fluency development has been established for decades (California State Department of Education, 2007; Cunningham & Stanovich, 1998;

Figure 2.17 Slow, Average, and Good Readers' Visual Word Groupings

SLOW READER:

A   very   slow   reader   who   often   also   has

poor   compre   hension   fixates   or   stops   at

every   single   word   and   even   divides   words

into   syllables   if   the   words   seem   too   long.

AVERAGE READER:

The average   reader   on the   other hand   tries to

see a   few words   each time   her eyes   stop   but does

so   in a helter-   skelter   way   and does   not get

much better   comprehension   than the   slow reader.

The average   reader stops   at   every few   words and

tries to   get meaning   from   them.

GOOD READER:

The efficient reader   usually fixates   in the middle

of a group of words   and reads thought units

during each fixation.   The better reader   does not read

single words.   She does not look   at the printed material

in a helter-skelter way.   She has trained her eyes

to perceive ideas   in meaningful chunks or groups.

SOURCE: From Wassman, R., & Rinsky, L., 1993. *Effective reading in a changing world.* New York: Prentice Hall. Reprinted by permission of Pearson Education, Inc.

Figure 2.18   Reading Levels of Eighth Grader (L1 Spanish, seventh-grade instructional level; L2 English, third-grade instructional level)

Grade Level	Spanish Reading Level (L1)	Grade Level	English Reading Level (L2)
12		12	
11		11	
10		10	
9		9	
8	**Frustrational** *(beyond student's current reach)*	8	
7	**Instructional** *(window of ideal instruction)*	7	
6	**Independent** *(recreational reading that supports fluency and automaticity)*	6	
5		5	
4		4	**Frustrational** *(beyond student's current reach)*
3		3	**Instructional** *(window of ideal instruction)*
2		2	**Independent** *(recreational reading that supports fluency and automaticity)*
1		1	
Primer		Primer	
Pre-primer		Pre-primer	

Krashen, 1996) and is an important link to vocabulary development (Biancarosa & Snow, 2004); however, teachers must not forget the importance of holding students accountable for independent reading. Both in elementary and secondary classrooms, students must be required to do something with their independent reading texts, whether that be keeping a log or designing a project from the text. Many schools have begun to use programs such as Accelerated Reader (AR), which matches students with appropriate independent reading texts, and then tests their comprehension of that text via computerized tests. Even when using technology such as AR, it is important for teachers to check in on comprehension and monitor reading before assessments are given. For example, teachers can ask students to orally retell the story's beginning, middle, and end, or ask students to complete a short book report. Such authentic assessments can ensure that students read the text with the amount of attention needed to comprehend. These authentic assessments also hold students accountable for something beyond a formal assessment measure that might only ask multiple-choice questions or provide "fill in the blank" responses.

Sadly, the average student is not readily developing fluency through independent reading, as the average student does not spend much of his or her free time reading. The average amount of time a primary child in school reads independently over the course of a school day is 7 or 8 minutes and for middle grades is about 15 minutes (Anderson et al., 1985), though studies vary. In addition, the amount of time children read during their free time at home has been shown to be a predictor of reading success; unfortunately, children may read only 4 minutes at home, yet have time to view an average of 130 minutes or more of television (Anderson et al., 1985). It is essential that ELLs and SELs have ample time to practice reading and to develop their fluency. Because they most often are acquiring English many years after their peers, it is urgent to spend sufficient time on task to solidify literacy skills and to close the literacy gaps.

ENGLISH LANGUAGE DEVELOPMENT

English Language Development (ELD) must be infused in every moment of the school day in order for ELLs to progress appropriately in literacy. However, be wary of only relegating 30 minutes of the day to isolated ELD exercises. Instead, acquire the mind-set that every moment of the day is an opportunity to immerse ELLs in an English language environment and mine every opportunity for English language mastery, providing ELLs and SELs the chance to build their receptive and expressive language ability. Vygotsky (1962) suggested that "children's language development is determined by shared meanings of the adult language that the child internalizes. From the beginning of a child's life, knowledge is socially influenced and constructed" (p. 301, quoted in Reis et al., 2008), a solid

Figure 2.19   English Language Development

Decoding					Comprehension			
Word Recognition Strategies			**Fluency**		**Academic Language**		**Comprehension Strategies**	
Concepts about print	Phonemic awareness	Phonics	Sight words	Auto-maticity	Vocabulary	Syntax -------- Text structure	Compre-hension monitoring	(Re)organizing text
English Language Development								
Background Knowledge								

SOURCE: Adapted from California State Board of Education, 2007.

argument for taking every opportunity to model Academic English language, inviting both ELLs and SELs to practice English in context-embedded conversations and academic study, thereby readily expanding their receptive and expressive language.

Receptive language involves listening and reading, whereas expressive language involves speaking and writing (see Figure 2.20). Effective literacy teachers move students in and out of receptive and expressive language opportunities throughout the day, and even in a given period, so as to maintain a high level of language engagement. Unfortunately, Kinsella (2006, citing August, 2004) indicates that "only 4% of an EL's day is spent engaging in L2 informal 'student talk'" and "only 2% of an English Learner's day is spent in engaging in L2 'academic talk.'" Kinsella contends that academic talk needs to be "routinely instructed and structured across the

Figure 2.20   Receptive and Expressive Language Processes

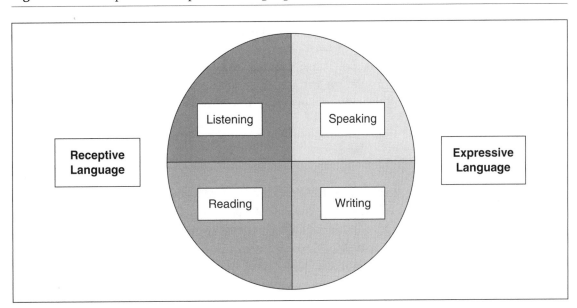

subject areas to ensure 'communicative competence' in English." Kinsella also believes that all students are Academic English as a Second Language Learners (AESLs) and observes that "[A]cademic English is not a natural language. . . . It must be explicitly taught, not merely caught." More about academic language will be addressed throughout the book.

BACKGROUND KNOWLEDGE

Background knowledge is of such significance to the English Language Learner and the Standard English Learner that Chapter 3 will be devoted to this topic. While ELLs and SELs can often mimic the progress of the native English speaker in acquiring the decoding branch of reading in the

Figure 2.21   Background Knowledge

Decoding					Comprehension			
Word Recognition Strategies				Fluency	Academic Language		Comprehension Strategies	
Concepts about print	Phonemic awareness	Phonics	Sight words	Auto-maticity	Vocabulary	Syntax -------- Text structure	Compre-hension monitoring	(Re)organizing text
English Language Development								
Background Knowledge								

SOURCE: Adapted from California State Board of Education, 2007.

primary grades, struggles often emerge around third grade as students begin to receive accelerated instruction in academic language. Academic language requires deep comprehension processing and culturally relevant background knowledge and experience to enable the ELL or SEL to maintain grade-appropriate progression in literacy skills.

SUMMARY

Keith Stanovich's (1986) Matthew Effects Model of students stepping up into success or stepping down into failure is a key model for visualizing literacy progress for all K–12, monolingual or bilingual, ELL or SEL students, and provides a strong visual model for summarizing this chapter. When a student has a clear understanding of phonemic awareness, he readily acquires good phonics skills (Yopp, 1992). With good phonics skills, he readily unlocks words and decodes, assuming no disability. Once he can decode, if he has heard the words he comes across in a book, has the words in his receptive language, and has the *schema* (background knowledge) for the text, he has a good chance of comprehending the text before him. When he comprehends text, he has the chance to enjoy reading. If he enjoys reading, he will likely read more. The more he reads, the better a reader he becomes (see Figure 2.22).

Unfortunately, the opposite is also true. An ELL or SEL student who struggles with phonemic awareness also struggles with phonics. If she struggles with phonics, she cannot readily decode words. If she cannot readily decode words, she does not know what the words say and, therefore, cannot comprehend text, as taxing mental energy is focused on decoding, rather than meaning. If she cannot comprehend text, she will not enjoy reading. If she does not enjoy reading, she reads less. If she reads less, she does not progress at the rate of her same-age counterparts. Hence, the "Matthew Effects Model" in Figure 2.22 illustrates students stepping up into success or

Figure 2.22 Keith Stanovich's Matthew Effects Model (adapted)

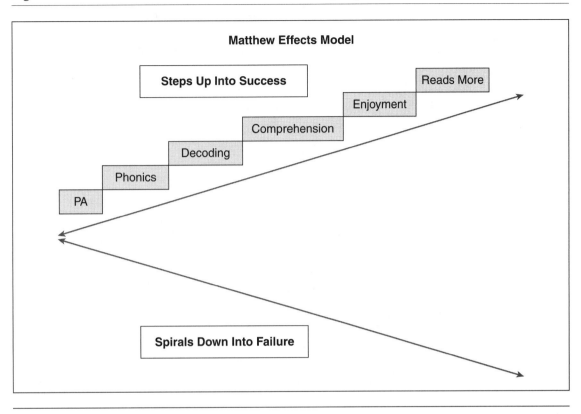

SOURCE: Adapted from Stanovich, 1986.

NOTE: PA = Phonemic Awareness

stepping down into failure. The population of English Language Learners is growing (NCELA, 2006, 2008; U.S. Census Bureau, 2004, 2006, 2008), and SELs historically continue to struggle with their achievement in school (Hollie, 2001a, 2001b). Emerging evidence indicates we have a crisis. It is the classroom teacher's responsibility to support ELLs and SELs, removing barriers and building bridges to ensure universal literacy access.

Claude Goldenberg (2006), author of *Successful School Change: Creating Settings to Improve Teaching and Learning* (2004) and member of the National Literacy Panel, writes,

> Phonological skills, including phonological awareness and decoding, are foundational. With good, structured, explicit teaching, English-language learners can make progress comparable to that of other students in the early stages of learning to read. Their language limitations begin to slow their progress as vocabulary and content knowledge become increasingly important, around third grade. It is thus critical that, from the very beginning, teachers work to develop these students' English-language skills, particularly vocabulary. . . . There can be little doubt that explicit attention to vocabulary development—everyday words as well as more specialized academic words—should be part of English-learners' school programs. (p. 23)

Therefore, even in the midst of focusing lessons on the decoding branch of reading, it is imperative that the instructor remember that it is *reading for meaning* all the way.

Now, with the foundation of decoding established, we will turn our attention to the importance of background knowledge and experience as a rich foundation on which an ELL or SEL teacher may base his or her instruction, as it is this background knowledge and experience from which ELLs and SELs create meaning from text.

REFERENCES

Anderson, R. C., Hiebert, E. H., Scott, J. A., & Wilkinson, I. A. G. (1985). *Becoming a nation of readers.* Washington, DC: U.S. Department of Education.

Armbruster, B. B., Lehr, F., & Osborn, J. (2001, September). *Put reading first: The research building blocks for teaching children to read.* Jessup, MD: National Institute for Literacy.

Biancarosa, G., & Snow, C. E. (2004). *Reading next: A vision for action and research in middle and high school literacy: A report to Carnegie Corporation of New York.* Washington, DC: Alliance for Education.

California State Department of Education. (2007). *Reading language arts framework: Kindergarten through Grade Twelve.* Sacramento, CA: Author.

Center for Applied Linguistics. (2006). *Project archive: National Literacy Panel on Language Minority Children and Youth.* Retrieved March 25, 2009, from http://www.cal.org.

Cole, R. (Ed.). (1998). *Educating everybody's children.* Alexandria, VA: Association for Supervision and Curriculum Development.

Cunningham, A. E., & Stanovich, K. E. (1998). What reading does for the mind. *American Educator, 22*(1 & 2), 8–15.

Francis, D. J., Rivera, M., Lesaux, N., Kieffer, M., & Rivera, H. (2006). *Practical guidelines for the education of English Language Learners: Research-based recommendations for instruction and academic interventions.* Portsmouth, NH: RMC Research Corporation, Center on Instruction.

Fry, E. (2001, Fall). What's so good about a word list? *Wisconsin English Journal, 43*(2), 4–8.

Goldenberg, C. (2004). *Successful school change: Creating settings to improve teaching and learning.* New York: Teacher's College Press.

Goldenberg, C. (2006, July 26). Improving achievement for English-Learners: What the research tells us. *Education Week, 25*(43), 34–36.

Guitiérrez, R. (2000). Advancing African-American, urban youth in mathematics: Unpacking success of one math department. *American Journal of Education, 109,* 63–111.

Hetzel, J. (1996). *Fingertip assessments.* Presentation to the Community Home Education Program teachers, Orange County Department of Education, Costa Mesa, CA.

Hollie, S. (2001a, September 22). Acknowledgement, affirmation, and accommodation: The non-standard language approach. *Language Teaching & Learning. Academic Exchange Quarterly,* 1096–1453. Retrieved September 22, 2008, from http://www.thefreelibrary.com/_/print/PrintArticle.aspx?id=80679270.

Hollie, S. (2001b, March). Acknowledging the language of African American students: Instructional strategies. *English Journal, 90*(4), 54–59. Retrieved September 22, 2008, from http://www.jstor.org/stable/821903?seq=1.

Ivey, G., & Broaddus, K. (2001). Just plain reading: A survey of what makes students want to read in middle school classrooms. *Reading Research Quarterly, 36*(4), 350–377.

Kinsella, K. (2006, July 26). *Rigorous and accountable academic discussion with the rBook*. Workshop at the Read 180 National Summer Institute, San Francisco. Retrieved September 19, 2008, from http://teacher.scholastic.com/products/read180/pdfs/Kinsella_NSI_07_rBooks.pdf.

Klemp, R. (2002). Peer-to-peer accountability through cooperative literacy. *IN Focus, 31,* 20–28.

Klemp, R., Hon, J., & Shorr, A. (1992). Cooperative literacy for the middle school: A learning strategy–based approach. *Middle School Journal, 42*(19), 26.

Krashen, S. (1996). *Every person a reader: An alternative to the California Task Force on Reading.* Burlingame, CA: Language Education Associates.

Michigan Department of Education. (2007). *Helping your child read.* Retrieved March 28, 2009, from http://www.michigan.gov/mde/1,1607,7-140-5233-23207--,00.html.

Moll, L. C., & Gonzalez, N. (2004). Engaging life: A funds of knowledge approach to multicultural education. In J. A. Banks & C. A. M. Banks (Eds.), *Handbook of research on multicultural education* (2nd ed., pp. 699–715). San Francisco: Jossey-Bass.

National Clearinghouse for English Language Acquisition. (2006). *How has the English language learner population changed in recent years?* Washington, DC: Author. Retrieved April 1, 2008, from http://www.ncela.gwu.edu/expert/faq/081eps.html.

National Clearinghouse for English Language Acquisition. (2008, April). *ELL demographics by state.* Washington, DC: Author. Retrieved April 1, 2008, from http://www.ncela.gwu.edu/stats/3_bystate.htm.

National Literacy Panel. (2006). Washington, DC: US Government Printing Office. Available online at www.cal.org/calwebdb/nlp.

National Reading Panel. (2000). *National Reading Panel report.* Washington, DC: U.S. Government Printing Office. Available online at http://www.nationalreadingpanel.org.

Perfetti, C. A. (1985). Some reasons to save the grapheme and the phoneme. *Brain and Behavior Sciences, 8*(4), 721–722.

Reis, S. M., Eckert, R. D., McCoach, D. B., Jacobs, J., & Coyne, M. (2008, May/June). Using enrichment reading practices to increase reading fluency, comprehension, and attitudes. *Journal of Educational Research, 101*(5), 299–314.

Schoenbach, R., Greenleaf, C., Cziko, C., & Hurwitz, L. (1999). *Reading for understanding: A guide to improving reading in middle and high school classrooms.* San Francisco: Jossey-Bass.

Shefelbine, J. (1998). *Academic language and literacy development.* Paper presented at the Reading and English-Language Learner Forum, Sacramento, CA.

Stanovich, K. E. (1986). Matthew effects in reading: Some consequences of individual differences in the acquisition of literacy. *Reading Research Quarterly, 21*(4), 360–407.

U.S. Census Bureau. (2004). *U.S. Census Bureau factsheet.* Washington, DC: U.S. Government Printing Office. Available online at http://www.census.gov.

U.S. Census Bureau. (2006). *U.S. Census Bureau factsheet.* Washington, DC: U.S. Government Printing Office. Available online at http://www.census.gov.

U.S. Census Bureau. (2008). *Fact sheet: Race, ethnic, or ancestry group.* Washington, DC: Author. Retrieved April 1, 2008, from http://factfinder.census.gov/servlet/SAFFFacts CharIteration?_submenuId=factsheet_2&_sse=on.

Vygotsky, L. (1962). *Thought and language.* Cambridge: MIT Press.

Wassman, R., & Rinsky, L. A. (1993). *Effective reading in a changing world.* Upper Saddle River, NJ: Prentice Hall.

Williams, C. (2008). *Sight word sentence building frames.* Irvine, CA: Teach Brite. Retrieved December 22, 2008, from http://www.teachbright.com/activity.html.

Williams, R. (1994). *Round and round the seasons go.* Huntington Beach, CA: Creative Teaching Press and Youngheart Music.

Wutz, J., & Wedwick, L. (2005). Scaffolding book selection for independent reading. *Reading Teacher, 59*(1), 16–32.

Yopp, H. K. (1992, May). Developing phonemic awareness in young children. *Reading Teacher, 45*(9), 696–703.

Yopp, H. K. (1997, April 25). *The role of phonemic awareness in reading acquisition.* Presentation to the Community Home Education Program teachers, Orange County Department of Education, Costa Mesa, CA.

3

Background Knowledge and Experience

Gibbons (2002) describes four roles of the effective reader: code breaker, text participant, text user, and text analyst. A common experience among ELL teachers as well as SELs is that students will master the alphabetic principle, establish knowledge of phoneme–grapheme relationships, and decode English words, yet after reading a passage aloud have minimal understanding of the passage. In other words, when ELLs or SELs read a passage, they often can pronounce the words but are unable to comprehend the meaning due to a gap in background knowledge and experience; they are, in essence, word callers. It therefore becomes imperative for ELL and SEL teachers to clearly understand common barriers between the student and the text as they relate to background knowledge and experience that enable the students to connect with, visualize, and experience the story in the text (see Figure 3.1).

Most effective teachers get to know students in and out of school in order to build new learning on what students actually know or find interesting (Gutiérrez, 2000; Sleeter, 2008), deliberately accessing students' knowledge and background experience to link it with academics (Moll & Gonzalez, 2004). Without sufficient background knowledge, the ELL or SEL will waiver as a text participant, text user, and text analyst. As a text participant, the reader connects information in the text with background

Figure 3.1 Gap #1: The Gap Between the Student and the Text

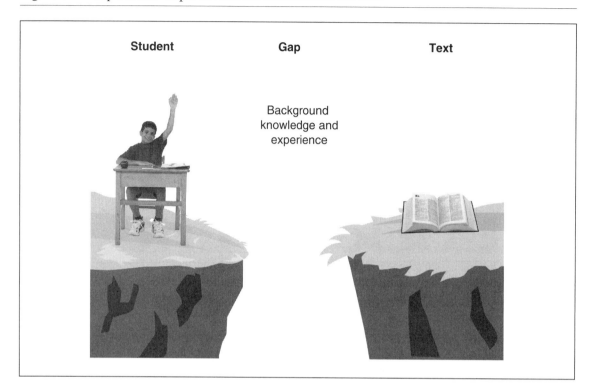

Figure 3.2 Four Roles of Effective Readers

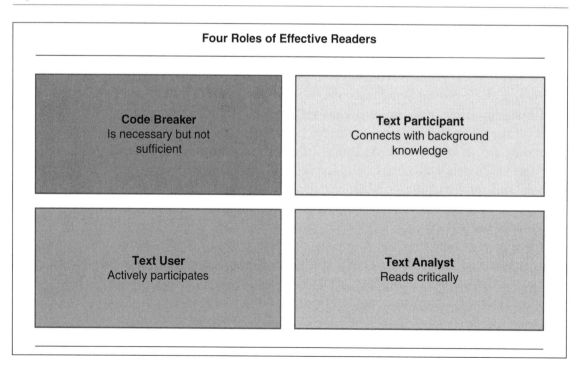

SOURCE: Adapted from Gibbons, 2002.

knowledge and experience. As a text user, the student actively participates in the reading process—asking questions, making predictions, and making connections (Keene & Zimmermann, 2007). As a text analyst, the student reads critically—analyzing the merits of what has been said, determining value and accuracy of material (see Figure 3.2). In order to launch the ELL or SEL reader from just a code breaker to a maturing, active reader, the astute classroom practitioner, particularly in the early years of the ELL's transition, must build bridges to the student's background knowledge to enhance his or her cognitive interaction with the text (Keene & Zimmermann, 2007). As illustrated in Figure 3.3, the teacher must consider code breaking as the launching pad, with text participant, text user, and text analyst as the destination.

Figure 3.3 The Literacy Journey: Launching Pad to Destination

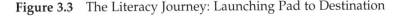

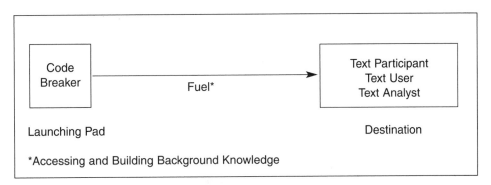

Accessing and building background knowledge become the fuel for this literacy journey as background knowledge forms the foundation for the reading framework as shown in Figure 3.4.

Accessing and building background knowledge occurs as ELL and SEL teachers ensure schema fit, appropriate context, and linkages during classroom literacy instruction. Later, as a mature reader, the student takes his or her own responsibility to ensure linkages, context, and schema fit by actively analyzing reading gaps during self-monitoring, taking charge of his or her own learning.

Figure 3.4 Key Components of Effective Language Arts Instruction

Decoding					Comprehension			
Word Recognition Strategies			**Fluency**		**Academic Language**		**Comprehension Strategies**	
Concepts about print	Phonemic awareness	Phonics	Sight words	Auto-maticity	Vocabulary	Syntax -------- Text structure	Compre-hension monitoring	(Re)organizing text
English Language Development								
Background Knowledge								

SOURCE: Adapted from California State Board of Education, 2007.

SCHEMA FIT: BECOMING A TEXT PARTICIPANT

Keene and Zimmermann (2007) claim that "proficient readers capitalize on six types of schema when comprehending text and learning new material: memories and emotions, text-to-world connections, text-to-text connections, knowledge of potential obstacles to comprehension, knowledge of their own reading preferences, and knowledge about the author/illustrator" (pp. 100–101). We would categorize schema fit for ELLs and SELs into four categories: experience, knowledge, language, and text structure.

Experience is everything when it comes to ELLs' and SELs' reading comprehension and discussion of schema. Experience encompasses day-to-day living, memories, emotions, culture, and text-to-world connections. These experiences become the lens through which the student interprets text. This *world knowledge,* as Hacker (2004) calls it, helps the reader monitor "sources of dissonance" (p. 762) when reading text, as well as monitor sources of agreement between experience and text. For example, an Asian American ELL who reads a short story on a Mexican American girl's *quinceañera* may struggle to understand what is happening in the story. Her background knowledge does not fit with the *quinceañera,* because she has had no experience with it. The astute teacher will look for potential schema fits and misfits and bring clarification prior to reading the text. For example, in this case, the teacher can explain to the Asian American ELL, who happens to be familiar with the American "sweet sixteen" party, the similarities and differences between the sweet sixteen celebration that some Americans enjoy and the *quinceañera* that many Mexican Americans enjoy. However, the teacher would explain that the *quinceañera* is a much more elaborate "coming of age" celebration and is deeply rooted in Mexican culture.

Knowledge of the specific topic in the passage is also critical for schemata. ELLs and SELs rely heavily on their understanding of vocabulary, in particular, as it greatly impacts access to text, the achievement gap, and the ability to comprehend a passage. The larger the vocabulary acquired in English on the specific topic, the more readily the ELL or SEL is able to comprehend the text. When the student has at least some familiarity with the topic, comprehension of the English passage comes more easily. For example, when author June Hetzel was visiting friends in Herzogenburg, a small village 30 minutes outside of Vienna, most of the conversations with her friends and their relatives the first evening occurred in German. Hetzel found herself lost in the language, missing quite a bit of content during the lengthy evening visit. However, the second evening, they visited another relative's house and the topic of music came up. A cousin pulled out his clarinet and began to play. Then, Hetzel played the song "Autumn Leaves" on the piano, followed by "Memory," from the

Broadway musical *Cats*. Fairly quickly, Hetzel found herself comprehending the conversation at a deeper level as the discussion centered around music. Hetzel more readily picked up cognates and familiar vocabulary in an area of specific interest to her. The same thing happens with ELL students in the context of our English-speaking classrooms. Vocabulary in L1, the student's primary language, enhances vocabulary in L2, the student's second language (Roberts, 2008). When a topic for which the ELL has deep content knowledge comes up in the text, the student's interest is piqued and vocabulary is readily recognized, acquired, and applied. The same happens for SELs and other students in your classroom.

Language plays a critical role for the ELL or SEL, as the more similar the language of the text is to the language of the ELL or SEL reader, the better "fit" it is for understanding. When the background schema allows for experiential understanding of the text, as well as deep vocabulary and conceptual understandings, comprehension readily comes. However, when experience, knowledge, and language (specifically, the vocabulary of the topic) are limited, comprehension is challenging. For example, read this short paragraph from an old college textbook, *Vector Mechanics for Engineers* (Beer & Johnston, 1977):

> A force represents the action of one body on another. It may be exerted by actual contact or at a distance, as in the case of gravitational forces and magnetic forces. A force is characterized by its point of application, its magnitude, and its direction; a force is represented by a *vector*. (p. 2)

More than likely, the reader was able to decode the preceding paragraph—but possibly may not be able to explain it, as the reader may have limited knowledge of the vocabulary used in this particular context if he or she is not an engineer or does not have a particular interest in engineering. However, if the reader has a deep knowledge of vector mechanics and is familiar with the language surrounding these topics, understanding of the passage is simple.

Finally, *text structure* plays a critical role in an ELL's or SEL's ability to understand text. Discussed in more detail in Chapter 4, text structure relates to how a passage is organized. The more familiar the passage organization, the more readily the student comprehends the text. So, for example, a Japanese American ELL might be familiar with haiku and readily read haiku poetry in English as the text structure fits previous schemata. However, another reader from a different background may have never heard of haiku. The structure of the poem might seem quite awkward at first and he or she might become "lost" in trying to interpret various haiku poems.

Another illustration of text structure familiarity and its ready assistance in comprehension is *story*. Nearly every ELL, regardless of his or her

L1, is familiar with the concept of story, oral or written. Therefore, when an ELL reads a story in English, he has a schema fit for story and how it generally goes—beginning, rising action, climax, falling action, and conclusion. However, when the ELL comes to a science chapter in the textbook, he or she may not be sure how the text will be organized, having less familiarity with characteristic textbook organizational structures, such as problem–solution or compare–contrast. Being less familiar with the structure of the passage, and also often less familiar with the technical vocabulary associated with the chapter, the ELL can flounder. Therefore, the ELL is initially dependent upon the teacher to assist in building scaffolds of understanding by defining text structure prior to reading the passage. The same applies for SELs.

In addition to general experience, knowledge, language, and text structure as it relates to schema fit, it is also important to remember that "effective readers call on particular kinds of culturally acquired knowledge to guide and influence comprehension" (Gibbons, 2002, p. 79). For example, a teacher was teaching English through a thematic insect unit to Arabic- and French-speaking second- and third-grade students in Africa. As she introduced students to the term *praying mantis*, she said to them, "Show me what we do when we pray," in an effort to help the children understand the common name of the insect in English and to give her students a clever memory device for the name. In response, all of her students immediately bowed low with palms facing the ground as would be appropriate for Muslim prayer. The startled teacher realized that her own Christian conception of prayer was two palms together in front of the body, the position of the praying mantis. In this scenario, the teacher immediately realized that the cultural conceptions she brought to the situation differed from her students and that she needed to make adjustments to bring in her students' cultural conceptions to enhance their schema fit, not her own. In this case, she needed to explain cultural differences through contrastive analysis to help her students understand the English name of the insect, praying mantis.

Often, such misfits in schemata are not readily apparent to the teacher, but must be uncovered to understand more deeply conceptual blocks between student and text. ELLs and SELs need teachers who can relate to their families, communities, and backgrounds in culturally accurate ways, reading them well (Murrell, 2001). Hence, the ELL teacher needs to approach the text from the ELL students' perspective, asking himself or herself questions in three areas—background experience, knowledge (e.g., conceptual understanding), and language labels:

1. What **background experiences** might *enhance* my ELLs' or SELs' understanding of the text?

2. What **background experiences** (or lack of background experiences) might *create a barrier* in my ELLs' (or SELs') understanding of the text?

3. What **concepts** in this passage might be *familiar* to my students?

4. What **concepts** in this passage might be *unfamiliar* to my students?

5. What **key vocabulary** in this passage might be *familiar* to my students?

6. What **key vocabulary** might be *unfamiliar* to my students?

One teacher, in bringing the text *G'Day, Australia!* (Sayre, 2003) to her students, realized as she previewed the book that the geographic terms of *continent, country, equator, Southern Hemisphere, Indian Ocean,* and *Pacific Ocean* were familiar to her students, because she had assessed her students on these terms in the previous social studies unit. However, in the book preview, she also realized that there were three significant conceptual schema misfits—her students did not understand *state vs. territory* and they were not familiar with *marsupials* (mammals with pouches on their abdomens) or *monotremes* (mammals that lay eggs). Utilizing the six questions listed previously, she organized her thinking around experience, concepts, and vocabulary (see Figure 3.5). She then made the instructional decision to show a short video about Australian animals, to assist in bridging the gap in students' conceptual understanding (schema misfit) and build background knowledge about Australian animals.

Figure 3.5 Action Plan for Schema Fit and Misfit for Sayre's *G'Day, Australia!* (2003)

Schema Fit	Schema Misfit	Action Plan
Experience We had a parent visit class who was a native of Australia.	**Experience** No one in the class has been to Australia.	**Experience** Show a short video on Australia, highlighting unique Australian animals. Invite Australian parent in to show brief narrated slide show.
Concepts Continent vs. country	**Concepts** State vs. territory Marsupials Monotremes	**Concepts** Introduces concepts through mapping exercise and video.
Vocabulary Continent Country Equator Southern Hemisphere Indian Ocean Pacific Ocean	**Vocabulary** platypus wombats wallabies koalas echidna	**Vocabulary** After video and map exercise, reinforce concepts through "picture map" game prior to introducing the text.

Another teacher, with primarily an Asian population of native Mandarin- and Cantonese-speaking students, introduced Gary Soto's book, *Too Many Tamales* (1996). Concepts and vocabulary in *Too Many Tamales* included schema fits and misfits as well (see Figure 3.6). Nearly all of the concepts of the story were familiar—family, cooking, mealtime, losing something, truthfulness, responsibility, and the desire to be "grown up"; however, the story was built around the process of making tamales, which was completely unfamiliar to this Asian population of ELLs. Much of the vocabulary was familiar to these Asian American students—*Christmas, ring, dough, meat,* and *family;* however, much of the vocabulary around making tamales was unfamiliar, such as *kneaded, masa,* and *corn husks.*

In this case, the teacher decided to invite a Hispanic community member to class to demonstrate *tamale* making in class. Students observed her *kneading* dough and actually got to try kneading the dough themselves. Children also got to place the *masa* in the *corn husks* and spoon meat into the center. Then, the community volunteer shared a *platter* of already prepared tamales with the children. When the children came to the text, they utilized

Figure 3.6 Action Plan for Schema Fit and Misfit for Gary Soto's *Too Many Tamales* (1996)

Schema Fit	Schema Misfit	Action Plan
Experience The three Spanish-speaking ELLs are familiar with tamales.	**Experience** The majority of class, Mandarin-speaking ELLs, are unfamiliar with tamales.	**Experience** Invite Hispanic member of community to demonstrate and narrate tamale making with students, sharing samples and allowing students to *knead* the *masa.*
Concepts Family Cooking Mealtime Losing something Truthfulness Responsibility Desire to be "grown up"	**Concepts** Process of making tamales	**Concepts** Students will gain experience in tamale making.
Vocabulary Christmas ring dough meat family stomach platter	**Vocabulary** tamales kneaded masa corn husks niña	**Vocabulary** Unfamiliar Spanish-origin words will be charted alongside the English words and the Chinese character equivalents.

their new background experience to comprehend the text, actively and enthusiastically participating in discussion. The classroom teacher readily bridged the gap by building background knowledge, vocabulary, and conceptual understanding to ensure schema fit with the passage.

Essentially, schema fit involves organizing information into neurological files for ready retrieval (Keene & Zimmermann, 2007). Connecting meaning and making sense of information can only occur as ELLs attach background knowledge and experiences to text through schema fit.

CONTEXT: BECOMING A TEXT USER (ACTIVE PARTICIPANT)

Context also becomes essential for the ELL, as it is easy to become "lost" or disoriented when you are in a second-language world. For example, when you are lost in a mall, where do you go? *To the directory.* What do you look for? *The "you are here" dot.* The "you are here" dot on the diagram provides the context for your whereabouts, orienting you to the next place you might want to go. In the same way, the English Language Learner or Standard English Learner must know the "you are here" dot of the reading passage—in other words, the *context*—so he or she can continue to make meaningful progress in the text.

For example, June Hetzel administered an informal reading inventory to a fifth grader. The boy read the third-grade passage and received a 98% score on word accuracy but a 20% score on comprehension. Intuitively, Hetzel sensed that the student simply did not have the background experience necessary to comprehend the passage. She chose to give him the fourth-grade passage even though this went against the directions of the reading inventory. The student scored 95% accuracy on word recognition and 75% on comprehension. It made no sense that the child would have 20% reading comprehension on the third-grade passage but 75% comprehension on the fourth-grade passage. However, the third-grade passage was about a rodeo, and the fourth-grade passage was on a familiar topic for the child. After the informal assessment was administered, the instructor asked the child, "Have you ever been to a rodeo?" The child responded, "No."

Hetzel had grown up going to rodeos every summer of her elementary school years. Corrals, cowboys, lassos, bulldogging, saddles, and Brahma bulls were common vocabulary and common sights in her childhood. Her Uncle Wilbur made his living working in the rodeos and her maternal grandfather, Vernon Wilder, had driven cattle from Missouri to Texas as a young man. When Hetzel read the rodeo passage, images of childhood swept across her mental screen, replaying scenes as if she were the central character.

Unfortunately, however, for the student without this background experience, there was no text-to-life connection. Nothing was playing on the mental screen other than a question mark, because there was no schema fit with the text, and the ELL's background experiences, conceptual understandings, and vocabulary were a misfit for the passage. (See Figure 3.7.) Hence, even when a teacher has made the text-to-student match (3.0 ELL reading ability matched to a 3.0 reading passage), there can still be a major disconnect or gap in understanding based on background knowledge and experience. The astute instructor recognizes the critical importance of ensuring that the ELL understands the context of the passage. If the ELL does not understand the context, the astute ELL teacher offers experiences to provide a context for learning. Strategies that build background experiences, conceptual understandings, and language include field trips, simulations, video clips, total physical response (TPR), demonstrations, and guest speakers. Cultural misunderstandings and schema misfits can occur with SELs, as well as with any student in a classroom, creating a gap in reading comprehension (see Figure 3.7).

Figure 3.7   Student and Gap: Bridge-Building Strategies for Background Knowledge, Experience, and Language

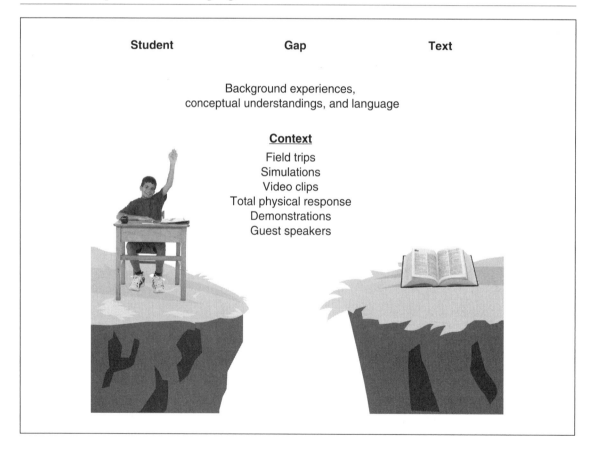

Field trips can be one of the most powerful background builders for student understanding of text. Such field trips can be large or small. For example, if your students are reading about the fire department, have them walk or take the school bus to visit the local fire department. If students are reading a story about a park, have them walk across the street to the local park. If students are reading a story about an ocean or lake, take them there—especially if it is close. Many schools choose to take their students on "traditional field trips" each year that tie in with their areas of study. This is particularly important for ELLs, and especially for low socioeconomic status (SES) students who may only know their immediate community environment. So, for example, one school conducts the field trips, shown in Figure 3.8, to build background knowledge.

Figure 3.8   Field Trips to Enhance Schema Fit

Grade Level	Field Trip(s)	Content Standards
1	Community: Visit the zoo, the park, and the library.	Science: Animals Social Studies: Community
2	Community Helpers: Visit the police department and the fire department.	Helpers
3	Westward Expansion: Visit the Southwest Indian Museum.	Social Studies/History: Westward Expansion, Native Americans
4	Sacramento/San Francisco (2-day trip), including Sutter's Fort, panning for gold in the Sacramento River, the Capitol Building, train museum SF: the mint, pier, Golden Gate Bridge, China Town	California History
5	Science Museum, Natural History Museum, Fullerton Arboretum, Observatory	Science: Space Science: Habitats
6	One-week Nature Camp	Science: Habitats, animals, and conservation

If field trips are unaffordable, *simulations* can be explored. For example, one fourth-grade teacher in Los Angeles, Brenda Wyma, could not take her students to the railway station or railway museum, yet she was about to have her students study the building of the transcontinental railroad. In order to build background knowledge prior to reading the text and to provide *context* for the history passage, the teacher declared a "Railroad Day," holding an incredibly elaborate, themed event. She herself arrived dressed as a railroad conductor. Photographs and sketches, collected over the years, adorned the walls. Children were taken out to the field to "build" the transcontinental railroad, utilizing tongue depressors as railway ties. The red team wore red bandanas and the blue team wore blue bandanas.

The race was on! Children feverishly "laid track" until they met at "Promontory Point," where the golden spike was hammered into the ground. (Mrs. Wyma literally used a railroad spike she had sprayed gold and drove it into the ground.)

When Mrs. Wyma returned to the room, she pulled down the U.S. map and showed the children exactly where the railroad was built and gave them the history of the transcontinental railroad. The children's "race to Promontory Point" on the school field helped them comprehend this period of history as they now had *experience, conceptual understanding,* and *vocabulary* to associate with the passage. Then, after carefully introducing key terms with *realia* (actual objects), she led her students through the chapter on the transcontinental railroad.

Video clips also effectively build background knowledge for ELLs, SELs, and native speakers alike. For example, you may anticipate your students reading a book on California gray whales, and while whale watching is a common field trip or experience in Alaska, Washington, Oregon, and California, it isn't in Iowa. A video clip or full-length video quickly fills in the students' experiential gaps as they view massive creatures of the deep, providing ELLs and SELs with a general context for learning and a neurological place to "file" new vocabulary and concepts. ELLs and SELs quickly grasp the enormity of the size of the whales as they see them next to other objects, such as boats, in the video.

Total physical response (TPR) is a strategy that requires the student to physically move and that can truly imbed into the ELL's or SEL's memory the size of the California gray whale. A gray whale is about the length of a school bus. Having the students walk along a school bus, counting their steps, will provide a physical experience to drive home the point. When asking the ELLs and SELs where the whale's blowhole is, have them point to the top of their heads. When asking the students how the tail of a whale, or fluke, moves, have them move their hands up and down in a wavelike fashion. This TPR teaching strategy can help build background knowledge and reinforce vocabulary, and later can be used to assess receptive and expressive language comprehension. Having the lesson taught in a vivid, hands-on context provides the ELL, in particular, with a head start in acquiring technical vocabulary.

Demonstrations can also be powerful for setting context. For example, one teacher wanted his students to write "How to" papers. He first walked through a demonstration speech of "How to Make a Grasshopper Pie": "First, you take Oreo cookies and crush them with a rolling pin." (He held up the cookies and then held up the rolling pin. As he crushed several cookies in a heavy plastic bag, the students enjoyed a sample cookie.) "Second, you mix melted butter to form pliable dough." (He showed the students the change in texture.) "Third, you press the cookie crust inside the pie tin." (He demonstrated the process and then magically pulled out a pie crust that he had prepared the night before.) "Fourth, you mix the ingredients: marshmallow cream, whipped cream, mint flavoring, and green food coloring." (He held up each ingredient as he called out its name, prior to measuring and mixing.) "Finally, you pour the 'grasshopper' filling into the pie crust, and there you have it—Grasshopper Pie!" (He pulls out a completed grasshopper pie and begins to serve.) As students enjoyed their Grasshopper Pie samples, the teacher showed the students a picture of a green grasshopper. "Are there grasshoppers in the pie?" he asked them. *(No, there are no grasshoppers in the pie.)* "Why do you think someone might call this Grasshopper Pie?" *(Because the pie is green. It is a fun name for the dessert.)* He then showed his students the written version of the "How to" on an overhead and walked through the example. This demonstration provided context and understanding for all learners, but particularly for English Language Learners. The demonstration, all the parts of it, provided important context for key vocabulary—specifically, ordinal words (e.g., first, second, third, fourth) that are essential for writing how-tos. From there, the ELLs began to think about what demonstration speech they would prepare and began formulating their plans for their "How to" papers.

Along with demonstrations, *guest speakers* can be powerful builders of background knowledge, setting the context for assisting ELLs and SELs in comprehending text passages. One teacher had a community volunteer speak about her Native American heritage. She did more than speak. She came dressed in authentic tribal clothes and discussed each aspect of her clothing. Then, she took the children to the school field where she had poles and material, and she erected a life-size teepee with the students' help. The students will never forget it. Every word she spoke was contextually embedded—a key to rapidly building conceptual understanding and language, particularly for ELLs.

As the ELL and SEL reader gains background knowledge, conceptual understandings, and vocabulary related to the passage, he or she increasingly experiences more schema fit and more readily interacts with text, reading critically and utilizing metacognitive strategies (see Figure 3.9).

Figure 3.9 Metacognitive Strategies

Metacognitive Strategies
(listening to the voice in your mind that speaks while you read)

Monitoring for meaning—knowing when you know, knowing when you don't know

Using and creating schema—making connections between the new and the known, building and activating background knowledge

Asking questions—generating questions before, during, and after reading that lead you deeper into the text

Determining importance—deciding what matters most, what is worth remembering

Inferring—combining background knowledge with information from the text to predict, conclude, make judgments, interpret

Using sensory and emotional images—creating mental images to deepen and stretch meaning

Synthesizing—creating an evolution of meaning by combining understanding with knowledge from other texts/sources

SOURCE: Reprinted from *Mosaic of Thought, Second Edition: The Power of Comprehension Strategy Instruction* by Ellin Oliver Keene and Susan Zimmerman. Copyright © 2007 by Ellin Oliver Keene and Susan Zimmerman. Published by Heinemann, Portsmouth, NH. All rights reserved.

These metacognitive strategies include monitoring for meaning, using and creating schemata, asking questions, determining importance, inferring, using sensory and emotional images, and synthesizing (Keene & Zimmerman, 2007). In essence, the ELL and SEL reader becomes a text participant as he or she actively interacts with text.

LINKAGES: BECOMING A TEXT ANALYST (READING CRITICALLY)

Linkages relate to connecting the known with the unknown (Keene & Zimmermann, 2007). Linkages involve the teacher assisting the ELL and SEL students in identifying background knowledge and context that will enhance their connection to the text, and also involves identification of gaps or dissonance. It is important to understand that "students can develop literacy in English more easily when reading and writing assignments tap into their cultural heritage" (Freeman & Freeman, 2003, p. 7). The Freemans studied culturally relevant texts with Hispanic students in Arizona, along the border of Mexico, and found that when these students read texts like *Family Pictures: Cuadros de Familia* (Garza, 1990) and *In My Family: En Mi Familia* (Garza, 1996), they related to the authors' experiences growing up Hispanic in the United States and demonstrated higher levels of proficiency with these culturally relevant texts. In other words, culturally relevant texts are assets in the comprehension process. Yet, as with any text, there can be disconnects. Therefore, it becomes essential for the ELL or SEL teacher to acquire and utilize strategies that identify connections or linkages with student background understandings, while also assisting in identifying missing links in understanding.

KWL charts and similar types of teaching strategies assist the ELL/SEL teacher in gathering student background knowledge prior to reading a text and linking students' understanding with text content by purposely identifying before, during, and after questions (Keene & Zimmermann, 2007). For example, if the teacher was about to introduce the picture book *Coming to America: The Story of Immigration* (Maestro, 1996), it would be helpful to draw the three-column chart as shown in Figure 3.10 and ask the students, "What do you know about coming to America or immigration?" The teacher would then fill in student responses in the chart. See Figure 3.11 for an example from Grade 2.

Notice how Juan and Geoffrey are aware of real details of modern-day immigrants. Notice how Sarah does not know what an immigrant is. She thinks anyone who comes to America is a pilgrim. Now the teacher moves to the second step: "What do I want to know about coming to America and immigration?"

Even in asking their questions, children reveal background experiences or the lack thereof. Antonio, in Figure 3.11, reveals knowledge of the

Figure 3.10   KWL Chart, Column One

"K" What do I know?	"W" What do I want to know?	"L" What have I learned?
"When you come to America, you have to get a lot of papers. Your uncles and cousins are happy to see you." —Juan		
"When you come to America, you ride in a boat. That is what my grandmother did when she came from Poland." —Geoffrey		
"When you come to America, you are a pilgrim." —Sarah		

Figure 3.11   KWL Chart I for *Coming to America* (Maestro, 1996)

"K" What do I know?	"W" What do I want to know?	"L" What have I learned?
"When you come to America, you have to get a lot of papers. Your uncles and cousins are happy to see you." —Juan	"I want to know how come you need all these papers. Why can't you just walk to California from Mexico? You could do it because there is land there." —Antonio	
"When you come to America, you ride in a boat. That is what my grandmother did when she came from Poland." —Geoffrey	"I want to know where the people are coming. How many countries of people do we have in America?" —Richard	
"When you come to America, you are a pilgrim." —Sarah	"I want to know about the Statute of Liberty and Ellers Island. Who was Ellers?" —Geraldine	

California/Mexico border. He knows they are connected by land. Richard reveals that he is curious. He has noticed a lot of different people in America. He wants to know about the various countries from which people emigrate. Geraldine reveals that she has heard of the Statue of Liberty and Ellis Island; however, she reveals in her question that she thinks someone named Ellers owns the island. These questions—"What do you know?" and "What do you want to learn?"—informally assess student knowledge and background experiences.

After reading the text *Coming to America: The Story of Immigration* (Maestro, 1996), the teacher then asks the final question, "What did we learn?" The students respond, and the teacher records their responses in the third column (see Figure 3.12).

After filling in the third column, students may also observe that they may have had some misconceptions, and those misconceptions or gaps are corrected (whether or not they were recorded in the first column).

Anticipation guides are another way to informally assess ELLs' and SELs' prior background knowledge and experience and vocabulary, linking them to text content. For example, if students were about to read the book entitled *If You Traveled on the Underground Railroad* (Levine, 1998), a teacher might prepare the Anticipation Guide in Figure 3.13 to determine students' background knowledge and experience and how they link to the text's academic content.

The Anticipation Guide would immediately pique student interest and reveal to the teacher where linkages and learning gaps existed in background knowledge. After reading the text, the students would go

Figure 3.12 KWL Chart II for *Coming to America* (Maestro, 1996)

"K" What do I know?	"W" What do I want to know?	"L" What have I learned?
"When you come to America, you have to get a lot of papers. Your uncles and cousins are happy to see you." —Juan	"I want to know how come you need all these papers. Why can't you just walk to California from Mexico? You could do it because there is land there." —Antonio	"I learned that people came to America in all different ways. Some people, like the Native Indians, already lived here. Some people came on a boat because they wanted to. Some people were forced to come here from Africa." —Sam
"When you come to America, you ride in a boat. That is what my grandmother did when she came from Poland." —Geoffrey	"I want to know where the people are coming. How many countries of people do we have in America?" —Richard	"I learned that some people were sick and when they came to Ellis Island, the government made them go home." —Randall
"When you come to America, you are a pilgrim." —Sarah	"I want to know about the Statute of Liberty and Ellers Island. Who was Ellers?" —Geraldine	"I learned that people that came to America a long time ago were also trying to learn English." —Karim

Figure 3.13   Anticipation Guide for *If You Traveled on the Underground Railroad* (Levine, 1998)

Anticipation Guide
. . . . *If You Traveled on the Underground Railroad*

<u>Directions</u>: Mark "T" for true or "F" for false on each line.
Before   After

____   ____   1   The Underground Railroad provided transportation from London to Paris and was important during World War II.

____   ____   2.   The Underground Railroad was a secret path to escape from slavery in the southern part of the United States.

____   ____   3.   The Underground Railroad was mostly used between 1830 and 1860.

____   ____   4.   The Underground Railroad was a real railroad.

____   ____   5.   The Underground Railroad included many forms of transportation, including railroads, horse-drawn carts, carriages, and boats.

____   ____   6.   People who helped those traveling on the Underground Railroad were called "railroad workers."

____   ____   7.   People who took care of you, fed you, and gave you a place to sleep were called "station masters."

____   ____   8.   Many slaves who used the Underground Railroad traveled all the way to Canada where they would be free.

____   ____   9   Harriet Tubman was a famous conductor on the Underground Railroad and helped thousands of fugitives escape slavery.

____   ____   10   Harriet Beecher Stowe, who had a station on the Underground Railroad, wrote a famous book called *Uncle Tom's Cabin.*

---

back and respond to the same 10 statements. The teacher would then place the overhead of these statements on the board and have students provide correct responses. The teacher could then follow up with his students, asking questions such as "What did you think before you read the book that changed after you read the book? What misconceptions were cleared up? What new understandings do you have?" Anticipation Guides are powerful tools to identify linkages, demonstrate before/after learning, and bridge gaps of understanding. In addition, these guides can be written for entire books, chapters, or sections of chapters. Anticipation Guides are particularly powerful for content area text, though they can be applied to fiction text as well by anticipating plots and character analysis.

Vocabulary knowledge self-assessments can be critical exercises prior to reading fiction and nonfiction texts. Kate Kinsella (2003) utilizes these pre-assessments on a regular basis to assist ELLs with academic vocabulary development. One of our favorites is shown here in Figure 3.14:

Figure 3.14 Vocabulary Self-Assessment

Vocabulary Word	"I've never seen the word in my life."	"I've seen the word or heard of the word, but I don't know what it means."	"I know a little bit about this word."	"I could get up right now and teach the rest of the class what this word means."
Immigration	X			
Slavery				X
Freedom				X
Nationality			X	

SOURCE: Adapted from Kinsella, 2003.

This powerful assessment strategy heightens the ELLs' or SELs' self-awareness as to which vocabulary has linkages with their background knowledge and understanding and which vocabulary words require additional study. The *vocabulary knowledge self-assessment chart* can be summarized as a class profile on an overhead to highlight words that are most familiar to students (linkages) and most foreign to students (gaps).

SUMMARY

The effective ELL and SEL teacher provides fuel for the "code breaker" to launch into text participant, text user, and text analyst by accessing and building background knowledge, experience, and language. He does this by first starting with the student, getting to know his student, and identifying his or her schema, so that the ELL or SEL has an opportunity to connect the known with the unknown. Second, he establishes the context of the passage to enable the student to become a text participant, successfully interacting with the passage. Finally, he identifies gaps and linkages between the student's schema and the content so that the student has the foundation for thinking critically and analyzing the text (see Figure 3.15). Over time, students experience *flow* in reading (Csikszentmihalyi, 1990), connect the known with the unknown, and participate in questions and answers through metacognition (Smith, 2004). Eventually, ELLs and SELs build independent skills that provide successful foundations in literacy, enabling them to analyze and use text for real-life purposes.

Figure 3.15 Schema, Context, and Link

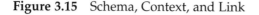

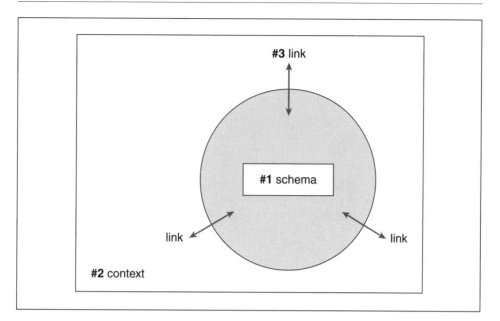

REFERENCES

Beer, F. P., & Johnston, E. R., Jr. (1977). *Vector mechanics for engineers.* New York: McGraw-Hill.

California State Board of Education. (2007). *Reading/language arts framework for California public schools: Kindergarten through Grade Twelve.* Sacramento: California Department of Education.

Csikszentmihalyi, M. (1990). *Flow theory: The psychology of optimal experience.* New York: Harper & Row.

Freeman, Y., & Freeman, D. (2003, Fall). Struggling English language learners: Keys for academic success. *TESOL Journal, 12*(3), 5–16.

Garza, C. L. (1990). *Family pictures: Cuadros de familia.* San Francisco: Children's Book Press.

Garza, C. L. (1996). *In my family: En mi familia.* San Francisco: Children's Book Press.

Gibbons, P. (2002). *Scaffolding language, scaffolding learning: Teaching second language learners in the mainstream classroom.* Portsmouth, NH: Heinemann.

Guitiérrez, R. (2000). Advancing African-American, urban youth in mathematics: Unpacking success of one math department. *American Journal of Education, 109*(1), 63–111.

Hacker, D. (2004). Self-regulated comprehension during normal reading. In R. B. Ruddell & N. J. Unrau (Eds.), *Theoretical models and processes of reading* (5th ed.). Newark, DE: International Reading Association.

Keene, E. O., & Zimmermann, S. (2007). *Mosaic of thought: The power of comprehension strategy instruction* (2nd ed.). Portsmouth, NH: Heinemann.

Kinsella, K. (2003, March 21). *Dynamic strategies to improve comprehension.* Keynote address, Claremont Reading Conference, Claremont, CA.

Levine, E. (1998). *If you traveled on the underground railroad.* New York: Scholastic.

Maestro, B. (1996). *Coming to America: The story of immigration.* New York: Scholastic.

Moll, L. C., & Gonzalez, N. (2004). Engaging life: A funds of knowledge approach to multicultural education. In J. A. Banks & C. A. M. Banks (Eds.), *Handbook of research on multicultural education* (2nd ed., pp. 699–715). San Francisco: Jossey-Bass.

Murrell, P. D., Jr. (2001). *The community teacher: A new framework for effective urban teaching.* New York: Teachers College Press.

Roberts, T. A. (2008). Home storybook reading in primary or second language with preschool children: Evidence of equal effectiveness for second-language vocabulary acquisition. *Reading Research Quarterly, 43*(2), 103–130.

Ruddell, R. B., & Unrau, N. J. (Eds.). (2004). *Theoretical models and processes of reading* (5th ed.). Newark, DE: International Reading Association.

Sayre, A. P. (2003). *G'Day, Australia!* Brookfield, CT: Millbrook Press.

Shefelbine, J. (1998). *Academic language and literacy development.* Paper presented at the Reading and English-Language Learner Forum. Sacramento: California Reading and Literature Project.

Sleeter, C. (2008, May/June). An invitation to support diverse students through teacher education. *Journal of Teacher Education, 59*(3), 212–219.

Smith, F. (2004). *Understanding reading: A psycholinguistic analysis of reading and learning to read.* Mahwah, NJ: Lawrence Erlbaum. (Original work published 1971)

Soto, G. (1996). *Too many tamales.* New York: Putnam & Grosset.

4

Comprehension

Academic Language, Vocabulary, and Passage Comprehension

Moving from the foundational role of background knowledge, experience, and language and how those affect ELLs' and SELs' comprehension, our focus will now turn to the right branch of the reading diagram depicting the key components of effective language arts instruction (Figure 4.1) in comprehension. The *comprehension* branch includes *academic language* and *comprehension strategies*.

Figure 4.1 Key Components of Effective Language Arts Instruction

Decoding					Comprehension			
Word Recognition Strategies			Fluency		Academic Language		Comprehension Strategies	
Concepts about print	Phonemic awareness	Phonics	Sight words	Auto-maticity	Vocabulary	Syntax -------- Text structure	Compre-hension monitoring	(Re)organizing text
English Language Development								
Background knowledge								

SOURCE: Adapted from California State Board of Education, 2007.

Academic language involves understanding of *vocabulary, syntax* (word order), and *text structure.* Syntax and text structure are also a critical part of comprehension, as is vocabulary, though it is not shown this way in the original model (see Figure 2.4). Text structure becomes critically important for comprehension as students learn organizational patterns of text, particularly nonfiction textbooks. Patterns include sequential or chronological order, comparison/contrast, cause and effect, definition or explanation, simple listing, and problem–solution (Tompkins, 2000).

Comprehension strategies involve teachers facilitating each student's ability to monitor his or her own comprehension through a variety of strategies as the student progresses from a novice reader to a seasoned reader. As a student becomes a well-developed, lifelong reader, he learns to (re)organize text to make it his own. Therefore, a discussion of student/text match for appropriate readability level is a very complex one, particularly for the English Language Learner. Figure 4.2 highlights major considerations for a comprehension gap between an ELL and the text he is assigned to read.

Teaching ELLs and SELs to comprehend a passage can be a challenging task—more daunting than teaching a child to decipher the relationship between phonemes and graphemes (decoding skills). Much of the complexity of teaching comprehension is due to the complex nature of comprehension itself, as well as the fact that comprehension is *not* a visible process, whereas decoding *is* visible. A teacher can "see" or hear the accuracy of oral decoding. As the student orally reads to the teacher, the instructor can easily determine strengths and weaknesses in the decoding process. Errors and accuracy of oral decoding are clearly visible to the teacher. However, if an ELL or SEL has fluent oral reading ability, he may sound like he understands the passage because he has mastered the decoding process; however, the learner's reading comprehension is still not fully visible to the instructor in this context. The instructor may gain glimpses of an ELL's or SEL's understanding through prosidy, dialogue, and questioning, but the student's complete understanding of the passage is not known by the teacher. The teacher attempts to see as much of the picture as possible through questioning and dialogue; however, it is only part of the picture because the ELL, in particular, is limited in being able to verbalize or write about his full understanding of the text. Also, because interpretations of passages vary, the determination of whether or not a child is truly comprehending a passage is, at best, a subjective activity because passage comprehension varies from reader to reader, depending upon the background knowledge, experience, and cultural values that the reader brings to the text.

Reading is not primarily a visible activity, though it is based on a visual activity—with obvious exceptions, such as tactile reading (Braille) or auditory reading (Morse code). Reading comprehension is what happens behind the eyes (in the brain) as the reader "digests" the written passage. Because reading comprehension is thinking, that is, processing ideas in the brain that are represented in print, it is challenging for the teacher to

Figure 4.2 Comprehension Gap

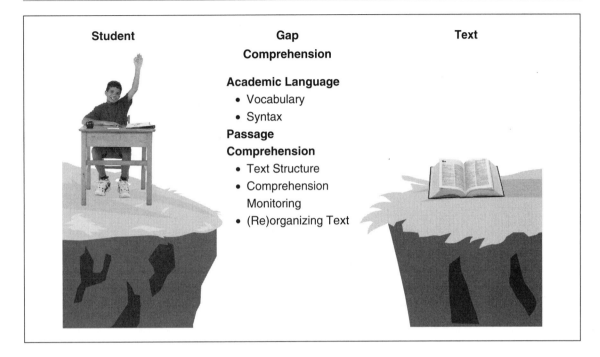

determine whether or not a child is truly understanding the intent of a passage. Yet, from a reading instructor's perspective, passage comprehension of the ELL or SEL *must* become "visual" so that the teacher can determine what the student is bringing to the text (prior knowledge), what the student understands in the text, and gaps of knowledge (vocabulary, concepts, or experiences) that block comprehension for the student. When the gaps between the student and the text are identified, this informs the instructor regarding the "next step" in the instructional process of helping the student become a more developed, proficient reader.

Reading comprehension is multifaceted. It involves the intent and clarity of the writer as he or she attempts to harness thoughts in words. Comprehension also involves the interpretation of the text by the reader as well as myriad other variables, such as the reader's background knowledge, experience, cultural understandings, language background, and subject area expertise. Comprehension is largely dependent upon the reader's ability to interact with the text, ask questions, make predictions, find answers, and thoughtfully explore the author's intent. Frank Smith (1971) describes reading comprehension as a series of predictions: question-prediction-answer-question-prediction-answer. If a student is simply calling out words, she is not comprehending. Passage comprehension involves deep interaction with the text, including understanding of academic language.

One way to assist ELLs and SELs with comprehension is via the use of think-alouds and metacomprehension. *Metacomprehension* is similar to metacognition (thinking about one's thinking) in that it allows students to hear or think through the thinking process that goes on while one is reading. In this manner, the reading process comes alive for the student, and he or she is presented with a model of what effective readers do and do not do. Typically, metacomprehension is utilized along with an *instructional read-aloud* (IRA) where the teacher models a particular comprehension strategy while reading a text aloud. Reading a text aloud permits students to access grade-level or more difficult texts, as they can focus on creating meaning from what is read instead of decoding each word. For example, while a teacher is reading the picture book *Grandfather's Journey,* by Allen Say (1993), he can model metacomprehension with the comprehension skill of making connections. When author Ivannia Soto-Hinman taught this process in her university secondary reading course to her preservice teachers, she made text-to-text, text-to-world, and text-to-life connections. As the grandfather in the text traveled to the new world, Soto-Hinman connected to what it must have been like for her own parents to have traveled to a new world from Costa Rica (text-to-life connection). Specifically, she made a connection to one of the last few lines of the book, which states, "The funny thing is, the moment I am in one country, I am homesick for the other." Soto-Hinman shared with her students how her mother had often told her that she still often feels this way, even though she has now been in the United States longer than she was in Costa Rica. The specific text-to-life connection was that Soto-Hinman's mother felt that when she was in Costa Rica, she did not fully belong, and when she was in the United States, she also felt like she did not fully belong. The power of metacomprehension comes with unveiling specific reading processes so that they become second nature to students. Although teachers cannot fully see what occurs during the comprehension component of the reading process, the use of *metacomprehension,* via think-alouds, allows ELLs and SELs to have a model of those thinking processes so they can successfully apply them.

ACADEMIC LANGUAGE

According to Shefelbine (1998), academic language involves the study of at least three areas: *vocabulary, syntax,* and *text structure.* In a broader sense, academic language also encompasses the language of school, texts, and testing. Preliminary curricular frameworks and guidelines—such as those developed by Diaz-Rico and Weed (2002), Dutro and Moran (2002), Girard (2005), and Scarcella (2003)—list topics to address when focusing on academic English (e.g., adverbial forms, conditional sentences, prepositions, words that express relationships). Similarly, Goldenberg (2006) suggests that specific features of academic English include tense agreement, plurals, and proper use of adjectives and adverbs. Most scholars agree that ELLs need not master conversational oral English in order to be taught the features of academic English. Instead, instruction in academic English must be "done early, consistently, and simultaneously across content areas—[and] can make a difference in English learners' ability to understand the core curriculum and that its importance increases as children enter upper grades" (Gersten et al., 2007). In addition, Gersten et al. suggest that there are specific benefits of academic English to the domains of reading and writing when it is infused into instruction early on:

- Reading—gaining perspective on what [is] read, understanding relationships, and following logical lines of thought.
- Writing—developing topic sentences, providing smooth transitions between ideas, and editing writing effectively.

Each content area and text type also carries academic language of its own, further making the acquisition of such language more difficult for the ELL and SEL, as he or she also acquires the basics of Standard Academic English. Gersten et al. (2007) also suggest the following: "Reading, discussing, and writing about texts needs to be a central part of the English language development instruction dispersed throughout the day" (p. 36).

In the following three sections, practical methodologies for strengthening ELLs' and SELs' vocabulary, syntax, and text structures will be discussed, including strategies for embedding these skills throughout the school day. Considerations for teaching these elements are critical, as they present potential barriers or bridges to ELLs' and SELs' comprehension.

Vocabulary

Vocabulary acquisition forms the foundation for comprehension. According to the Center on Instruction (Francis, Rivera, Lesaux, Kieffer, & Rivera, 2006),

Vocabulary instruction rarely occurs despite the fact that it is the academic language of classrooms and texts that prove most difficult for ELLs and in spite of the fact that ELLs—and their classmates—need between 12 and 14 exposures to a word and its meaning, across multiple contexts [different texts, classroom discussions, writing activities], in order to gain a deep understanding of a word. (p. 20)

The missing link, with ELLs and students who struggle with the reading process, such as SELs, often is receiving those multiple exposures to words in a variety of ways, and more important, practicing those words in context enough times to gain mastery. Here again, the role of oral language development is essential. Students must be exposed to words several times in several ways, but also must apply them often enough to internalize and solidify these new words in long-term memory.

English vocabulary can be studied and readily retained through hands-on experiences, picture walks, and a focus on technical vocabulary.

Hands-on experiences can include such activities as experiments. One high school physics teacher had his students studying water displacement. Instead of talking about the concept from a theoretical perspective, he had

Figure 4.3 Vocabulary

Decoding					Comprehension			
Word Recognition Strategies				**Fluency**	**Academic Language**		**Comprehension Strategies**	
Concepts about print	Phonemic awareness	Phonics	Sight words	Auto-maticity	Vocabulary	Syntax -------- Text structure	Compre-hension monitoring	(Re)organizing text
English Language Development								
Background knowledge								

SOURCE: Adapted from California State Board of Education, 2007.

his students build foil boats, predict the weight each boat could carry, and then proceed with the experiment. As students watched the initial demonstration and then tried it themselves, all the key vocabulary was used in context. This context-embedded scaffold was essential for Korean English Language Learners in the classroom.

Picture walks build context for reading, creating semantic concepts and categories for new vocabulary words encountered in the text. *Grandfather's Journey* (Say, 1993), a book used in a prior example, is a Caldecott Medal book with exquisite illustrations that provide visual schemata for the written text. When the teacher shows the book to the class, turning each page, discussing each picture, but not reading the text, students have an opportunity to "see" the vocabulary, and they start making connections between visual schemata and terms heard auditorily but not yet encountered in their reading. Picture walks build semantic understanding of individual words as well as semantic categories for words. For example, in *Grandfather's Journey*, terms that describe places, such as *Pacific Ocean, deserts, farms, mountains, cities,* and *seacoast,* suddenly have context, meaning, and category through vivid imagery. Students are able to connect their understanding of these concepts from their L1, transferring the concept to their L2 with a new label (e.g., *montaña* to *mountain, ciudad* to *city,* and so forth). This approach can be used in tandem with picture dictionaries where students create a visual to go along with a word, select a sentence from the text that uses the word in context, and then create their own definition from the two. An example of this is found in Figure 4.4.

The role of *technical vocabulary* in the comprehension of text, especially within a content area, is critical. For example, if a student is going to read an expository passage about the California gray whale, it will be essential that she understand technical terms such as *mammal, baleen, calf, spouting, spyhopping, migration, flukes, filter feeder,* and so forth. Without understanding these technical terms, it will be difficult to comprehend a California gray whale passage. The astute instructor sees these potential literacy gaps

Figure 4.4 Student-Authored Picture Dictionary Example

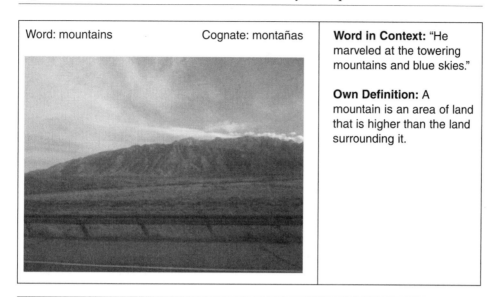

| Word: mountains | Cognate: montañas | **Word in Context:** "He marveled at the towering mountains and blue skies." |
| | | **Own Definition:** A mountain is an area of land that is higher than the land surrounding it. |

SOURCE: Ivannia Soto-Hinman.

between student and text and introduces the vocabulary ahead of the passage, providing literacy bridge-building strategies such as photographs, drawings with labels, and video clips that help students independently conceptualize the meanings of the technical vocabulary, transferring L1 concepts and labels to L2 concepts and labels, as students receive context-embedded instruction. For example, when one teacher taught ELLs whale units in Los Angeles County, she would take them whale watching for California gray whales in the Pacific Ocean. Students would observe these creatures with great excitement. She would also take her students to a marine museum where they could continue to acquire technical vocabulary in context. In addition, the teacher would also provide illustrated word banks for students so that key terms became common in their everyday vocabulary and were collected in their notebooks. Finally, prior to each lesson, all technical vocabulary was reviewed with use of gestures and hand motions that the students would imitate. In this example, the teacher has utilized several scaffolds, or accommodations, critical to ELL *and* SEL literacy development (Center for Applied Linguistics, 2006) to extend vocabulary knowledge, including filling in prior knowledge or background experiences; providing students with word banks for facility and assistance with the language; and creating opportunities for multiple use of the language, both orally and in writing.

Students need to know that words extend beyond one context and can have multiple meanings. Using a multiple meanings approach to vocabulary development can create further access to language for the ELL. Teaching one word at a time is simply an inefficient approach to vocabulary development, and requires additional time that the ELL students do not have. For example, in the California gray whale expository text example described previously, additional technical terms, such as *mammal, baleen, calf, spouting, spyhopping, migration, flukes,* and *filter feeder,* were taught in association with the specialized term. Multiple meanings of calf and fluke(s) included the following:

> Calf: whale baby (in the sea); cow's offspring (on land) (e.g., The cow gave birth to a calf.)

> Flukes: whale tail; unusual happening (e.g., It was a fluke that she won the race.)

Another approach to teaching vocabulary and related words is to assist students in determining examples and non-examples associated with a target word (see Figure 4.5). Examples of cetaceans would include killer whales, porpoises, and dolphins. Non-examples of cetaceans would include amphibians, such as a frog, toad, or salamander, which are cold-blooded vertebrates.

Teaching students both examples and non-examples of words and multiple meanings allows students to access language beyond learning terms one word at a time. Students create categories and mental files for groups of words instead of memorizing individual words. In fact, teaching one word at a time is one of the most inefficient ways to address vocabulary development, especially with ELLs who often need additional time and instruction in order to "catch up" with their peers.

Figure 4.5   Cetacean Examples and Non-Examples

Key Term	Examples	Non-Examples
Cetaceans	Killer whales Porpoises Dolphins	Frogs Toads Salamanders

Syntax

Syntax refers to word order, which relates to grammar. Native and non-native English speakers easily transfer aspects of syntax that are similar. However, differences in syntax between the student's oral language in L1 and L2 and the student's textbook will create a gap or challenge. For example, a child who grows up speaking non-Standard English will have some trouble comprehending a typical reading text. In the United States, some African American children who grow up speaking non-Standard English are quickly challenged by the mismatch between their home language and the academic language of their textbooks when they enter school. For example, typical English syntax might be, "Henry doesn't care," whereas in African American Vernacular English (AAVE), a child might say, "Henry, he don't care."

Figure 4.6 Syntax

Decoding					Comprehension			
Word Recognition Strategies			Fluency		Academic Language		Comprehension Strategies	
Concepts about print	Phonemic awareness	Phonics	Sight words	Auto-maticity	Vocabulary	Syntax -------- Text structure	Compre-hension monitoring	(Re)organizing text
English Language Development								
Background knowledge								

SOURCE: Adapted from California State Board of Education, 2007.

Non-native English speakers are challenged by grammar differences as well. In English, we would say *the blue house*, whereas Spanish speakers would say *la casa azul* (the house blue). Naturally, then, the native German speaker would easily translate *das blaue Haus* to *the blue house*, because the word order is familiar, but the native French or Spanish speaker would need to make a syntactical adjustment. The knowledgeable instructor sees the "gap" and supports the student in leaping over the chasm through intentional teaching of contrasts in language structure.

A bridge-building strategy to assist is acknowledging and discussing the syntactical differences so that the student processes the differences in the context of support for both home and school languages. However, it is of critical importance that discussing and handling these grammar differences be sensitively communicated. Situations vary between L1 and L2 and non-Standard English speakers. For example, in Henry's case, discussed in the preceding paragraph, a teacher could ask, "How many ways can we say that Henry doesn't care?" The teacher then writes student responses on the board:

Henry, he don't care.

Henry, he don't care at all.

Henry doesn't care.

Henry does not care.

The teacher can then explain that all of these sentences communicate what the speaker is trying to convey, and so are correct in their own systems. However, when speaking or writing to a diverse audience, it is appropriate to use Standard English, which would be the third and fourth sentences in the example.

Explicit discussion assists with language labels, but immersing the students in Standard English through oral reading and retellings embeds grammar patterns in long-term memory. Children need to be immersed in the syntactical patterns of the new L2 through read-alouds, modeling, and books on tape so that the grammar/syntax patterns become intuitive, even when students are unable to place the appropriate grammar label on their new patterns in the mainstream language. Memory of text—scripts, poetry, and passages—can assist in training the brain in the subtleties of language without conscious knowledge of embedding these new grammar patterns (Pudewa, 2005). For example, when Andrew Pudewa was trying to learn Japanese, he decided to memorize children's stories. He shares that memorizing these stories helped imbed in his mind many of the syntactical patterns of the Japanese language.

Text Structure

Because some children are either read to from an early age or told stories (in the oral tradition), they generally have an intuitive sense about the structure of fiction texts (e.g., story plot). After listening to stories read or told to them by parents or teachers throughout childhood, they usually have a grasp of story beginnings, settings, characterization, rising action, climax, falling action, conclusion, and story endings. However, students often do not have a good sense about how *nonfiction* text is organized because they have not read as much of this sort of text. For this reason, ELLs frequently feel overwhelmed by dense language often utilized across content-area expository textbooks. Generally speaking, however, there are only a few common nonfiction text patterns found in academic books: sequential or chronological order, comparison/contrast, cause and effect, definition or explanation, simple listing, and problem/solution (Tompkins, 2000).

Figure 4.7   Text Structure

Decoding					Comprehension			
Word Recognition Strategies			**Fluency**		**Academic Language**		**Comprehension Strategies**	
Concepts about print	Phonemic awareness	Phonics	Sight words	Auto-maticity	Vocabulary	Syntax -------- Text structure	Compre-hension monitoring	(Re)organizing text
English Language Development								
Background knowledge								

SOURCE: Adapted from California State Board of Education, 2007.

Sequential or chronological order is a typical overarching pattern in history book chapters. However, within an individual history text chapter, one often finds comparison and contrast, cause and effect, or problem and solution patterns used. Consider the following brief passage on whales, which is organized in a compare-and-contrast format. Before the teacher had the students read the passage, he would provide the chart in Figure 4.8.

Figure 4.8   Compare/Contrast Chart on Whales

	Toothed Whales	Baleen Whales
Blowholes		
Feeding		
Migrating		

The teacher would introduce the text structure—comparison and contrast—with a graphic organizer and invite the students to fill out the chart as they read or just after reading the following passage:

There are two large groupings of whales, toothed and baleen. Though whales are all cetaceans, the toothed and baleen whales have a number of distinctive differences. The toothed whales have one blowhole while the baleen whales have two, giving their spouts a heart-shaped spray. Toothed whales, of course, have teeth and are meat eaters, whereas baleen whales have baleen and are filter feeders. Baleen whales feed primarily on small creatures, such as krill, whereas a toothed whale, such as a killer whale, might attack larger animals like sea lions. Baleen whales tend to be much larger and migrate for longer distances than toothed whales.

After or during the reading of the passage, the students would fill out the chart. Using a graphic organizer such as this allows students to organize information and the teacher to scaffold the text using a process of comparing and contrasting toothed and baleen whales. It is important to note that students must be taught explicitly how to use the graphic organizer with sufficient modeling before they can successfully do so on their own. For example, one reader responded to the passage as shown in Figure 4.9.

Figure 4.9   Filled-in Compare/Contrast Chart on Whales

	Toothed Whales	Baleen Whales
Blowholes	One blowhole	Two blowholes
Feeding	Teeth, large animals	Baleen, filter feeder, krill
Migrating	Shorter migrations	Longer migrations

The reader's ability to organize pieces of information in the passage into a cohesive whole demonstrates his or her understanding of key points in the text. The teacher later required a written sample:

This passage was about wales. Some wales have teeth and some have baleen. The whales with teeth have one hole on top of their head and they breathe through it. They are large animls that migrate a lot of places, but not as far as the baleen wales. The baleen wales have two blowholes and the blowholes are like are noses in a way. The baleen wales don't have teeth and that is very strange. But, they eat a lot of little animals and that adds up to a lot of food in the end. I know it doesn't say it in the book right now, but I read in another book (its pretty intersting) that the baleen wales kind of spit out the water with these teeth like baleen pieces in the way and that's how they catch their food and then swallow the food. That's what it means to be filter feeder. And the baleen whales eat little krill fish and there big travel farth than the Killer wales. I do like the way killer whales look and I seen one at the Sea world. Have you?

Clearly, a student who could write something like this was able to bring complex language down to simple terms with the help of the graphic organizer. The sample also shows deeper understanding of the content, reference to another book on whales, and first-hand experience with killer whales at Sea World—all great background knowledge that would enhance his understanding of a difficult passage, packed with content vocabulary. The passage itself, however, would be extremely difficult for most ELLs unless the teacher did significant background building by showing photos of toothed and baleen whales; showing maps of whale migration routes; and pointing out specific whale anatomy, such as the blowholes, teeth, and baleen. Once this background knowledge and vocabulary were built and reinforced, the student would most likely be able to successfully navigate the passage, fill out the chart, and write a summary.

PASSAGE COMPREHENSION

For the purposes of our discussion, *passage comprehension* will be defined as the ability of a student to interpret large chunks of texts in a sensible, defendable fashion. This means that a young child in first grade can retell a story in sequence, accurately capturing the basic plot and qualities of the characters. Passage comprehension might mean, for a fifth-grade child, the ability to retell a passage of her history book, capturing the essence of the Revolutionary War, and synthesizing critical issues and events on both sides. For a middle school or high school ELL or SEL, passage comprehension for a novel might mean the ability to not only describe a sequence of events, plot, and characters, but also to discuss broad themes that run throughout the passage. Or, in comprehending a content-area textbook, a secondary ELL or SEL who has deeply comprehended a passage would be able to describe multiple perspectives that led to the battle, including rationale on both sides of the conflict. As we discuss passage comprehension, we will first examine comprehension monitoring and then move on to the student's ability to (re)organize text.

Comprehension Monitoring

Explicitly practicing and teaching comprehension-monitoring strategies are essential for developing literacy success. Bridge-building strategies

Figure 4.10 Comprehension Monitoring

Decoding					Comprehension			
Word Recognition Strategies			Fluency		Academic Language		Comprehension Strategies	
Concepts about print	Phonemic awareness	Phonics	Sight words	Auto-maticity	Vocabulary	Syntax -------- Text structure	Compre-hension monitoring	(Re)organizing text
English Language Development								
Background Knowledge								

SOURCE: Adapted from California State Board of Education, 2007.

that assist all learners in the area of comprehension monitoring include appropriate questioning strategies that probe their thinking, such as the threefold view, QAR, and Bloom's taxonomy, described further below. Basically, these strategies are meant to help the students learn to monitor their comprehension through asking questions and reflecting on their own thinking about the passage. (see Figure 4.11).

Threefold View of Comprehension

While teaching reading in the elementary or secondary classroom, it can be difficult to hold the six levels of Bloom's taxonomy in one's mind and ensure that each student is being asked to reflect on meaning at each of these levels. Because of this, many classroom teachers find it easier to think of reading comprehension in three broad categories: "on the lines," "between the lines," and "beyond the lines."

Apply these three layers of passage comprehension—"on the lines," "between the lines," and "beyond the lines"—to an adolescent's ability to read a car manual in her driver's education course. The ELL or SEL who can simply regurgitate sentences from the car manual on how to use jumper cables when a car battery dies may reflect some rudimentary comprehension of the text, but regurgitation of a passage is not enough. In the event that the manual is not explicitly clear, the individual must be able to infer various concepts, such as location of the car battery, positive and negative jumper cable clips, the critical nature of appropriately sequencing the steps, "clipping the cable to the engine head," the concept of grounding, and so forth. So a person who can read "between the lines" interprets at a deeper level and is able to jump her car battery based upon the written directions (assuming a fairly clear writing of the manual). However, an ELL or SEL who could read only "on the lines" might miss the seriousness of keeping the positive and negative clips from touching each other and have an electrifying experience! The person who is reading "between the

Figure 4.11 Comprehension Monitoring

Student	Gap	Text

Comprehension Monitoring
Bridge-Building Strategies

Questioning
Threefold view
QAR
Bloom's Taxonomy
Interactive techniques
Think-aloud strategy
Bet lines
Writer response journal

lines" has some background knowledge about how a car runs and the role of the battery.

ELLs and SELs who read "beyond the lines," however, may have picked up myriad additional ideas that are related but beyond the scope of the text. A car manual can be a very motivating text for a reluctant secondary male reader. When the learner is able to connect with the text, the teacher will observe a heightened level of comprehension that may extend well beyond the content of the text.

Clearly, the reader who is able to comprehend at all three levels—"on," "between," and "beyond the lines"—demonstrates mental dexterity and cognitive interaction with the passage. But the reader who comprehends at all three levels has also brought some background to the text. When the background (e.g., cars) is not there, the reader will struggle to comprehend unless the teacher provides some practical background knowledge prior to reading the text. As discussed earlier, with ELLs and SELs, as with all students, it is essential to determine how much they already know about specific topics and what prior knowledge you must fill in so that the students are successful.

Interestingly, assessing students at the basic knowledge level of comprehension can be a misleading task. For example, note this nonsense passage:

The four burnzies fiborously frintztied the pulpiliptous purdles.

Below are basic knowledge–level, on-the-lines questions about this passage.

- How many burnzies were there?
- How did the burnzies frintzy?
- What kind of purdles were present?

If the reader looked back to the original passage, he or she was more than likely able to answer the questions correctly. (Answer 1: There were *four* burnzies. Answer 2: The burnzies *fiborously* frintztied. Answer 3: *Pulpiliptous* purdles were present.) The reader was able to answer these "on the lines" questions because of his or her knowledge of English syntax, though the reader probably had no idea what the nouns *burnzy* or *purdle* meant. In addition, the reader was probably in the dark about the adverb, *fiborously,* and the adjective *pulpiliptous.* Yet, a student, even an ELL or SEL who has mastered Standard English syntax, who was only asked on-the-line reading comprehension questions, would more than likely successfully answer these questions. Many of our ELLs, SELs, as well as native English-speaking students who may be word callers can correctly answer basic knowledge–level questions when, in reality, they do not understand the passage's meaning. Insightful teacher practitioners, aware of this phenomenon, avoid limiting passage comprehension questions to just on-the-line, factual recall. Higher-level questioning is necessary for the teacher to have accurate insight into whether or not the young learner is processing the deeper meaning of the text.

QAR: Question–Answer Relationship

A fourfold view of passage comprehension is represented by the question–answer relationship (QAR) reading comprehension strategy developed by Taffy Raphael (1986). *Right there* and *think and search* are categories of text-oriented questions, whereas *author and you* and *on my own* are reader-oriented questions. The four levels of questioning represent four types of strategies for assisting students in processing text meaning, and these can be easily applied to fiction and nonfiction text (see Figure 4.12).

Right-there questions are factual, on-the-line questions. For example, in the story of *The Three Little Pigs,* "How many pigs were there?" or "What kind of house did the first pig build?" are right-there, factually oriented questions. An example of a right-there history question would be, "In what year did the Revolutionary War begin?" Notice that these questions are more oriented toward tiny bites of factual recall as opposed to comprehending a large passage of text. Keep in mind that these facts can often be accurately regurgitated by ELLs, SELs, and Standard English speakers who are able to decode and have a strong sense of English syntax; however, they still may not have a deep understanding of the passage. The astute instructor must probe beyond the right-there or factual level of understanding, also asking *think-and-search, author-and-you,* and *on-my-own* questions. These categories assist students in practicing responses to typical

Figure 4.12 QAR Examples

Text-Oriented Questions	"Right There" What year did Mother Teresa begin serving in India?	"Think and Search" Describe three major accomplishments of Mother Teresa during her lifetime.
Reader-Oriented Questions	"Author and You" What areas of needs have you observed in your community? How are these needs similar to those that Mother Teresa served?	"On My Own" Tell about a time when you saw someone in need. How did you feel? Did you take action? What happened?

assessment questions they might encounter. The scaffold of the walk-through heightens the student's understanding of the types of questions that he or she might be asked.

Bloom's Taxonomy

Bloom's levels of questioning (Bloom & Krathwohl, 1956) reflect a six-fold model: knowledge, comprehension, application, analysis, synthesis, and evaluation. Though the most precise definitions of these categories overlap, the more generally accepted definitions that follow invite a rich opportunity for monitoring comprehension, keeping in mind that the ultimate goal is that the student will ask herself these types of questions as she reads, probing deeply into the material and driven by curiosity and an intrinsic drive to learn.

Knowledge-level questions are factual recall, right-there, on-the-line questions. Key words such as *who, what, when, where, why, identify,* and *find* clue the reader into the type of on-the-line, factual information that the teacher is seeking. Students can answer knowledge-level questions without fully understanding the passage; however, knowledge-level questions are the starting point for comprehension in that basic facts must be identified first. For example,

1. Who were the main characters?

2. Who was the protagonist?

3. Who was the antagonist?

A critical point to keep in mind is that newcomers may or may not have the vocabulary associated with some of your knowledge-level questions (e.g., *character, protagonist, antagonist*). It will be important to clarify terms prior to having the students work on their own.

The *comprehension level* of Bloom's taxonomy requires the ELL or SEL to reflect on the intent of the passage. The reader does not provide exact facts or information, but processes the information in his or her own words. Cue words, such as *explain, paraphrase, distinguish, interpret, defend,* and *summarize,* let the reader know that a higher level of processing is required to reflect his or her own personal comprehension of the passage. An ELL or SEL cannot fake passage comprehension and desperately needs mastery of academic terms, such as the cue words listed above, in order to be able to comprehend academic language (Center for Applied Linguistics, 2006; Kinsella, 2003). The following are examples of comprehension-level questions:

1. Explain why the Gold Rush created such a "gold fever."

2. Defend the author's argument for school choice.

3. Summarize the four major sections of the book.

The comprehension level is where ELLs often begin to struggle. One reason for this is that they cannot picture in their mind verbs such as *explain, defend,* or *summarize* as readily as they can picture nouns such as *bicycle, mountain,* or *flower.* It is critical to explicitly teach high-utility words, particularly high-utility *academic verbs* (e.g., *explain, defend, summarize*), and to provide guided practice in responding to these types of questions so that all learners will be successful in responding to classroom questions and standardized assessment items. Word Walls with verbs, meaning, anchor sentences, and memory images are extremely helpful for discussion for ELLs and provide ready reference to high-utility academic verbs. For example, sentences posted might look like Figure 4.13.

Application-level questions require the reader to take the ideas of the passage and to apply them in another context. Cue words such as *infer, construct, imagine, what if, associate,* or *chart* force the reader to apply the ideas to a new context. For example,

1. What principles can you infer from the consequences of the main character's behavior?

Figure 4.13   Word Walls for High-Utility Words

Word	Meaning	Anchor Sentence	Memory Image
Strutted	To walk confidently about	The rooster strutted around the yard.	
Defend	To protect or provide reasons for an opinion	Dave defended the frogs, giving reasons to protect their habitat.	

SOURCE: Photos by June Hetzel.

2. Construct a graphic organizer to show what you learned from this passage.

3. Imagine yourself in a similar situation. How would you respond and why?

Again, key utility vocabulary can become the barrier that keeps an ELL from success, and Word Walls for these high-utility words at the application level are extremely helpful for all learners.

The *analysis level* of questioning requires the reader to break down the ideas into elements. Cue words such as *categorize, classify, analyze, compare,* and *simplify* force the reader to break down information into "chunks." Examples of analysis questions include the following:

1. Classify the characters according to their behavior.

2. Analyze the actions of the protagonist.

3. Compare the reasons Sally and Rex gave for working in the convalescent home.

Use of graphic organizers easily assists students in formulating visual images of their thinking (comprehension) about the passage. For example, one teacher discussed the character qualities of the four children in *The Lion, the Witch and the Wardrobe* (Lewis, 1950), utilizing multiple examples from the text. Then, she had students analyze and rate characters based upon their virtues (see Figure 4.14). After using the scaffold of the discussion and chart, the ELLs wrote an essay defending their scores.

The *synthesis level* of questioning requires the reader to put the elements of the passage into a new whole. Cue words such as *revise, associate, reconstruct, write,* and *prepare* help the reader reorganize information. For example,

1. Write a short newspaper article reporting on the first Olympics.

2. Reconstruct the novel in three to six paragraphs.

3. Prepare a series of overheads for the social studies passage to make it easy for a young child to understand.

Figure 4.14 Responding to Literature

	Honesty	Cooperation	Determination
Lucy	1	1	2
Susan	1	1	1
Edmund	5	2 & 5	4
Peter	1	1	1

1 = Excellent, 2 = Good, 3 = Satisfactory, 4= Unsatisfactory, 5= Unacceptable

SOURCE: Adapted from Hetzel, 2002.

Synthesis is critical to preparing ELLs and SELs for college-level success, because every literature review required at the university demands synthesis of multiple sources. Synthesis activities, such as writing a newspaper article or preparing a series of overheads to express comprehension of the social studies chapter, truly reveal the reader's deepest understandings of the passage. ELL and SEL teachers will scaffold this process with intermediary support structures so students clearly understand the process. Writing scaffolds include multiple grade level–appropriate models (both process and end products), use of rubrics, illustrated vocabulary banks, opportunities to work in pairs and small groups, and multiple opportunities for revision and feedback.

The *evaluation level* of questioning asks the reader to make a judgment about the ideas in the passage. This requires the reader to call upon his or her values as well as background information from the story. Cue words such as *support, explain, argue, defend, determine,* and *differentiate* help elicit this level of understanding. The following are some examples:

1. Identify the wisest character and support your selection.

2. Did you think the ending of the story was fair? Explain your viewpoint.

3. Provide three arguments to justify Nathan's unusual decision.

Evaluation is a powerful line of questioning because it reveals the reader's values and background understandings as well as gaps in understanding.

Interactive Techniques

The think-aloud strategy, bet lines, writer-response journals, and sketch-to-stretch are all interactive techniques to involve the reader by providing ongoing interaction with the text, rather than just a reader response at the end of a lengthy passage.

Think-Aloud Strategy

The *think-aloud* strategy is a technique where the teacher reads a passage aloud and thoughtfully unveils his or her thinking, as the teacher is reading, including questioning, making personal connections, predicting, evaluating, and clarifying. This is a helpful technique for the teacher to model what comprehension monitoring looks like for a seasoned reader, and the technique can later be adapted by the students as they monitor their own comprehension. For example, if the teacher reads *The Tale of Mr. Jeremy Fisher* by Beatrix Potter (1908/1987), he might read aloud the story, inserting comments, as follows:

Once upon a time there was a frog named Mr. Jeremy Fisher. (I love frogs! They are cute little amphibians. Here is a picture of a frog.

Mr. Jeremy Fisher is quite a fancy name for a little frog.) *He lived in a little damp house* (Damp means moist or sort of wet. That's okay for frogs.) *among the buttercups on the edge of a pond.* (Buttercups are flowers and a pond is a small lake. Frogs usually live by the edge of ponds, at least that's where I always saw frogs when I was a kid.) *The water was all slippy sloppy in his kitchen and by his back door.* (Slippy sloppy, slippy sloppy. I love the sound of those words. Slippy sloppy reminds me of the way pond water lightly laps the ground around the pond's edges.) *But Mr. Jeremy liked getting his feet wet. Nobody ever scolded him, and he never caught a cold!* (Oh look! The illustration shows Mr. Jeremy Fisher sitting in his house reading the newspaper and he's letting one of his feet dangle in the slippy sloppy water. Too cute. I wonder if something is going to happen to him. Like maybe he'll fall into the water. That happened to me once when I was dangling my feet in the slippy sloppy water off the side of a boat. Hmmm, let's see what happens next. What do you think will happen next?)

The think-aloud is a metacognitive approach that verbalizes the actual thinking about the text that goes on in a fluent reader's head. The think-aloud strategy is one of the few strategies that actually allows the struggling ELL or SEL to get a visual-auditory glimpse of how it works inside the proficient reader's head. Interestingly, many teachers and parents intuitively go about a similar dialogue when reading aloud to young children.

The important thing to remember with the think-aloud strategy in the context of teaching ELLs, however, is that you are adding even more potentially unknown "text" with all of your comments. If the ELL doesn't have the basic vocabulary of the passage to start with, the think-aloud may not add any more clarity unless you emphasize the meanings of words as you go, with *synonyms, gestures,* and even *visuals* to make the meaning context-embedded. Note the following passage about Jeremy Fisher with additional context-embedded clues:

Once upon a time there was a frog named Mr. Jeremy Fisher. (I love frogs! They are cute little amphibians. Mr. Jeremy Fisher is quite a fancy name for a little frog. [The teacher pulls a stuffed frog out of a bag and points at it when he uses the word frog]) *He lived in a little damp house* (Damp means moist or sort of wet. That's okay for frogs . . . [The teacher runs over to the water faucet and holds his hand under the water when he says the word "damp" . . . then he draws a simple little sketch of a house on the board and emphasizes the word "house" as he labels it.)] *among the buttercups on the edge of a pond.* (Buttercups are flowers and a pond is a small lake. Frogs usually live by the edge of ponds, at least that's where I always saw frogs when I was a kid. [The teacher draws a quick little sketch of a pond on the board and labels it. Then, he draws some simple flowers and labels the flowers as well.]) *The water was all slippy sloppy in his kitchen and by his back door.* (Slippy sloppy, slippy sloppy. I love the sound of those words. Slippy sloppy reminds me of the way pond water lightly laps the ground around the pond's edges. [The teacher points to the water and rhythmically moves his hand back and forth along the water's edge as he says, "slippy-sloppy, slippy-sloppy."]) *But Mr. Jeremy liked getting his feet wet. Nobody ever scolded him, and he never caught a cold!* (Oh look! The illustration shows Mr. Jeremy Fisher sitting in his house reading the newspaper and he's letting one of his feet dangle in the slippy sloppy water. [The teacher points to his feet and then to Jeremy Fisher's feet in the illustration in the book.] Too cute. I wonder if something is going to happen to him. Like maybe he'll fall into the water. [The teacher tips to one side as he says the word "fall."] That happened to me once when I was dangling my feet in the slippy sloppy water off the side of a boat. Hmmm, let's see what happens next. What do you think will happen next?)

As you can see from the preceding passage, the think-aloud strategy is scaffolded for the ELL to ensure comprehension through contextual gestures, book illustrations, board sketches, and word labels. Even if the ELL does not comprehend everything that you have said, she has her receptive vocabulary stretched, she has several new words to add to her vocabulary bank, and she can begin to understand the idea of *thinking about her thinking* in the context of the reading process.

Bet Lines

Bet lines are key stopping points (text lines) where teachers ask students to dialogue about what they have just read and make predictions about the future. Similar to the think-aloud, the bet line promotes individual and group interaction about the content of passages and can be utilized in personal monitoring of comprehension as well.

Teachers often introduce bet lines with a short story. The short story is duplicated with blank lines inserted following certain key paragraphs. Students are instructed to fold back their paper at the first line and *not* to read ahead. Everyone shares reading the first section aloud (*unison, round robin, popcorn reading,* or *oral cloze*) and stops at the bet line. Students make predictions about what will happen next, supporting them from story content or personal experiences. After the discussion finishes, the class folds their paper down to the next bet line. The next section is read and predictions are confirmed or refuted based upon story content. Further predictions about what will happen next then follow.

The bet line strategy elicits more and more dialogue as time goes on, and the children can hardly wait to read the next section of the text. The bet line encourages highly interactive group dialogue, increasing cognitive curiosity as suspense in the story plot grows (e.g., "I bet this will happen next . . ."). Through the course of the classroom dialogue, summarizing, clarifying of vocabulary, making connections with personal experiences, questioning, and predicting all come into play. The bet line simply couches these interactive strategies of proficient reading within a different context, providing another nice way to reinforce these critical skills of proficient readers. As students gain practice with oral bet lines, they see how proficient readers think and begin to monitor their own comprehension through interactive metacognitive strategies.

Writer-Response Journal

The *writer-response journal* is another method of promoting interaction with the text in the form of predicting, clarifying, making personal connections, questioning, and evaluating; however, in this case, the predominant interaction is through written language (see Figure 4.15). The journal entries can be handled in a variety of ways, and the students determine whether or not their responses to the text will include a question, a prediction, and so forth. The students may be directed to make a journal entry following each page of reading, each section of reading, or particular query points indicated by the teacher. The writer-response journal helps the ELL or SEL continue to cognitively interact with the passage, connecting the reading and writing processes.

Figure 4.15   Writer-Response Journal Based on DeJong's *The Wheel on the School Bus* (1972)

Chapter, Text Page #s, and/or Quotes	Writer Response
Chapter 1: Do You Know About Storks?	This is interssting chptr. Like the storks. Holland is the country. But one student wants to shoot the storks.

Sketch-to-Stretch

A variation on the writer-response journal is the *sketch-to-stretch* technique where the reader responds to the passage intermittently through drawing pictures instead of writing words (see Figure 4.16). This can be helpful for the English Language Learner, as recalling the specific word labels in the new language can be daunting in the early stages of literacy, and receptive understanding (listening, reading) is generally 2 years ahead of writing vocabulary.

(Re)organization of Text

(Re)organization of text involves the student making the text his or her own by actually changing its form (e.g., rewriting a story in simpler register for younger children, taking a short story and writing a Reader's Theater script). (Re)organization of text enhances the ELL's or SEL's processing of text and assists in providing student ownership and understanding of text for long-term memory. There are many approaches for

Figure 4.16 Sketch-to-Stretch Journal Based on DeJong's *The Wheel on the School Bus* (1972)

Chapter, Text Page #s, and/or Quotes	Sketch to Stretch
Chapter 1: Do You Know About Storks?	

Figure 4.17 (Re)organization of Text

Decoding					Comprehension			
Word Recognition Strategies			Fluency		Academic Language		Comprehension Strategies	
Concepts about print	Phonemic awareness	Phonics	Sight words	Auto-maticity	Vocabulary	Syntax -------- Text structure	Compre-hension monitoring	(Re)organizing text
English Language Development								
Background knowledge								

SOURCE: Adapted from California State Board of Education, 2007.

assisting ELL or SEL students with comprehension through (re)organization. Because reading is a receptive literacy process, strategies for (re)organizing text will include expressive literacy processes—writing and speaking. Writing strategies might include historical timelines, journals, and outlines. Speaking strategies for (re)organizing text might include pair-shares, pair-squares, and oral summaries. However, (re)organization of text is also greatly enhanced through illustrations, models, diagrams, and graphic organizers. Combining writing, speaking, and other expressions of understanding and (re)organizing (e.g., drama, art), teachers can inspire students to express their understanding through multitudinous approaches (see Figure 4.18).

While multitudinous approaches for (re)organizing text exist, we will limit bridge-building strategies to oral strategies, written strategies, artistic strategies, and combination approaches (see Figure 4.19).

Oral Bridge-Building Strategies

Effective oral strategies for (re)organizing text include pair-share, pair-square, and oral summaries. *Pair-share* is a paired student verbal interaction

Figure 4.18 (Re)organization Strategy Bank

(Re)organization Strategy Bank	
☐ Cartoon	☐ Model (e.g., clay, pipe cleaners)
☐ Chart	☐ Murals With Key Words Outline
☐ Computer Graphics	☐ Outline
☐ Concept Diagrams	☐ Pair-Share
☐ Correspondence	☐ Pair-Square
☐ Diagram	☐ Picture Dictionary
☐ Diorama	☐ Play
☐ Display	☐ Poetry
☐ Drama	☐ Poster
☐ Film	☐ Rewrite
☐ Glossary	☐ Series of Illustrations
☐ Graphic Organizer	☐ Songs
☐ Illustration	☐ Speech
☐ Illustration Chart	☐ Summary
☐ Illustration Text and Chart	☐ Timeline
☐ Journals	☐ Video
☐ L1 Summary	☐ Vocabulary Diagrams

NOTES:

Figure 4.19 Comprehension Monitoring

Student   Gap   Text

(Re)organization
of Text

Bridge-Building Strategies
Oral Strategies
Written Strategies
Artistic Strategies
Combination Strategies

invited at a critical stopping point in the text. For example, the teacher might conduct a shared reading of a few paragraphs and then conduct classroom discussion utilizing pair-share responses (see Figure 4.20).

Notice how the pair-share invites opportunity for all students in the classroom to practice their oral language skills while also (re)organizing the text in their own minds, utilizing vocabulary they understand. Depending on the students' level of proficiency, they may need additional scaffolding via language stems to assist them with their conversation. These can include the following:

- *I agree with . . . but would like to add . . .*
- *I disagree with . . . because . . .*
- *I need clarification on . . .*
- *I am confused by . . .*

Figure 4.20 Classroom Pair-Share

Teacher	Students
"Share with your partner what the last two paragraphs were about."	
	Anisa to Zineb: "I think this tells the desert, but I don't know desert."
	Zineb to Anisa: "The desert is hot dry place. You know, sand. The sun. Also, we read animals that live in desert."
	Anisa to Zineb: "And plants."
"Tell your partner what it is like in the desert."	
	Anisa to Zineb: "Okay. Hot and, and . . ."
	Zineb to Anisa: "Dry. That means no water. No rain. The desert is hot and dry."
"What kinds of plants and animals are in the desert?"	
	Anisa: "I don't know the names, but scorpion. Scorpion lives in desert."
	Zineb: "The scorpion is dangerous. Its sting kill you."
	Anisa: "I see a scorpion in the desert."
	Zineb: "There are cactus. Needles are sharp."
	Anisa: "I know cactus."

The *pair-square* is quite similar to the pair-share except the teacher asks partners to partner up with another pair so there are four in each group (see Figure 4.21).

Figure 4.21 Classroom Pair-Square

Teacher	Students
"Now, pair-shares join friends and become a pair-square. Now there are four of you. In your groups, try to remember all of the characteristics of a desert. Have someone record your answers."	
	Ghita: "I remember that deserts are near the equator."
	Anisa: "What is equator?"
	Fatim-Zahra: "It's the line. Here. (Points to the equator on the map.) It's hot near the equator."
	Anisa: "Oh."
	Fatim-Zahra: "The sun is closer to the equator."
"What else did we read about the desert? I heard you say that deserts are often near the equator."	
	Zineb: "What else did we read? We need more ideas about the desert."

Oral summaries provide opportunities for students to verbally give a short statement about the main idea of a paragraph or passage (see Figure 4.22). This can take place in the context of a pair-share or pair-square

Figure 4.22 Oral Summary

Teacher	Students
"You now have had several minutes to discuss in your groups what we read about the desert. Take turns describing the most important ideas about a desert from this passage."	
	Fatim-Zahra: "I know, I know. Let me do it." (The other girls consent.)
	Fatim-Zahra: "A desert is a hot place. Many deserts near the equator which closer to the sun. Many plants, like cactus. Many animals, like scorpins."
	Anisa: "No! Scor-*pi*-on."
	Fatim-Zahra: "Okay, scor-*pi*-on."
"Who is ready to stand up in their group and summarize this passage on the desert?"	
	(Fatim-Zahra waves her hand and volunteers.)

as described previously. Oral summaries come more naturally after the students have had time to socially construct the summary.

Written Bridge-Building Strategies

Effective written strategies to (re)organize text include historical time-lines, graphic organizers, and rewritten text. *Historical timelines* are a logical opportunity for students to highlight in their text or record key events in a given historical passage. This timeline, which can be recorded on paper with pen, pencil, or colored markers; created on a computer screen; or provided in text form on a bulletin board, assists the learner in (re)organizing his thinking related to the passage. For example, ELL students read a passage entitled "First in Flight" and recorded their timeline (see Figure 4.23).

Figure 4.23 Flight Timeline

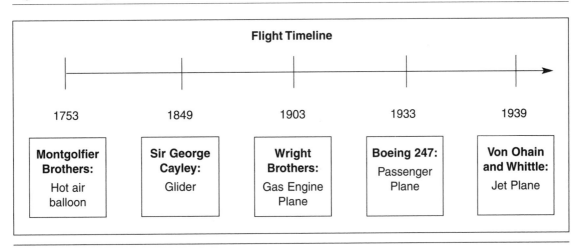

SOURCE: Adapted from Hetzel & Wyma, 1995.

The historical timeline may be the assessment by which the ELL teacher desires to determine the ELLs' understanding. However, she may also want the ELLs to compose a paragraph summarizing the timeline. In this summary, she might focus on use of ordinal words (first, second, third, etc.) and use of commas (see Figure 4.24).

Figure 4.24 Sample Paragraph of Historical Timeline

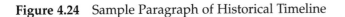

Name: Abdel

The first flights history is very interesting. First, in 1753, Montgolfier Brothers fly in hot air balloon. Second, in 1849, Sir George Cayley fly a glider. Third, in 1903, the Wright brothers fly a gas plane with engine. Fourth, in 1933, the first passenger plane fly. Fifth, in 1939, a German man and an English man fly the jet plane. When I am man, I will fly my own plane. I will have two. I will have one for me and one for best friend.

Graphic organizers are another powerful way for ELLs or SELs to (re)organize text. For example, students might read a passage about camping. The teacher builds background knowledge by bringing in *realia* (actual objects) related to the topic of camping (e.g., tent, sleeping bag, canteen, mess kit, water bottle, fishing gear, etc.). She introduces each object prior to the students reading the passage, demonstrating how each object is used in the context of camping. The teacher also shows students pictures of people camping and discusses each picture briefly, utilizes Q & A, and reinforces vocabulary. Following this, the students read the passage about camping. Then, students (re)organize the text by creating their own notes regarding the central idea of camping, including key ideas in the passage such as shelter, food, and activities (see Figure 4.25).

Figure 4.25 Camping Graphic Organizer

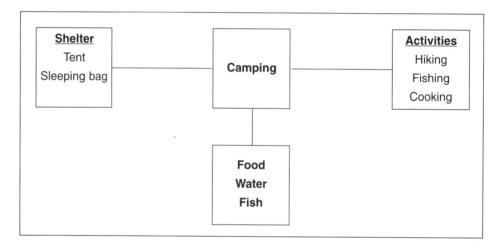

The graphic organizer may be all that the teacher wants if she is looking for just main ideas. However, the teacher may ask the students to demonstrate more complex language by writing their own summaries of the camping passage (see Figure 4.26).

Figure 4.26 Camping Narrative

Camping

If you camp you need many thing. You need shelter, food, and activity.

If you camp, you need a tent for over head. In night, you sleep there. You need also bag to sleep.

Food is fish. You cach the fish with stick. And drink the water, not from lake. Drink bottel.

Activities: You hike. You fish, You cook fish. Sleep in night, the tent.

That camping. I think fun.

Rewritten text is another way to help students (re)organize text into its essential points. During one summer, Hetzel was teaching native Arabic and French speakers. Her third graders read a photography book entitled *Horses* (Schwartz, 1999). Rewritten texts demonstrated clear understanding of the essential points in the narrative; in addition, the children's rewrites were (re)organized into their own words for long-term memory.

Artistic Bridge-Building Strategies

Memorable artistic strategies that assist learners in (re)organizing text include illustration series, murals with key vocabulary, cartoons, and illustrated charts. An *illustration series* might be the approach an ELL teacher takes to have his students first demonstrate their understanding of a passage. For example, if the teacher is having the students study germination, he will first provide his ELLs the opportunity to plant a bean in some soil to allow for firsthand observation of seed germination over several days. Later, he will have the students read a passage on germination from their science textbook. The ELL teacher then might require an illustration series for students to demonstrate their understanding of the passage on germination.

The students illustrate the seed from the point of the primary root emerging, to the appearance of the plant above soil, to the emergence of the *plumule* (the developing bud), to the emergence of the first leaves. A student illustration that approximates this clearly demonstrates the ELL's understanding of germination, that is, the process of a seed changing from a seed to a seedling.

Using *murals with key vocabulary* is another way to assist ELLs, particularly Beginning and Early Intermediate students, in demonstrating their understanding of the content topic at hand. In these particular murals, the teacher has provided space on her bulletin boards for students to illustrate three biomes: rain forest, desert, and prairie. The students create the mural and add key words. As the students build the mural, the teacher directs conversation to build English language acquisition (see Figure 4.27). Artistically oriented children also enjoy illustrating their understanding of text through *cartoons*. Cartoon illustrations are a fun way to motivate students and clearly demonstrate comprehension and (re)organization of passages.

Illustrated charts are yet another alternative to assist ELL students in (re)organizing text, particularly with technically dense content-area vocabulary found in expository texts. For example, ELL students might be studying a plant unit and, in particular, reading a passage on *monocots* and *dicots,* such as the expository selection in Figure 4.28.

Despite the fact that experienced educators can clearly see this passage has dense technical vocabulary, these types of passages are often what the ELL student is confronted with, particularly Advanced Intermediate and Advanced ELLs in middle school and high school. In this strategy, realia (real-life objects) are first utilized to introduce the unfamiliar concepts and

Figure 4.27 Teacher–Student Conversation on Rain Forest Mural

Teacher	Students
"Sarah, can you point to the forest floor in the rain forest mural?"	(Sarah points to the forest floor.)
"What is this called?"	"F-f. . ."
"Forest floor."	"F-forest f-floor."
"Yes, this is the forest floor. The forest floor is the ground that we walk on."	"Ground?"
"Yes, ground. The ground or floor of the rain forest." (The teacher gestures to the ground.)	
	(Sarah excitedly points to the mural.) "Here is forest floor. The forest floor is ground. Animals walk on ground. Animals walk on forest floor. People walk on forest floor."
"Well done!"	

Figure 4.28 Expository Selection

Flowering plants are divided into two broad divisions—monocots and dicots. Monocots, such as the iris and the palm tree, have one cotyledon or seed leaf, fibrous roots, narrow leaves with parallel veins, and flowers whose petals occur in multiples of three. Dicots have two cotyledons or seed leaves, tap roots, leaves with branched veins, and petals that occur in multiples of four or five. A violet and a maple tree are both examples of dicots. Scientists use these two broad divisions, monocots and dicots, to classify flowering plants all over the world.

SOURCE: Hetzel, Miller, & Wyma, 1995, p. 21.

key terms (e.g., *seeds, roots, stems, leaves, flowers, monocots, dicots*) and to build background knowledge and oral language. The teacher then exposes the ELL students to the passage. He then introduces a two-column chart with monocots and dicots as headers (see Figure 4.29). Students work in teams to illustrate and explain the difference between monocots and dicots. Illustrations and explanations demonstrate understanding.

Combination Bridge-Building Strategies

Powerful combination strategies that assist ELL as well as SEL learners in (re)organizing text include displays, concept diagrams, vocabulary diagrams, and picture dictionaries. *Displays* are hands-on opportunities that require three-dimensional responses to student learning, including written

Figure 4.29   Two-Column Monocots and Dicots Chart

	Monocots	Dicots
Seeds		
Roots		
Stems		
Leaves		
Flowers		

	Monocots	Dicots
Seeds	one cotyledon or seed leaf 	two cotyledons or seed leaves 
Roots	branched, fibrous roots all of similar size 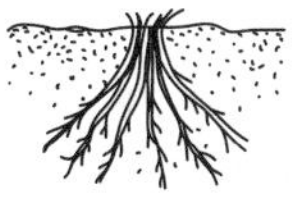	long, slightly branched tap root that grows deep into the soil 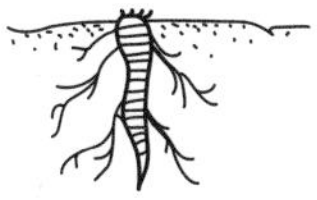
Stems	usually herbaceous stems with tissues randomly arranged throughout stem 	both woody and herbaceous stems with tissues arranged in a circular pattern 
Leaves	leaves are narrow with parallel veins and there is a sheath around the part of the stem near the leaf 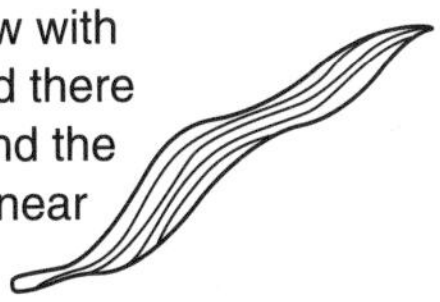	leaves are broad with branched veins 
Flowers	petals occur in multiples of three; sepals and petals are difficult to tell apart 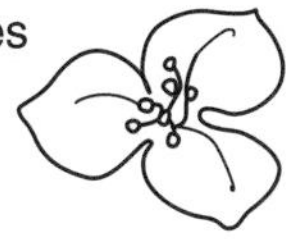	petals occur in multiples of four or five; petals and sepals are easily distinguished 

SOURCE: Hetzel, Miller, & Wyma, 1995; illustrations by Diane Valko.

explanations and illustrations. In Figure 4.30 you see three young students and their science displays, which (re)organize their learning of aerodynamics. Both displays record their study of multiple sources and experimental design as well as models and scientific journals.

Concept diagrams are labeled illustrations that students compose to express their understanding of a particular concept. For example, Figure 4.31 shows a sketch of an airplane with the headwind at 30 mph, the airspeed at 80 mph, and the ground speed at 50 mph. Clearly, the student understands the concept, and the illustration not only (re)organizes the concept

Figure 4.30 The Scientific Method

SOURCE: Hetzel & Wyma, 1995; illustrations by Diane Valko.

in her own mind, but imbeds it in long-term memory. In addition, the teacher has evidence of student learning related to airspeed, the speed or velocity of a flying machine in relation to the air around it.

Vocabulary diagrams are labeled illustrations that demonstrate students have heard and understood the basic vocabulary of the unit of study. For example, in the flight unit, the students drew a diagram of a plane and

Figure 4.31 Headwind/Airspeed

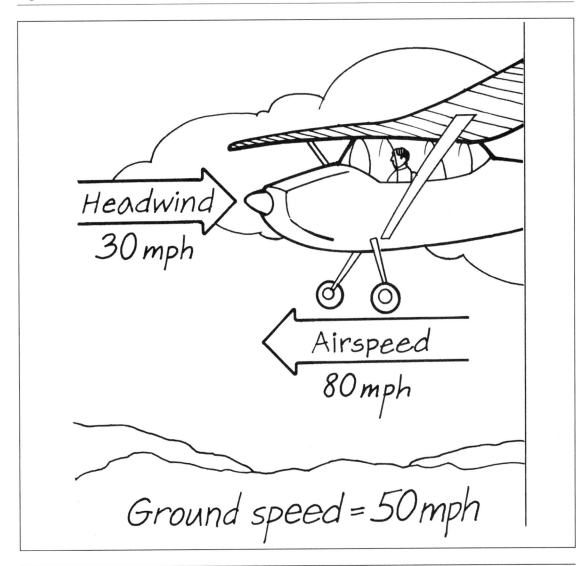

SOURCE: Hetzel & Wyma, 1995; illustrations by Diane Valko.

labeled key vocabulary: *fin, rudder, elevators, flaps, spoilers, tail plane, engine,* and *slats* (see Figure 4.32). ELL students enjoy this type of activity, and they are readily successful at it. It provides an illustrated vocabulary bank for them and an easily accessible assessment of basic conceptual understanding for the teacher.

However, labeled diagrams may not be enough to ensure comprehension. *Picture dictionaries* are also helpful in (re)organizing key concepts from content-area lessons. For example, Figure 4.33 shows a student's recording of key flight terms—*aeronautics, envelope,* and *fin*—with the meaning written out as well as a simple sketch. This (re)organization of key concepts in text in both linguistic and artistic terms provides two venues of reinforcement for long-term recall.

Figure 4.32   Labeled Vocabulary Diagram of Plane

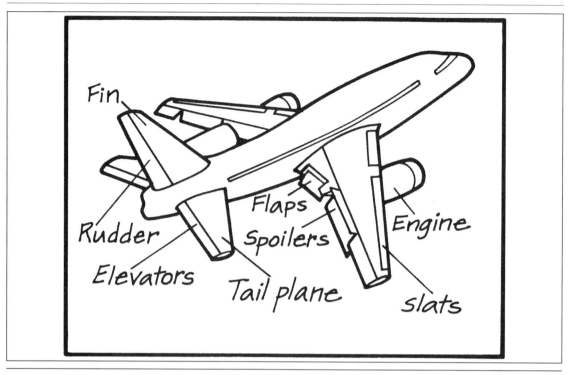

SOURCE: Hetzel & Wyma, 1995; illustrations by Diane Valko.

Figure 4.33   Illustrated Flight Terms

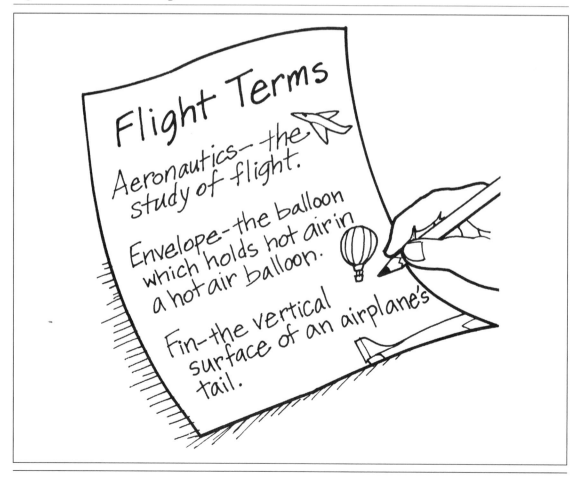

SOURCE: Hetzel & Wyma, 1995; illustrations by Diane Valko.

SUPPORTING ELD AND BACKGROUND KNOWLEDGE AND EXPERIENCE

Finally, let us look at a classroom scenario to better understand how the instructor applies meaning-making strategies while simultaneously supporting English language development (ELD) and practicing pedagogy that takes into account ELLs' and SELs' background knowledge and experiences. For example, a teacher might plan for students to read *The Gardener*, a picture book by Sarah Stewart (1997) about a young girl, Lydia Grace Finch, who must leave her parents during an economic depression and go to live with her Uncle Jim, a cantankerous baker who never smiles. Lydia Grace, the young gardener, makes her new goal to bring joy and beauty to Uncle Jim's drab bakery and high-rise by providing beautiful flowers for his bakery and customers. Her masterpiece, however, is a surprise rooftop garden for Uncle Jim. The young heroine has optimism and determination and endears the reader to her generous spirit. So, in preparation for this lesson, the ELL teacher needs to think about the foundational ELD skills needed by the students in her classroom. In this case, her upper-elementary ELL students are working on the ELD comprehension skills in Figure 4.34.

Figure 4.34 Comprehension Strategies and Applications for Upper-Elementary Class

English Language Development (ELD) Level	Strategies and Applications
Beginning: 5 students	Answer simple questions with one- to two-word responses.
Early Intermediate: 5 students	Ask and answer questions by using phrases or simple sentences.
Intermediate: 10 students	Listen attentively to stories and information, and identify important details and concepts by using both verbal and nonverbal responses.
Early Advanced: 8 students	Listen attentively to more complex stories and information on new topics across content areas, and identify the main points and supporting details.
Advanced: 2 students	Listen attentively to stories and information on topics; identify the main points and supporting details.

SOURCE: Strategies and application text taken from California State Board of Education, 1999, *English-Language Development Standards for California Public Schools, K–12.*

The teacher then considers the context-embedded teaching strategies that she will use to help provide meaning for all four literacy strands (reading, writing, listening, speaking) as she develops her lesson and plans to move in and out of these strands throughout the hour (see Figure 4.35).

In addition to infusing listening, speaking, reading, and writing throughout the lesson or hour, she also thinks through what "gaps" could prevent her students from comprehending the meaning of the text (see Figure 4.36).

Figure 4.35   Literacy Around the Clock

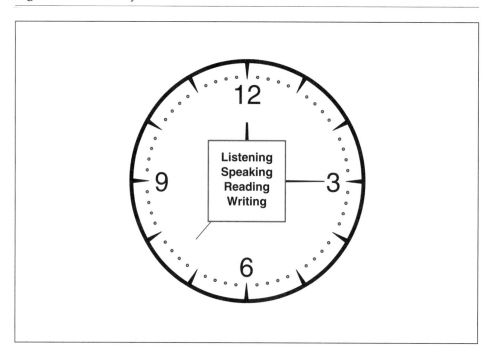

Figure 4.36   Potential Gaps Between Student and Text

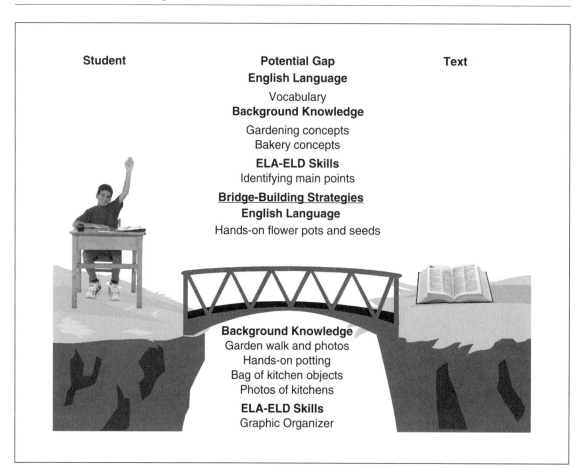

Using the "gaps" model as a springboard, she develops a multiday lesson plan that is tailored to the specific needs of her ELL students, focusing on English language development. This particular model is an adapted Madeline Hunter lesson plan format with ELL accommodations and scaffolds embedded (see Figure 4.37).

Figure 4.37   Lesson With ELL Adaptations by June Hetzel, 2008

LESSON PLAN, GRADE 4, READING

State Standard: 3.0 Literary Response and Analysis
3.2 Identify the main events of the plot, their causes, and the influence of each event on future actions.

Lesson Objective:

Comprehension: The learners will identify and discuss the main events of the story.
Decoding: phonemes, blends, digraphs in context of "sounding out" new vocabulary

Key Vocabulary:

Garden Vocabulary: Garden, gardener, pot, soil, dirt, flower, window boxes, catalogue, seeds, bulb, plants, radishes, onions, lettuce, spring
Family Vocabulary: uncle, aunt, niece, mother, father, mama, papa, grandma, daughter
Bakery Vocabulary: baking, baker, bakery, bread, knead, dough, cake pans, tea cups, store, customer, cake, lunch
Locations: city, country, train, travel, house, apartment, high-rise, rooftop, upstairs, downstairs
Miscellaneous: smile, frown secret, happiness, beauty, imagine, retire, homesick
School: letter, envelope, write, schoolwork, homework

Materials:

31 copies of *The Gardener;* graphic organizers; illustrated word banks; pots, soil, seeds, flowers, water; bakery items—pans, tea cups, spoons, etc.; mix-and-match illustrated cards; copies of graphic organizers; Picture Bingo cards for garden and picture vocabulary

Class Profile:

Background Knowledge: Most children have gardening experience; several parents are migrant workers
Language Background: Spanish and Hmong; all English Language Learners; 2 advanced ELLs above grade level in Spanish reading
ELD Levels: 10 Beginning and Early Intermediate ELLs; 18 Intermediate and Early Advanced ELLS; 2 advanced ELLs
Literacy Levels: Two newcomers (unknown); reading range .5 to 2.9 reading levels

INSTRUCTIONAL PLAN

	Rationale
Anticipatory Set 1. **Walk About:** Walk children through the school garden. Utilize garden vocabulary in Q & A. 2. **TPR:** Provide Total Physical Response exercise. Each child has a small pot, seeds, and access to water and soil. Step-by-step planting exercise 3. **Visuals:** Share several photographs of flowers, gardens, vegetables, etc. Ask for one- to two-word responses.	Build background knowledge and receptive and expressive vocabulary
Communication of the Objective "Today, we will read *The Gardener* (teacher holds up book) and learn about a girl, Lydia Grace (teacher points to picture of Lydia) who brings happiness (teacher smiles) through her garden (teacher points to drawing of garden). After reading the book (teacher points to book), we will identify the main points of the story by identifying what happened first, second, and third (teacher holds up one finger, then two, then three fingers)."	

Instructional Input	
1. **Picture Walk:** Walk through the picture book, page by page, briefly discussing each page, pointing to pictures, asking questions, etc.	
2. **New Concept:** Introduce the concept of "main point" by introducing "first, then, last" or "first, second, third," or "beginning, middle, and end."	
3. **Introduce Bakery Vocabulary:** Share several kitchen objects by pulling them out of the bag, one at a time. Repeat names of objects, sounding out each individual phoneme (e.g., /b/ /a/ /k/ /r/) Invite students to repeat in unison. Use each word in a sentence. Q & A. Leave items on the table.	
4. **Decoding Exercise—Kitchen:** Write names of kitchen items on the board. Invite students to match the item with the written word. Emphasize phonemes, blends, digraphs as students orally decode the words. Stretch out each word so students can hear and repeat each phoneme correctly: /t/ /e/ /k/ /u/ /p/.	
5. **Decoding Exercise—Garden:** Review garden vocabulary. Write names of objects on the board. Invite students to match words and objects. Emphasize phonemes, blends, digraphs as students orally decode the words.	
Guided Practice	
1. **Shared Reading:** Read the book aloud to the students using oral cloze (students fill in words orally when you pause), alternating with unison reading.	
2. **Oral Language:** Discuss pictures on each page.	
a. TPR for newcomers and Beginning ELD. Invite everyone to follow directions on the page.	
i. "Point to Uncle Jim."	
ii. "Point to Lydia Grace."	
iii. "Point to the flowers."	
iv. "Point to the bakery."	
b. Beginning students, particularly newcomers, may not be ready to produce speech. Allow for just listening and TPR (Total Physical Response).	
c. One- to two-word responses expected for Early Intermediate and Intermediate; however, phrase back more expanded responses and allow time for expanded responses.	
i. "How old do you think Lydia Grace is?" "Why?"	
ii. "Is Lydia Grace happy?" "How do you know?"	
iii. "Is Uncle Jim happy?" "How do you know?"	
iv. "How does Lydia Grace spend her time?" "Why?"	
v. "How does Uncle Jim spend his time?" "Why?"	
d. Sentence responses for Early Advanced and Advanced:	
i. "Why do you think Uncle Jim is grumpy?"	
ii. "What makes Lydia Grace plant flowers?"	
iii. "What do you like about Lydia Grace?"	
3. **Graphic Organizer:**	
a. Discussion: "Identify the main points of the story. What happened first? Second? Third?"	
b. Board Work:	
i. Model: Write the main points in the graphic organizer on the board as students verbally respond.	
ii. Model: Write a summary of the main points in a paragraph format on the board while eliciting responses from the students.	

Independent Practice

Students may go as far as they are able with the assignments below. The ☆ indicates the minimum desired competency for the ELD level.

Exercise	Beginning	Early Intermediate & Intermediate	Early Advanced & Advanced
Match picture cards with words.			→
Listen to books on tape related to garden and kitchen stories.			→
Draw pictures of the three main events in the graphic organizer.	★		→
Draw pictures of the three main events and write a sentence below each picture.		★	→
Write a paragraph about the three main events in *The Gardener*.			★

The teacher rotates around the room while the children are working on their independent practice, discussing the main events with each student and recording each student's ability to articulate the three main events of the story, comprising the beginning, middle, and end. The instructional assistant or volunteer tutor is assigned to work with the beginning ELL students on individualized work.

Closure/Assessment

1. **Oral Review:** Review the story with the whole class. Review the concept of "main events." Review what happened first, second, and third.
2. **Pair-Share:** Ask students to tell their neighbor what happened first, second, and third.
3. **Pair-Share:** Ask the students to tell the "main events" of the story.
4. **Vocabulary Game:** Play Picture Bingo with garden and kitchen vocabulary words.
   a. Each student has a Bingo card and chips.
   b. Invite students to pull a word from the hat, read it, and use it in a sentence. Model the pronunciation and sentence usage of the word as needed.
   c. Reinforce phoneme/grapheme relationships in the context of Bingo and utilizing the board.

Reinforcement:

- Listening station with books and earphones.
- Computer station with a variety of leveled literacy programs.
- Tutor matches: Continue individual work with newcomers and Beginning ELLs to ensure mastery of the 44 phonemes of English and graphic representations. Reinforce "main events."

Teachers build receptive and expressive understanding of language by immersing their ELLs, as well as their SELs, in environments rich with Standard English language. Teachers provide books, magazines, posters, labels of objects in the room, and rich oral language. As can be seen in the preceding *The Gardener* lesson and as summarized in Figure 4.38, the teacher provided a plethora of opportunities for listening, speaking, reading, and writing throughout the lesson that reinforced decoding skills, English language development, and comprehension skills while building upon background knowledge as discussed in detail in Chapter 3.

Figure 4.38 Literacy Scaffolds for English Language Learners and Standard English Learners

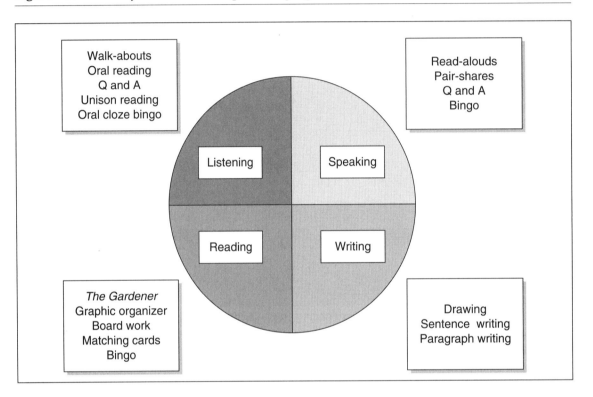

Teachers read daily to their ELLs and SELs and provide print text for their students to follow along. Students generally acquire a receptive or listening vocabulary 2 years above their speaking vocabulary, which benefits the student as she approaches text. She decodes the word (e.g., *garden*) and remembers the meaning from the walk through the garden, the experience potting flowers, the teacher's demonstration lessons with garden photos, from her own prior experiences, or from the reading of text accompanied by illustrations. She attaches the meaning of the word *garden* to the written word and continues to move through the text. If she does not know the meaning of the word, she begins to develop strategies to decipher the meaning, such as use of context clues, illustrations, picture dictionaries, and asking a friend.

In reviewing potential gaps, we clearly see that the teacher was aware that the English vocabulary related to gardening and bakery experiences was an essential prerequisite in order for the students to comprehend the text. She also recognized background experiences and concepts she could build upon. In addition, she utilized ELD strategies throughout her lesson.

Hence, the teacher skillfully developed scaffolded experiences to support English Language Learners' comprehension. Figure 4.39 shows how each experience moved the student from the concrete to the connecting abstract language link, and then finally to the written text.

Figure 4.39 Context-Embedded Language Linkages

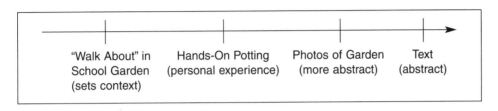

SUMMARY

The *comprehension* branch of Key Components of Effective Language Arts Instruction includes *academic language* and *comprehension strategies*, as shown in Figure 4.40.

Figure 4.40 Key Components of Effective Language Arts Instruction

Decoding					Comprehension			
Word Recognition Strategies			Fluency		Academic Language		Comprehension Strategies	
Concepts about print	Phonemic awareness	Phonics	Sight words	Auto-maticity	Vocabulary	Syntax -------- Text structure	Compre-hension monitoring	(Re)organizing text
English Language Development								
Background Knowledge								

SOURCE: Adapted from California State Board of Education, 2007.

Vocabulary instruction is key for the English Language Learner (Center for Applied Linguistics, 2006), and the teacher must remain attentive to English language development and background knowledge, scaffolding learning along the way. Many aspects of syntax are readily transferable from the student's L1, whereas the structure of nonfiction text can be particularly challenging. Critical to a maturing reader is the ability to monitor his or her own comprehension as well as (re)organize text for long-term memory. An English Language Learner is just as ready as any other student to learn to read; however, he or she requires the sensitive, systematic instruction of a caring teacher who understands good instruction, emphasizes vocabulary development, utilizes research-based meaning-making strategies, applies scaffolds to context-embedded teaching, and holds high expectations for all students. Similar to the English Language

Learner's needs, the Standard English Learner also benefits from the bridge-building strategies outlined in this chapter, though SEL language needs may not be as intense as the newcomer who is acquiring the English language and is immersed in an English-speaking environment for the first time.

REFERENCES

Beck, I. L., McKeown, M. G., & Kucan, L. (2000). *Bringing words to life: Robust vocabulary instruction.* New York: Guilford.

Bloom, B. S., & Krathwohl, D. R. (1956). *Taxonomy of educational objectives: The classification of educational goals, by a committee of college and university examiners. Handbook 1: Cognitive domain.* New York: Longmans.

California State Board of Education. (1999, July). *English-language development standards for California public schools, K–12.* Sacramento, CA: Author.

California State Board of Education. (2007). *Reading/language arts framework for California public schools: Kindergarten through Grade Twelve.* Sacramento: California Department of Education.

Center for Applied Linguistics. (2006). *National Literacy Panel on Language-Minority Children and Youth.* Washington, DC: US Government Printing Office. Available online at http://www.cal.org/calwebdb/nlp.

DeJong, M. (1972). *The wheel on the school bus.* New York: Harper Trophy.

Diaz-Rico, L. T., & Weed, K. Z. (2002). *The cross-cultural, language, and academic development handbook: A complete K–12 reference guide.* Boston: Allyn & Bacon.

Dutro, S., & Moran, C. (2002). Rethinking English language instruction: An architectural approach. In G. Garcia (Ed.), *English learners reading at the highest level of English literacy.* Newark, DE: International Reading Association.

Fillmore, L. W., & Snow, C. E. (2002). What teachers need to know about language. In C. T. Adger, C. E. Snow, & D. Christian (Eds.), *What teachers need to know about language* (pp. 7–54). Washington, DC, and McHenry, IL: Center for Applied Linguistics and Delta Systems.

Francis, D. J., Rivera, M., Lesaux, N., Kieffer, M., & Rivera, H. (2006). *Practical guidelines for the education of English Language Learners: Research-based recommendations for instruction and academic interventions.* Portsmouth, NH: RMC Research Corporation, Center on Instruction.

Gersten, R., Baker, S. K., Shanahan, T., Linan-Thompson, S., Collins, P., & Scarcella, R. (2007). *Effective literacy and English language instruction for English learners in the elementary grades: A practice guide* (NCEE 2007–4011). Washington, DC: National Center for Education Evaluation and Regional Assistance, Institute of Education Sciences, U.S. Department of Education.

Girard, V. (2005). English learners and the language arts. In V. Girard (Ed.), *Schools moving up: A WestEd initiative.* Retrieved November 8, 2006, from http://www.schoolsmovingup.net/cs/wested/view/e/140.

Goldenberg, C. (2006). *Improving achievement for English learners: Conclusions from 2 research reviews.* Retrieved April 8, 2009, from http://www.colorincolorado.org/article/12918.

Hetzel, J. (2002) *Responding to literature: Activities to use with any literature selection* (2nd ed.). Huntington Beach, CA: Creative Teaching Press and Youngheart Music.

Hetzel, J., Miller, S., & Wyma, B. (1995). *Plants.* Cypress, CA: Creative Teaching Press.

Hetzel, J., & Wyma, B. (1995). *Flight.* Cypress, CA: Creative Teaching Press.

Kinsella, K. (2003, March 21). *Dynamic strategies to improve comprehension.* Keynote address, Claremont Reading Conference, Claremont, CA.

Lewis, C. S. (1950). *The lion, the witch and the wardrobe.* London: Geoffrey Bles.

Potter, B. (1987). *The tale of Mr. Jeremy Fisher.* London: Frederick Warne. (Original work published 1908)

Pudewa, A. (2005). *Writing inservice* [Writing workshop]. La Mirada, CA: Biola University.

Raphael, T. E. (1986). *The contents of school-based literacy.* New York: Random House.

Say, A. (1993). *Grandfather's journey.* Boston: Houghton Mifflin.

Scarcella, R. (2003). *Accelerating academic English: A focus on the English learner.* Oakland: Regents of the University of California.

Schwartz, D. M. (1999). *Horses.* Huntington Beach, CA: Creative Teaching Press.

Shefelbine, J. (1998). *Academic language and literacy development.* Paper presented at the Reading and English-Language Learner Forum, Sacramento, California.

Smith, F. (1971). *Understanding reading: A psycholinguistic analysis of reading and learning to read.* Mahwah, NJ: Lawrence Erlbaum.

Stewart, S. (1997). *The gardener.* New York: Farrar, Straus & Giroux.

Tompkins, G. E. (2000). *Teaching writing: Balancing process and product* (3rd ed.). Columbus, OH: Merrill.

5

English Language Development and Academic English

English Language Development (ELD) as it relates to Academic English is a sensitive issue in a classroom of ELLs and SELs. Chapter 5 guides the teacher, step-by-step, through the process of sensitive language mentorship for these two groups of students. In addition, this chapter will discuss the language similarities and differences between ELLs and SELs, as well as provide an instructional framework for addressing both of their needs in a heterogeneous classroom.

SPECIALIZED LANGUAGE NEEDS OF ELLS

The R30 Census (U.S. Department of Education, 2000) defines ELLs as "Students whose primary language is not English and whose English language skills are not sufficient to allow them to function fully in academic English" (p. 1). Although ELLs bring with them a rich resource from their home language and culture, they often do not receive the specific support they need because they have all been lumped into the same category,

Figure 5.1 English Language Development Gap

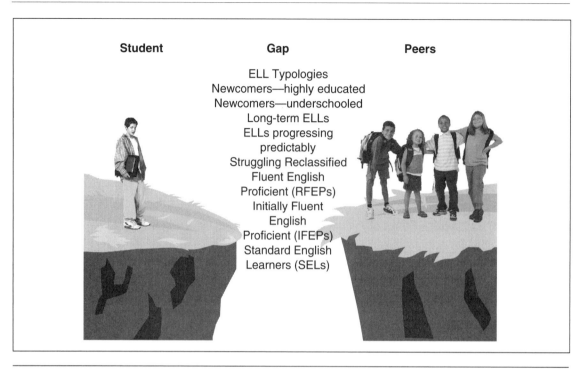

SOURCE: Typologies from Olsen, 2006.

without careful attention to their level of language proficiency or Academic English needs. For example, the instructional needs of a newcomer who enters the country with little to no schooling is vastly different from those of a newcomer who comes with schooling and is literate in his or her first language. According to Olsen (2006) of California Tomorrow, there are five different kinds of ELLs, with specific and unique language needs (see Figure 5.1). These ELL types include the following:

1. Newcomers who are highly educated and literate

2. Newcomers who are underschooled

3. Long-term ELLs in U.S. schools 6 years or more

4. ELLs progressing predictably through a developmental sequence

5. Struggling Reclassified Fluent English Proficient (RFEPs) and Initially Fluent English Proficient (IFEP) students

Each of the above groups of ELLs has distinctive needs that must be addressed in order to see the kind of progress in English needed. Historically, we have treated ELLs as a homogeneous group of students who require a one-size-fits-all approach, when in fact, they do not. Each of these groups of ELLs can benefit from instructional practices and adaptations that are specific to their needs. As such, ELLs would benefit from the adaptations in Figure 5.2, according to their distinctive needs.

Figure 5.2 ELL Distinctions

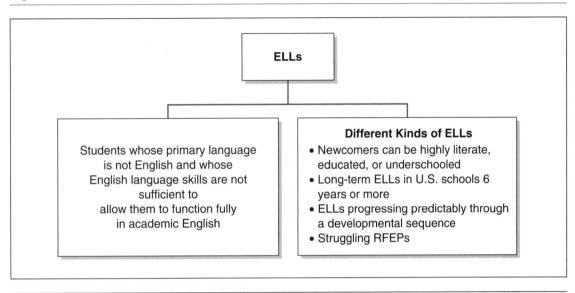

SOURCE: Olsen, 2006; U.S. Department of Education, 2000.

Newcomers Who Are Highly Educated and Literate

ELLs who come to this country with proficiency in L1 and schooling from their home countries often experience rapid progress in L2. This occurs because these students have a schema for language learning, which transfers easily from one language to another. In addition, since such students have had schooling in their home countries, they can acclimate to their new educational settings quickly. Due to the fact that ELLs in this category experience rapid language growth, they would benefit from accelerated English Language Development with specific emphasis on oral language development. For example, highly literate newcomers would be able to quickly gain proficiency in the forms and functions of English from their primary language, but would need ample opportunity to practice these components of language orally.

ELLs with strong L1 skills typically are able to transfer reading and writing skills more quickly than speaking or listening skills. This is because there has been a framework for literacy established in their primary language. In other words, many of the key skills in reading and writing have been introduced, including basic decoding skills (especially if the two languages are phonetically similar) and the grammatical components of writing (although targeted differences between the two languages may need to be addressed). For example, although decoding skills are often strong with highly literate newcomers, they may struggle with grammatical inversions in written and oral language. In other words, slight touchups in reading and writing can be made, whereas oral language development must be given ample time and practice, especially as the distinctions between social and academic talk are targeted.

A newcomer who is highly educated and literate would also benefit from immediate introduction to academic language development across the content areas. Since basic English skills will be acquired quickly, newcomers who are educated and literate would benefit from instruction in multiple-meaning words (e.g., in math—*product, multiply, times,* etc.), function words (e.g., *therefore* and *however*), and new labels in English vocabulary, because they often will already be familiar with concepts. For example, a highly literate ELL may have comprehended the concept *metamorphosis* in her home language, but will need additional English labels or vocabulary for the concept such as *form, structure, change,* and *transformation.*

Newcomers Who Are Underschooled

ELLs that are newcomers and underschooled would benefit from both acclimation to schooling in the United States, such as classroom expectations and a typical school schedule, as well as ELD. Since these students come to school with little English, they will need explicit and intensive instruction in the forms and functions of English, in a meaningful, contextually based setting where they can be practiced. That is, it is essential to teach the basics of English in the context of authentic reading and writing. A *language function* is a task accomplished by way of language. Examples of language function include describing, debating, comparing, contrasting, evaluating, explaining, asking for information, discussing, expressing an opinion, or telling a story. *Language forms* are the tools used to accomplish the language tasks or functions, such as sentence components, comparative adjectives, or past-tense verbs. For example, using Figure 5.3 below, a teacher would explicitly teach an ELD lesson demonstrating that when one expresses needs and likes, he or she would use indirect and direct objects, subject-verb agreement, and pronouns.

Figure 5.3   Forms and Functions of Language (English Learner Professional Development, 2008)

Language Functions	Language Forms
Expressing needs and wants	Indirect/direct object, subject–verb agreement, pronouns
Retelling/relating past events	Past-tense verbs
Describing spatial and temporal relations	Prepositional phrases
Making predictions	Verbs: future tense, conditional mode

SOURCE: Santa Clara County Office of Education, 2008.

The teacher might also use a sentence stem, such as, "My favorite food is _____ because _____." In addition, the teacher can ask a student to pair-share with a partner and then summarize his or her response with the following stem: "_____'s favorite food is _____ because _____." Newcomers who are underschooled also need to know how to use forms and functions in the context of their own writing and the texts they are reading. As teachers see that students are struggling with particular forms in their writing or speaking, they can target such skills using mini-lessons. Teachers can place students' own writing errors on the board (without their names on them) and have the class collectively discuss how to make the response better. Orally, teachers can recast student responses.

Long-Term ELLs in U.S. Schools 6 Years or More

Students who have been in the country for more than 6 years will benefit from intensive and accelerated ELD, while also receiving challenging Academic English development—the specialized language of each discipline, which is also used across the content areas. In contrast to only teaching the basic forms and functions as in the example above, these ELLs would benefit from learning the differences between social and academic purposes when using language functions in speech or writing. For example, whereas one might give instructions in a social setting, such as how to open a can, an academic purpose for giving instructions could include explaining the process of formulating conclusions after a lab experiment in science.

Figure 5.4 demonstrates how language functions can be expanded upon from the earlier example where ELLs were merely asked to describe basic needs. Notice that making a request in a social setting translates into classifying objects or ideas in an academic setting, such as in science. ELLs who have been in the country 6 years or more will benefit greatly from acceleration of ELD skills they may not have received, as well as expanding those skills with more cognitively demanding content knowledge in the academic setting.

Figure 5.4 Social and Academic Functions (English Learner Professional Development, 2008)

Social Purposes	Academic Purposes
Giving instructions	Describing processes (Math or Science)
Introducing ourselves	Comparing and contrasting (Language Arts or History)
Making requests	Classifying objects or ideas (Science)

SOURCE: Soto-Hinman, 2008.

ELLs Progressing Predictably Through a Developmental Sequence

Although this group of students is progressing as it should, it is important that as they learn skills in ELD, they are also challenged with cognitively respectful materials and receive academic language support across the content areas. ELLs who are progressing successfully should be introduced to more and more Academic Language Development (ALD), while also accelerating ELD. They must be exposed to the nuances of language and syntactical structures across a school day, and in a variety of content areas. In order to be successful in reading and writing, ELLs must be exposed to varied linguistic and textual differences between narrative and expository texts. For example, ELLs progressing predictably need to know that a history textbook is written in a linear format, with a focus on chronology, facts, and figures. Although science textbooks are also informational in nature, these texts focus on process thinking such as predictions or hypotheses, investigations, and interpretations. Explicitly teaching ELLs how to approach such texts differently—perhaps with a timeline in a history textbook versus a scientific method outline in science—will allow access to information across the content areas.

The scientific method outline in Figure 5.5 is a tool that can assist ELLs in analyzing science as a discipline. For example, as students read scientific texts or lab manuals, they can begin to internalize the steps and process taken when conducting a science experiment or lab.

Figure 5.5   Scientific Method Outline

Step	Description	Notes
Question	What does the scientist want to learn about?	
Research	Gathering information	
Hypothesis	An educated guess of an answer to a question	
Procedure/Method	Written and carefully followed step-by-step experiment designed to test the hypothesis	
Data	Information gathered during the experiment	
Observations	Written description of what was noticed during experiment	
Conclusion	Was the hypothesis correct or incorrect?	

Struggling RFEPs and IFEPs

Reclassified and initially fluent English proficient students (RFEPs and IFEPs, respectively) need academic language support to be successful at their grade level and beyond. They must be intensively and explicitly exposed to academic language across the content areas. It is important to remember that students who have been reclassified or were identified as initially fluent English proficient may not have been, and often still are not, at grade-level proficiency. Instead, they continue to need additional support and scaffolding to be brought up to grade-level language needs.

These students would benefit from the continued use of visuals, graphic organizers, and vocabulary development across the school day and content areas. Such strategies allow ELLs to have access to specifics regarding content areas and academic disciplines.

NEEDS OF STANDARD ENGLISH LEARNERS

Standard English Learners are students who speak a variation of English, often not used in an academic or professional setting, and are learning mainstream English. Although associated with African American Vernacular English, SELs encompass a wide group of language variations including Chicano English and Hawaiian Pidgin. It is important to note, however, that not all African American or Mexican American students are SELs. Although there is currently no language assessment in place to identify SELs, these students are typically identified by the following characteristics (LeMoine, 2006):

1. They speak a variation of English.

2. They tend to have the lowest scores on standardized achievement tests.

3. They experience barriers to their education due to teacher attitudes toward their language and culture.

Although such variations are often viewed in the pejorative, there is a rich language structure and resource in these non-native forms of English. According to LeMoine (2006), SELs have "Combined their intuitive knowledge of their indigenous language structures with newly acquired English vocabulary and created new languages that proved quite functional in their new surroundings" (p. 12). In essence, SELs have learned to function linguistically and culturally in two worlds. In an educational setting, SELs need to be guided into transferring those rich linguistic skills into academic English. Kinsella (2007) describes all students as Academic English as Second Language (AESL) learners. It is important to note that for many students, but especially ELLs and SELs, Academic English is not a natural language or one that is often used. For ELLs, another language is often spoken at home and, often, the only English they hear is in school. The same is true of SELs who hear a variation of English at home rather than Standard English or Academic English. For both groups, then, it is essential that Academic English be explicitly taught and modeled throughout the school day. Both of these groups must also have ample opportunities to practice Academic English within a school day.

Kinsella (2007) asserts that the essential components of Academic English include vocabulary, syntax, grammar, and register (see Figure 5.6). Each of these components will be discussed at length in subsequent chapters, but Figure 5.7 includes a brief definition of each term.

Figure 5.6   What Is Academic English?

What Is Academic English?

ALL students are AESL
(Academic English as a Second Language)

- Academic English is not natural language. It must be explicitly taught.
- Essential components of Academic English Language:

  —Vocabulary

  —Syntax

  —Grammar

  —Register

SOURCE: Kinsella, 2007.

Figure 5.7   Definitions From Public Broadcasting Company
http://www.pbs.org/speak/about/guide/#Grammar (retrieval
date 7/18/09)

Academic Language Component	Definition
Vocabulary	The words of a language. Differences in vocabulary are among the most noticeable contrasts between language varieties. Language change involving vocabulary items can occur more quickly than changes in grammatical structure or the sounds of a language.
Syntax	The study of rules and patterns for the formation of sentences and phrases.
Grammar	How a language is structured. Although *grammar* is popularly used to refer to the language forms and constructions that are considered to be correct, linguists use this term to refer to the knowledge that native speakers implicitly have about the structure of their own language—for example, how to arrange words into sentences.
Register	Specialized use of a language for a defined situation or occasion. A common example is the baby talk register. This is a very specialized style that involves high pitch and particular vocabulary items. It is used when talking to a baby, an animal, or sometimes a significant other, but it would probably be considered inappropriate in other contexts.

SOURCE: PBS, 2005.

SELs also often come to school with a rich oral and storytelling tradition. Although narrative discourse patterns differ from those used at home, they can be used as segues to explicit teaching of the academic register, as well as the discourse patterns of school and the workplace. Language assets such as storytelling must be viewed as foundational and acknowledged where there may be gaps in early literacy experiences, instead of assuming that SELs do not come to school with their own foundational linguistic and narrative discourse pattern richness. Addressing students in this manner, and acknowledging their own rich linguistic histories, will go a long way when teaching students who speak non-standard variations of English. One way to do this is by affirming students regarding their rich language histories. For example, LeMoine (2006) suggests "Infusing information on the origin and historical development of standard and non-standard languages into the instructional curriculum" (p. 14).

One way to access SELs' rich linguistic resource is by using texts, such as *Flossie and the Fox,* by Patricia McKissack (1986), to both validate and contrast various language traditions. Such a text can assist *all* students in exposing them to other variations of English. *Flossie and the Fox* honors the oral tradition and folktales, and reverses stereotypical roles by portraying the "cunning" fox as unable to outwit Flossie. Teachers can use this text to teach contrastive analysis in which grammatical features can be compared, such as "He going" in African American Vernacular English and "He is going" in Standard English. When reading the text, students can work through a translation exercise in which they reenact and repeat lines from the text, embodying each character. Students can then respond to each other the way that the other character would, using the language variation that that character would use. Figure 5.8 includes an example of this instructional scenario.

By utilizing the translation exercise, students begin to value the language usage of each of the characters in the text. They can also begin to think about where each language can be used—non-Standard English in social situations and Standard English in school and the workplace. Students can also reenact each of these scenes with props and the language from the text using a modified Reader's Theater model.

While we know that there are many different types of SELs (e.g., African American, Native Hawaiian, Mexican American), there currently exists no systematic way of identifying SELs. For example, although ELLs in California are identified using the California English Language Development Test (CELDT), there is no such assessment in place to identify SELs. There is also no systematic approach for addressing SELs' academic language levels and progression from year to year (See Figure 5.9.). Because SELs themselves are not systemically identified, even though best practices have been developed, this group of students often does not receive the type of instruction needed. The following section will discuss commonalities in language needs between ELLs and SELs, and how approaches for ELLs might also be appropriate for SELs.

ELL and SEL Commonalities

Classroom teachers can bridge the gap between SELs and ELLs by understanding where the commonalities between the two groups exist,

Figure 5.8 Non-Standard/Standard English Comparative Chart

Non-Standard English (McKissak, 1986)	Standard English (Soto-Hinman, 2008)
Flossie: "I be Flossie Finley," she answered with a proper curtsy. "I reckon I don't know who you be either."	**Flossie:** "I am Flossie Finley," she answered with a proper curtsy. "I reckon I don't know who you are either."
Big Momma: "Take these to Miz Viola over at the McCutchin Place," she say reaching behind her and handing Flossie a basket of fresh eggs. "Seem like they been troubled by a fox. Miz Viola's chickens be so scared, they can't even how lay a stone."	**Big Momma:** "Take these to Miss Viola over at the McCutchin Place," she said, reaching behind her and handing Flossie a basket of fresh eggs. "It seems like they have been troubled by a fox. Miss Viola's chickens are so scared, they aren't even able to lay a stone."
Flossie: "Come to think of it," she said matter-of-fact-like, "rats got long pointed noses." She snapped her fingers. "That's it! You a rat trying to pass yo'self off as a fox."	**Flossie:** "Come to think of it," she said matter-of-factly, "rats have long pointed noses." She snapped her fingers. "That's it! You're a rat trying to pass yourself off as a fox."

and thus be better able to approach those needs in a heterogeneously grouped classroom. Due to the fact that both groups have been identified as students with linguistic needs, ELLs and SELs often have the lowest achievement scores. In addition, educator attitudes toward language differences between these two groups or their cultures often set up barriers to success in schools (LeMoine, 2006). Both of these factors, as well as the distinctions introduced previously, perpetuate the achievement gap, but can also assist an educator in making important educational decisions (see Figure 5.10).

For example, since we know that educator attitudes create a barrier to ELL and SEL success, it is important for districts and schools to target professional development around these key components. In the Hayward Unified School District in California over the last 4 years, there has been a focused, systemic approach to training around meeting the needs of both ELLs and SELs. Both administrators and teacher leaders meet once a month for professional development, which they then take back to their own school sites. In addition, teacher leaders have worked with departments and grade levels to design instructional read-alouds (IRAs) that are both linguistically and culturally appropriate. These teacher leaders, called *partner teachers,* have also demonstrated culturally and linguistically responsive instructional read-alouds (IRAs) in classrooms, so that all teachers within the system become comfortable with designing and implementing them.

Effective Instructional Practices With SELs and ELLs

Since we know that SELs and ELLs have similar linguistic and educational needs, teachers can begin to use the following framework by

Figure 5.9 SEL Distinctions

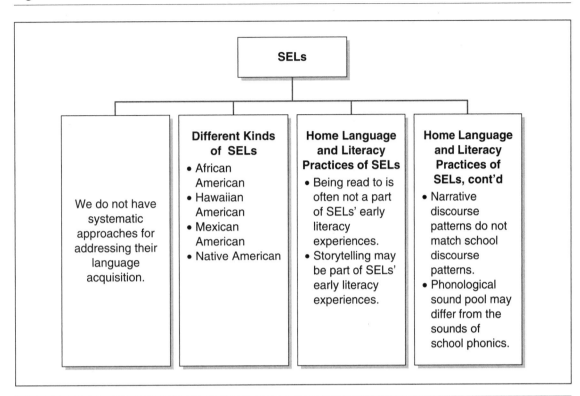

SOURCE: LeMoine, 2006.

Figure 5.10 ELL and SEL Commonalities

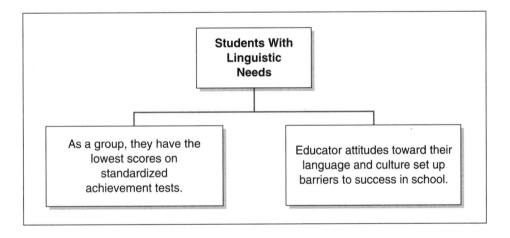

SOURCE: LeMoine, 2006.

LeMoine (2006) to design lessons that are responsive to both groups' needs. The framework features include the following:

• Enhance positive attitude toward non-standard language varieties—This component includes having high expectations for SELs and ELLs. They must not be judged by their language abilities, but must be instructed as students with language resources and needs. Educators must acknowledge their own beliefs and biases toward language variations, dialects, and accents, and learn ways to move beyond them in order to assist students in becoming proficient in Academic English. Having high expectations also means using cognitively appropriate and respectful materials. Just because students are in language transition does not mean that they should not be introduced to higher-order thinking skills and interesting text. SELs' and ELLs' language abilities should not sentence them to meaningless drills and watered-down instructional materials that impede their rapid progress in English language acquisition.

• Integrate linguistic knowledge about non-standard language into instruction—It is important for teachers to understand both the historical and linguistic origins of non-standard forms of English in order to better understand and meet the instructional needs of their students. In a global society, SELs and ELLs will need to know how to communicate academically and cross-culturally. This means they must be taught Academic English explicitly, as well as the rules and norms of interacting with a variety of people and in a variety of contexts.

• Use appropriate second language acquisition methods to support acquisition of school language and literacy—LeMoine (2006) suggests that SELs also benefit from methods such as visuals, productive group work, graphic organizers, media, and manipulatives. Although many say that these approaches are "just good teaching," both ELLs and SELs *rely* on these scaffolds for success. In other words, other students might be able to comprehend or access concepts without such scaffolds, but these two groups need them in order to make language and achievement gains. Moreover, if these approaches *were* "just good teaching," we would see them used more often, especially systemically across classrooms, schools, and districts.

• Build on the learning style and strengths of SELs through culturally responsive pedagogy to enhance learning—*Culturally responsive pedagogy* can range from methods that acknowledge and honor the student's home culture, to utilizing diverse texts, to introducing a variety of historical perspectives. Cultural responsiveness allows both SELs and ELLs access to content by allowing them to make connections, interacting with concepts they might not have been able to otherwise, and providing engagement throughout an entire lesson or unit. Cultural responsiveness also becomes important for *all* students as an entire class builds their collective repertoire around learning and experiencing life from multiple perspectives, and extends their global community arsenal so that they are able to positively interact with a variety of people.

The above framework can be used as a guide when planning lessons for both SELs and ELLs in the classroom. In the Hayward Unified School District, teachers have been using LeMoine's (2006) framework as a lesson-planning guide in order to begin to internalize the effective instructional practices that should be used with both groups of students. Figure 5.11 is a standards-based lesson plan sample using the Intro, Through, and Beyond approach, as well as the "Effective Instructional Practices With SELs and ELLs" framework.

Figure 5.11   Effective Instructional Practices With SELs and ELLs

I. Enhance teacher's knowledge, understanding, and positive attitude toward non-standard language varieties and the students who use them.	*III. Use appropriate second language acquisition methods to support acquisition of school language and literacy.*
II. Integrate linguistic knowledge about non-standard language into instruction.	*IV. Build on the learning styles and strengths of Standard English Learners through Culturally Responsive Pedagogy to enhance learning.*

SOURCE: LeMoine, 2006.

ACADEMIC LANGUAGE DEVELOPMENT LESSON PLAN

The following IRA was developed for the text *Jazz*, by Walter Dean Myers (2006). The book, illustrated by Myers' son, Christopher, honors the history of jazz music via poetry. Special features, such as a glossary of jazz terms and timeline of important jazz events, make the book accessible to children. Note the skills that have been emphasized in the lesson plan below.

Notice that the lesson design in Figure 5.12 on the next page specifically includes the four components of LeMoine's (2006) effective instructional practices for SELs. A similar IRA was presented schoolwide in each classroom at Schafer Park Elementary School in Hayward, California. Before going into classrooms with the IRA, however, the principal planned an assembly featuring Latin jazz musician John Santos. Since the Schafer Park Elementary School has a large Latino population, Soto-Hinman attempted to make a connection between jazz and its influences on Afro-Cuban music through the assembly. In addition, the assembly provided students with both background knowledge and a contextualized experience with jazz music before the text was introduced.

After the literacy coach and the principal read the text aloud to classes of students, they followed a sequence of splitting students into groups of five and six, giving them a particular type of jazz to listen to and having them analyze the type of jazz heard according to the information provided during the IRA. Specifically, students analyzed the music for improvisation, rhythm, and African/European influences. Students then enjoyed performing the particular style of jazz that they had just heard using drums and instruments.

Figure 5.12   Jazz IRA

Academic Language Development Lesson Plan

Content Area(s): English/Language Arts
Suggested Length: 50 min.

Grade: 5th
Text: *Jazz,* by Walter Dean Myers

Strategies: Tap Prior Knowledge, KWL chart, Timeline chart, Think-Aloud, Think-Pair-Share

CA ELA Standards Addressed: *Reading 1.1:* Read aloud narrative and expository text fluently and accurately and with appropriate pacing, intonation, and expression. *Writing 1.2—Organization and Focus:* Create multiple-paragraph expository compositions, which establish a topic, important ideas, or events in sequence or chronological order.

Applicable CA Content Standards: *Music 3.4:* Describe the influences of various cultures and historical events on musical forms and styles.

Objective of the Lesson: Students will actively listen to an IRA in order to identify jazz terms and the timeline of important jazz events. Students will write a multi-paragraph essay with jazz terms and events in chronological order.

Into:

- KWL chart: Identify what students already know about jazz by charting student responses and having students write them on KWL graphic organizers.
- Play a jazz piece, and ask students to write down what they further want to know about jazz.

Through:

- Teacher fluently reads the first jazz poem, thinking aloud when she comes to key dates and terms related to jazz.
- Students use their timeline graphic organizers to write down important dates as they are also written on the board by the teacher.

Beyond:

- Think-Pair-Share: Students share with partner what they notice about the development of jazz through time.
- Students write a three-paragraph composition about three of the key chronological events, using their timeline as a resource.
- KWL chart: Teacher asks students to write down what they learned about jazz, specifying key terms and dates.

Expectations/Beliefs (*How will students know you have high expectations?*):	**Linguistic Component** (*Contrastive analysis, Standard English exposure*):
*Grade-level text with appropriate scaffolding embedded. *Culturally responsive and relevant text and methods used. *Grade-level standards addressed. *Students are expected to utilize key terms in writing and listen for key events in order to write a multiple-paragraph composition.	*Standard English exposure via read-aloud by the teacher. *Teaching academic language via key jazz terms.
SDAIE/ELD Techniques (*Visuals, manipulatives, graphic organizers, media*):	**Culturally Responsive/Relevant Techniques** (*Diverse texts, productive group work*):
*KWL chart *Sample jazz selection to create a plan for learning *Timeline graphic organizer *Think-pair-shares	*Diverse text: *Jazz* *Think-Pair-Share *Culturally-relevant historical perspective

SOURCE: Developed by Soto-Hinman, 2008.

This IRA lesson design explicitly took into consideration the notion of holding high expectations for SELs and ELLs; specifically taught linguistic skills via fluency of the poetry performances from the book *Jazz;* used multisensory techniques such as instruments, as well as other scaffolds to contextualize the text; and was culturally responsive in its historical introduction and perspective. Similarly, the text and school assembly honored diversity and allowed it to come alive, while also teaching higher-order thinking skills of analysis.

SUMMARY

This chapter unpacked the complexity of language transfer in a classroom of ELLs and SELs by guiding the teacher, step-by-step, through the process of sensitive language mentorship at a variety of language levels. This chapter also discussed the language similarities and differences between ELLs and SELs, and how to meet both of their needs in a heterogeneous classroom setting. In addition, an instructional framework of expectations/beliefs, linguistic components, second language acquisition methods, and culturally responsive/relevant techniques was presented to meet the specific language needs of both ELLs and SELs.

REFERENCES

Kinsella, K. (2007). *Academic language development presentation for Mountain View School District,* El Monte, CA.

LeMoine, N. (2006). SELs: Advancing language and learning in Standard English Learners. *The Ladder: A Magazine About Future Teachers.*

McKissack, P. (1986). *Flossie and the fox.* New York: Dial Books for Young Readers.

Myers, W. D. (2006). *Jazz.* New York: Holiday House.

Olsen, L. (2006). Ensuring academic success for English learners. *UCLMRI Newsletter.*

Public Broadcasting System. (2005). *Do you speak American?* [Viewer's guide]. Retrieved July 18, 2008, from http://www.pbs.org/speak/about/guide/#Grammar.

Santa Clara County Office of Education. (2008). *English learner professional development curriculum.* Santa Clara, CA: Author.

Soto-Hinman, I. (Ed.). (2008). *Professional Development Collaboration for Teachers of EL (PDCTEL) (6–12).* Santa Clara, CA: U.S. Department of Education.

U.S. Department of Education. (2000). *R30 Language Census.* Washington, DC: Author.

6

Perceptions and Expectations

One of the goals of the No Child Left Behind (NCLB) Act of 2001 has been to illuminate and improve academic achievement for all subgroups, including English Language Learners, one of the fastest-growing populations in the United States. According to the National Literacy Panel (Center for Applied Linguistics, 2006), 5 million public school students, which represents 1 in 9 students, are limited in their English proficiency. Similarly, according to the U.S. Census Bureau (2005), whereas the general population has grown by only 12%, the ELL population has grown by 169%. With this subgroup, there is also a growing achievement gap between ELLs and their native English-speaking peers. Further complicating the matter is that most ELLs who struggle academically have, in fact, been enrolled in U.S. schools since kindergarten, illluminating the need to examine and restructure instructional practice for this subgroup.

If not carefully considered, the gap between the teacher and student widens when educators are not sensitive to their own perceptions and expectations of student performance, differences in cultural and socioeconomic status between student and teacher, and language variables between student and teacher. This chapter will address a theoretical framework as well as practical strategies for closing the gap between teacher and student, promoting the teacher's role as a bridge builder in the learning context as it relates to perceptions and expectations (see Figure 6.1).

Figure 6.1 The Gap Between the Student and Teacher

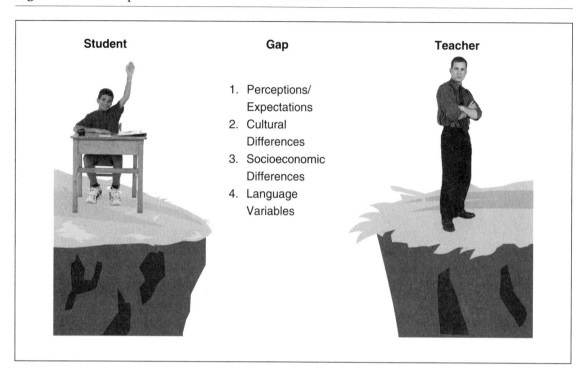

Establishing and holding high expectations for all students is an essential component to successfully meeting individual needs and is a guiding principle of the No Child Left Behind Act of 2001 (August & Hakuta, 1997; August & Pease-Alvarez, 1996; Brisk, 2005; Education Trust, 2003). Moreover, teachers' expectations of students are inextricably linked to their perceptions about students' abilities, their own pedagogical skills, and their content knowledge (Ferguson, 1998; Howard, 1995; Wenglinsky, 2001). When educators are not well-informed regarding the population and needs of the students they instruct, they can unknowingly hinder, rather than further, educational progress.

Research reported by Dusek and Joseph (1986) suggests that teachers of African American and Mexican American students do not expect them to perform as well as white students. Even though lowered expectations may not be intentional, they exist nevertheless and must be intentionally addressed. Low expectations can be overtly or covertly communicated to students by teachers and can become a self-fulfilling prophecy. According to Brophy (1983), teachers with low expectations of certain students demonstrated this by doing the following: calling on those students less frequently; providing less time to respond when called upon; giving students the answer rather than helping them to solve the problem themselves; criticizing them more often and praising them less; and paying less positive attention, but disciplining them more strictly. These expectations create a gap between student and teacher as shown in Figure 6.2.

Figure 6.2 Perceptions and Expectations

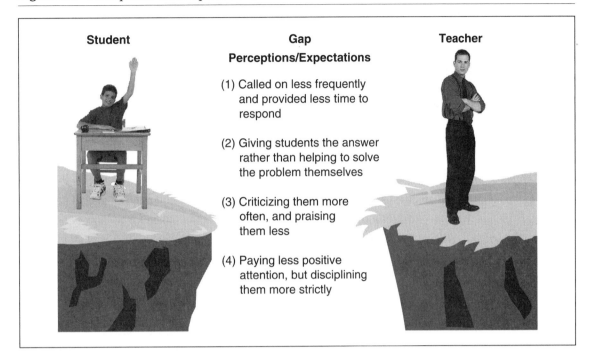

STUDENTS CALLED ON LESS FREQUENTLY AND PROVIDED LESS TIME TO RESPOND

Students who were called on less frequently were often overlooked, or were the recipients of inequitable treatment when called upon. For example, Irvine (1990), when comparing teacher expectations between white and black children, found that teachers hold more negative attitudes about black children's ability, language, behavior, and potential. Similar studies have documented the same perceptions with Latino students (Nieto, 1992). Specifically, on average, when students were provided with less time to respond, they were only given 1 to 2 seconds of wait time versus the 5 to 7 seconds needed for most ELLs to create a well-formulated response. It is essential that students be given more time to formulate coherent responses, but even more so for our ELLs. Typically, ELLs need time to process both the content and the language. For example, if one were teaching native English speakers physics in Spanish, it would take much more time for students to process the cognitively demanding task of physics itself as well as the specialized vocabulary usage of the content area.

The quadrants in Figure 6.3 represent Cummins's (1979) language grid. Quadrant A represents the least demanding of the language requirements because it includes less cognitively demanding material such as physical education, music, or art, which are subjects that are less language dependent, and incorporate many visual and/or auditory clues. Quadrant B is more language dependent, but provides some clues through visual demonstration, such as in science with a lab demonstration. Quadrant C is more language dependent than Quadrants A and B, but builds in context to make the message more comprehensible. Lastly, Quadrant D, the most cognitively demanding and language dependent, supplies the fewest clues. A physics example, where students are learning both the Spanish language and specialized science language, would fit under Quadrant D, especially if visual scaffolds were not used.

One technique that can be used to ensure that students formulate coherent responses is think-pair-share. The *think-pair-share* technique is an oral language scaffold where students get to first take time to formulate their thoughts, share those thoughts with a partner (a safer social setting), and then finally share in a whole-group discussion. This verbal scaffold not only benefits ELLs; it is also a way to ensure that teachers get the best thinking out of all students, not just confident students who quickly formulate verbal responses. Specifically, a verbal scaffold utilizes prompting, questioning, and elaboration to facilitate students' movement to higher levels of language proficiency, comprehension, and thinking.

Teacher-guided reporting (TGR) is an example of a verbal scaffold, as it initiates more extended time on task and layered discussions with ELLs. In addition, the process—which begins with an open-ended question, followed by teacher clarification, encouragement, and paraphrasing—allows for equity regarding academic language practice in the classroom for all students, creating an apprenticeship of language that builds with specific support (Gibbons, 2002).

Figure 6.3 Cummins's Language Grid Bridge-Building Strategies

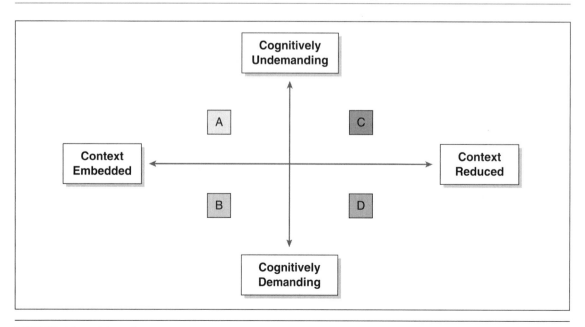

SOURCE: Adapted from Cummins, 1979.

Types of Scaffolds

Other kinds of scaffolds include those that are procedural and instructional. Procedural scaffolding includes the use of appropriate grouping, coaching, and modeling to facilitate learning. Procedural scaffolds utilize an instructional framework that involves explicit teaching, modeling, and practice opportunities with others, and embeds expectations for independent application. Other features of procedural scaffolding include one-on-one teaching, coaching, and modeling (see Figure 6.4).

Figure 6.4 Scaffolding for Increasing Independence—Teach to Apply

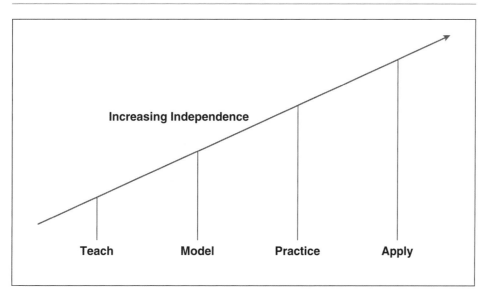

Procedural Scaffolding

Procedural scaffolding can include small-group instruction with children practicing a newly learned strategy with another more experienced student. Similarly, partnering or grouping students for reading activities, with more experienced readers assisting those with less experience, is an example of a procedural scaffold (see Figure 6.5).

Instructional Scaffolds

Instructional scaffolds can be tools such as graphic organizers to prepare students to comprehend and organize text content. Such scaffolds may also come in the form of simplifying language (e.g., reducing sentence length; reducing length of text; simplifying vocabulary; using present tense only; utilizing simple sentence structure, such as subject-predicate; placing less text on each page). Other examples of instructional scaffolds include tapping prior knowledge/personal experience to preview a reading passage or writing assignment (e.g., explicitly teaching students how to make text-to-text, text-to-life, and text-to-world connections via clustering or a journal/sentence prompt).

Figure 6.5   Scaffolding for Increasing Independence—Whole Class
to Independent Work

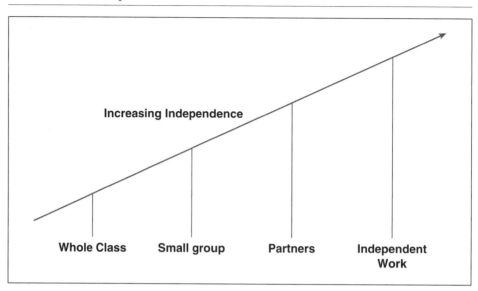

STUDENTS GIVEN THE ANSWER RATHER THAN HELPED TO SOLVE THE PROBLEM THEMSELVES

Typically, the students of teachers with low expectations were given answers rather than being allowed to solve problems themselves. They were also asked lower-level questions (e.g., What was the main character's name?), rather than higher-level questions based on Bloom's taxonomy (e.g., What motivated the protagonist?). These students were also often given the answers, in lieu of time to formulate a response of their own. ELLs, in particular, are often relegated to what is described as *initiation-response-feedback* (IRF) patterns (Gibbons, 2002). IRF represents those times when students are prompted with closed-ended questions, which often require only one-word responses, and where a potential language-rich dialogue is truncated. For example, when questioning is not carefully planned for, teachers may settle for scripted questions, which yield "yes" or "no" responses as shown in Figure 6.6.

Figure 6.6   Teacher–Student Conversation With "Yes" and "No" Responses

Teacher	Student
"Did the character in the novel feel scared?"	"Yes."
"Was he put in a difficult situation?"	"Yes."
"Does he feel like he's going to be hurt?"	"He will be."
"Good, Sam."	

In the dialogue recorded in Figure 6.7, the teacher begins with a closed-ended question, which only requires a one-word response. Once the student responds with a one-word answer, the teacher does not follow up with a question that would elicit a more detailed response, such as, "What makes you think that the character was scared? What actions and words from the text demonstrate that?" Instead, the teacher in this scenario is doing all of the work and all of the talking. The teacher, probably having the best of intentions, does not want to push the student, who may struggle with the language, but unless the teacher does so, he or she may never understand what the student actually knows and is able to do.

Figure 6.7   Teacher–Student Conversation Eliciting More Than "Yes"/"No" Responses

Teacher	Student
"Did the character in the novel feel scared?"	"Yes."
"Give me more detail about that, Sam. Did he share that he was scared with his big eyes?"	"Yes."
"Good. His eyes *were* big and he *ran* away."	

Instead, teachers need to plan for academic talk, promoting student verbal elaboration and allowing classroom dialogue to unfold according to students' individual needs. An example of an opportunity to promote student verbal elaboration is when a student is struggling with a particular grammatical form; the teacher can lead the student with a question that elicits an elaborated response, rather than a yes/no response.

If a student struggles with detailed responses in the context of subject matter content, the teacher might encourage the student to use language just presented in a lesson. Figure 6.8 is a dialogue example from a math class. Note how the teacher's questions in Figure 6.8 promote complex verbal responses from the student, rather than yes/no responses.

In the conversation recorded in Figure 6.8, the teacher leads the student to become clearer regarding the math moves that he took in order to solve the problem. By requiring elaborated verbal responses, the language processing itself helps solidify for the student his or her problem solving, as well as presents a verbal model for solving the problem for the rest of

Figure 6.8 Student/Teacher Conversation in Math Class

Teacher	Student
"How did you derive the answer to that math problem?"	
"What were the specific steps that you took? What did you do first?"	"I followed the formula that you showed us at the beginning of class."
"What specific math moves did you have to complete to get the variable 'x' by itself?"	"I tried to figure out how I could best get the 'x' by itself. So, I moved everything to the other side."
"Nice work. So, you had to divide and subtract in order to complete the problem. What was your solution?"	"First, I had to divide each side by 5 so that the 'x' was by itself. Then, I subtracted 2 from each side."

the class. The teacher begins with an open-ended question and then follows up by asking for more specific language regarding the steps taken. Notice that the teacher does not paraphrase student language until the end of the process so that the student is able to have more academic language practice throughout.

Bridge-Building Strategies for Academic Talk

Instead of the initiation-response-feedback (IRF) pattern, teachers can consider initiating dialogue using open-ended questions, which allows for multiple pathways into a conversation. *Open-ended questions* are those that cannot be answered with one-word responses. Open-ended questions allow students to have more language practice over time. Considering that, according to Diane August in a presentation to Los Angeles Unified School District's District 6 in 2002, ELLs spend less than 2% of their day in academic talk, it is imperative that teachers plan for language practice that includes longer stretches of time for student language application. In order for more academic language practice to occur in the classroom, it must be planned for and required in the classroom.

Opportunities for *academic talk* can range from something as simple as the think-pair-share technique where students first think about their own response, share that response with a neighbor, and then finally share their ideas with the entire class, to more technical group structures such as literature circles, where students read a common text and complete specific roles, in book study fashion, in preparation for an academic conversation with peers. *Literature circles* are organized discussions around a common text that students have read, usually with a list of questions to guide the discussion.

In literature circles, students take on a particularly active reading role, such as summarizing, connecting, questioning, or paraphrasing. These active reading roles allow students to engage in reading with a purpose, as well as help to guide the subsequent conversation that results. Once students have completed their own role, they engage in a conversation with their classmates in a small-group setting, which provides a time for academic language expression and in-depth analysis of the common reading selection. For example, when reading the poem "Harlem: A Dream Deferred" by Langston Hughes, students may understand the text by making a connection to a setback in their own life, and the types of setbacks described in the poem itself. Another student who represents the questioner might pose questions that he might ask the author about his use of imagery or rhetorical questions. Such a discussion might ensue as shown in Figure 6.9.

In the dialogue, we see a demonstration of the type of academic talk that is elicited by students discussing a common piece of text. Students take on discussant roles to structure the academic conversation. The discussant roles also assist in apprenticing students toward four comprehension tasks—*connecting, questioning, summarizing,* and *visualizing.* Students would then switch roles when they read a different piece of text, so that they gain practice in each of the roles equally. In this manner, academic talk is deliberately part of the lesson-planning process, and structured in such a way that students learn how to engage in academic discourse.

Figure 6.9   Student Conversation Based on Langston Hughes' "Harlem: A Dream Deferred"

Student #1: Connector	Student #2: Building on Connector Role
"I connect to Langston Hughes' experience with personal setbacks because when I first came to this country, my family really struggled to make their dreams come true. My father had to redo much of his education, as well as learn English, which set our family back financially for many years."	"Although my family didn't struggle the way that Miguel's did, I have had personal setbacks where I had to spend a year in continuation school to make up for poor grades. My dreams were almost entirely deferred when I thought about dropping out of high school."
Student #3: Questioner	**Student # 4: Response to Question Posed**
"The question I'd like to pose has to do with Langston Hughes' use of rhetorical questions in the poem. Why does he ask these questions and not bother to answer them? Why does each of the questions build the way that they do? It's like he's building suspense or something."	"I think Langston Hughes asks questions without answering them because they are very personal questions, and he wants us to consider them ourselves. He doesn't want to give us the answers because he wants us to struggle with them."

Figure 6.10   Literature Circle Paraphraser Template

Literature Circle: Paraphraser

Directions: *Your task is to make reference to a portion of the text that shows the point of view of the author. Copy the passage below and then paraphrase (put the text in your own words). You may paraphrase the text by replacing certain words or by changing word order (syntax).*

Passage:

_____

_____

_____

_____

Paraphrase: *(Remember that you can paraphrase by replacing words and/or changing word order.)*

_____

_____

_____

_____

SOURCE: Adapted from Daniels 2002.

When first instructing students in how to utilize and complete each of the four discussant roles, teachers would model how to complete each of the templates. They would then model for students how to use the information in the templates to have a literature circle discussion. In this manner, the templates themselves become scaffolds that lead up to the conversation. Once students know how to engage in each of the four discussant roles, they may no longer need the templates in order to have an academic conversation around a particular text.

STUDENTS CRITICIZED MORE OFTEN AND PRAISED LESS

In classroom cases where ELL students were criticized more often and praised less, many students received little to no positive feedback for their responses. Gibbons (2002) suggests the use of teacher-guided reporting to elicit academic talk with ELLs. One characteristic of TGR is the use of encouragement to build student talk, which also allows for more praise and fewer instances of criticism.

Bridge-Building Strategies

TGR is an oral language scaffold in which a teacher and student together build what a student may not be able to say on his or her own. This process is helpful when used with students just after a new concept has been learned—for example, when students have just read a short story and the teacher would like the student to retell the beginning, middle, and end of the story. A TGR oral language exchange might look like the one in Figure 6.11.

In the interaction recorded in Figure 6.11, the teacher begins the dialogue with an open-ended question about the vignette "My Name," from *The House on Mango Street* collection of stories by Sandra Cisneros (1984), which the class had just read together. The student begins with a short response to the teacher that includes very few details. As a result of the teacher asking the student for clarification in the way of specific details about the vignette, as well as using encouragement, the student's response in the end becomes much more thorough than the first response she provides for the teacher.

By working through an oral language scaffold, the student begins to unpack her own thinking and comprehension process. As she provides more and more detail, she realizes that she knows much more about the text than she might have realized. For example, the student begins very globally and does not provide many details on her own. As the teacher elicits more detail, however, it becomes clear that the student understands characterization and conflict in this vignette. With several more exchanges, the teacher might have brought the student to the theme as well as more detail regarding the character's internal conflict.

There are specific techniques that are critical to the success of TGR, of which several were used in the example above. One such technique includes the use of *encouragement*. Often, the importance of encouragement is taken for granted in the classroom. For ELLs and other struggling students, it is imperative that encouragement be used so that confidence with the language builds and additional language risks are taken. If we think back to our own process in acquiring a new language, the importance

Figure 6.11 Teacher-Guided Reporting Oral Exchange

Teacher	Student
"What was the story about?"	"A young girl who doesn't like her name."
"Tell me more about that. What is the girl's name, and why doesn't she like her name?"	"Her name is Esperanza, and she thinks her name is too long and harsh."
"Good. Keep going. What else does the author say about her name in the middle and at the end of the story?"	"She compares her name to other people's names. She likes her sister's name and would like to be renamed Xexe."

of *feedback* and encouragement may become more evident. For example, Soto-Hinman recalls her own experience of being encouraged to use her mother tongue, Spanish, when conversing with aunts and uncles. Although she was less proficient in Spanish than in English, the affirmation that she was using correct terms and tenses encouraged her to continue to practice.

The preceding example demonstrates this, as the teacher encourages the student to keep going with her response while at the same time asking for more detail in the story retelling itself. The use of encouragement puts the student at ease with the dialogue and helps build more confidence regarding language usage. In this manner, the teacher doesn't "save" the student by allowing short, truncated responses. Instead, she expects the student to use more language, and uses appropriate clarifying techniques to get her there, such as encouragement, feedback, recasting/paraphrasing, and wait time (see Figure 6.12).

STUDENTS PAID LESS POSITIVE ATTENTION BUT DISCIPLINED MORE STRICTLY

Finally, students of teachers with low expectations were often paid less positive attention and disciplined more strictly. In addition, these students were not given equitable treatment either for their positive or negative behavior. Research by Lopez (2003) demonstrates that Latino boys were more likely to be viewed by school personnel as "threatening" and potential "problem students." According to national data (Ginorio & Huston, 2001), Latino boys were 10% more likely to be suspended than Latina girls, who were suspended 4% of the time for similar offenses. In this manner, Latino males are often more strictly disciplined compared to Latinas who are guilty of similar behavior. Similarly, black students, particularly males, are more likely to be suspended from schools than whites for similar situations (Carter & Goodwin, 1994; Fine, 1991; Nieto, 1992). Likewise with Latinos, where a non-Latino student might be able to wear a hat in class

Figure 6.12   Elements of Teacher-Guided Reporting

Characteristic	Example
Encouragement	"You are doing well. Continue with that thought."
Feedback	(a) **Probing questions**—focus on content, not grammar (b) **Probing language**—asking for more detail/specificity in language
Recasting/paraphrasing	Summarizing or rephrasing in academic terms what the student just said
Wait time	Providing students with think time between 3 and 5 seconds

without fear of being labeled a troublemaker, Latino males are often assumed to be gang members when they wear such attire.

It is only when educators begin to unveil their expectations of students that they can start to change such treatment in the classroom. Strategies that can assist teachers in more equitable treatment of all students can include index cards with student names and information on them. In order to ensure that students are called upon equitably, the teacher can shuffle the cards and randomly select a student who will share with the whole group. Group work structures such as literature circles and techniques such as think-pair-share also ensure that all student voices are heard, even when not called upon formally in the whole-group setting.

Bridge-Building Strategies

In order to close the gap between the teacher and the student, educators must begin to unveil and examine their belief systems about the students they teach. As teachers begin this examination, they must also be open to ongoing reflective examination, clarifying their own belief systems. Often, this means stepping into a day in the life of their students, both at school and in the community. At school, teachers may engage in *shadowing projects* where they follow a particular student for several hours of the school day to gain understanding regarding their educational experiences, as well as obtain qualitative data about their academic lives. Such shadowing projects have been conducted in the Los Angeles Unified School District (LAUSD) and at Biola University (La Mirada, CA), in order to have educators and preservice teachers gain a glimpse into a day in the life of ELLs in their school settings. Participants have been trained using a protocol (see illustration that follows) where they monitor the domains of listening, speaking, reading, and writing at 5-minute intervals throughout a school day. It is important to note that participants are not ready to formally shadow ELLs until they have studied both the elements of academic talk in the classroom as well as the different forms of listening that they will monitor. At Biola University, students do not shadow an ELL until midway through the course, when they have amply studied academic speaking and listening. Figure 6.13 shows the ELL Student Shadow Study Observation Form.

Using the protocol above, participants monitor every 5 minutes who the primary speaker is—either the student or teacher—as well as who the primary speaker is speaking to. In addition, the type(s) of listening involved in the interaction is also monitored, whether it is one-way or two-way. One-way listening is an interaction where students are taking in information, such as a lecture. Typically, in one-way listening, there is no room for clarification or questions. In contrast, two-way listening allows for clarification to be made, because the interaction is dialogue-based. That is, the interaction is considered a conversation. Throughout the shadowing project, participants are often astounded by the fact that the teacher will do most of the talking, with much of the interaction being lecture-based,

Figure 6.13 ELL Student Shadow Study Observation Form

| Student First Name: _____ | Grade: _____ | ELD Level: _____ |
| Gender: _____ | School: _____ | |

Time	Specific Student Activity/Location of Student 5-minute intervals	Academic Speaking	Academic Listening 1-Way 2-Way	No Listening (Reading or Writing Silently)	Not Listening (Student Is Off-Task)	Comments

Primary Speaker	Mostly to Whom?	Primary Speaker	Mostly to Whom?
Your Student	1. Student	Teacher	5. Student
	2. Teacher		6. Small Group
	3. Small Group		7. Whole Class
	4. Whole Class		

Primary Listener	Listening Mostly to Whom?
Your Student	1. Student
	2. Teacher
	3. Small Group
	4. Whole Class

SOURCE: ELL Shadowing Protocol developed by Ivannia Soto-Hinman and Linda Carstens, 2002.

despite the fact that the teacher's primary duty is to develop ELLs' language skills. Figure 6.14 is an example of the shadow study form filled out for two intervals of a classroom interaction.

In the first language exchange at 10:20, we see that the ELL has just engaged in a song during English/Language Arts time. Therefore, academic talk has been coded as a 7, because the primary speaker is the student

Figure 6.14   ELL Student Shadow Study Observation Form

Student First Name: _____   Grade: _____   ELD Level: _____

Gender: _____   School: _____

⊙ Time	Specific Student Activity/Location of Student 5-minute intervals	Academic Speaking	Academic Listening 1-Way 2-Way	No Listening (Reading or Writing Silently)	Not Listening (Student Is Off-Task)	Comments
10:20	"Never Give Up" English/language arts song. Summing up— "make a long story short"	7	singing			Preparation for lesson B, paying attention, watching. Head nodding to "Ready?"
10:25	Instructional read-aloud of Miss Rumphius	10	2			

Primary Speaker	Mostly to Whom?	Primary Speaker	Mostly to Whom?
Your Student	1. Student	Teacher	5. Student
	2. Teacher		6. Small Group
	3. Small Group		7. Whole Class
	4. Whole Class		

Primary Listener	Listening Mostly to Whom?
Your Student	1. Student
	2. Teacher
	3. Small Group
	4. Whole Class

singing with the entire class. Singing has been noted in the two-way listening exchange, as the student is interacting through talk as well and not merely listening as he sings. Under the Comments section, the observer has written down any anecdotal notes important to the interaction. Here, specifically, the observer has noted that the student is attentive and nods that he is ready to sing.

In the 10:25 exchange, the student engages in an instructional read-aloud. Here, the exchange has been coded as a 2 under academic one-way listening because the student is taking in information and not asked to respond. Academic speaking has been coded 10 because the teacher is doing the talking while she reads the book aloud to the whole class. Students continued to code interactions this way, every 5 minutes for 2 to 4 hours.

The shadowing project allows students to begin to find patterns regarding who is doing most of the speaking in classrooms, and what kinds of listening ELLs are often asked to undertake. Students soon begin to notice that the primary speaker in classrooms is often the teacher, which is the second box under Primary Speaker (and numbers 5–7). Similarly, students find that the listening interactions are often one-way, or in lecture mode, with little room for questions or clarification on the part of the ELL.

In this manner, the shadowing project illuminates for teachers the absence of opportunities for ELLs' academic language practice in the classroom. Through this process, educators are able to reflect on their own instructional practices, and how such practices may positively or negatively impact student achievement. For example, one teacher in LAUSD's District 6 stated, "The person talking most is the person who is learning most . . . *and I'm doing most of the talking in my class!*" This process, then, creates an urgency for changing instructional practice across levels.

Teachers may also choose to videotape themselves while teaching in order to obtain additional information on who is doing the most talking in their classroom. They can use the same protocol form to analyze results in terms of academic speaking and listening, or they may choose to more broadly reflect on their teaching practices, such as the use of wait time or other elements they are striving to utilize in their teaching practice.

Community Bridge-Building Strategies

In addition to teachers needing to promote more student language application, they also need to promote more student-centered classrooms by getting to know students' lives outside of school. Teachers tend to bring their own culture and interests to the classroom, allowing their own perspectives to dominate the learning context. Bringing students' cultural context into the classroom can create a better sociocultural "fit" for learning, bridging the gap between teacher and student context. Teachers can get to know students by administering surveys about student backgrounds and interests; making home visits, where educators seek to open communication between school and home; and conducting community mapping projects, where educators seek to understand more about the assets of the community in which their students live.

By *surveying* student interests, educators can collect important background information, such as students' favorite authors or hobby interests. The survey in Figure 6.15 poses questions to students about how they view themselves as readers.

Figure 6.15 Student Reading Survey, "Me as a Reader"

1. Do you like to read? Why or why not?
2. Are you a good reader? Why do you think so?
3. What do you read at school? (Include reading you do in any language, not just English.)
4. What do you read outside of school? (Include magazines, text messages, and computer blogs.)

Student interests and hobbies listed in such surveys can then influence text selections, instructional techniques, and development of learning exercises in the classroom. In addition, the incorporation of personal interests into the curriculum increases student motivation. For example, if a teacher determines that a struggling reader in his classroom enjoys car magazines, he can encourage the student to select a book or magazine about cars for sustained silent reading time. The teacher might also be able to connect the student to information on the history of car production in the United States—from the Model T to present-day vehicles.

Home visits can allow educators to view their students in a more positive light, as well as build rapport and support between the home and school. Often, educators expect parents to work around teachers' schedules, meeting teacher expectations first before educators will meet their child's needs. In order to reach out to parents who cannot make it onto the school campus during school hours, or feel uncomfortable doing so, teams may choose to periodically meet parents in their homes. Home visits can consist of educators learning about their students' home lives in order to better meet their needs in the classroom, as opposed to negative parent conferences related to poor grades or classroom behavior.

The authors of this text view home visits as relational bridge builders. For example, one of the authors, Hetzel, enjoyed a home visit, including dinner, with one of her Latina students. At this home visit, Hetzel met her student's family, heard about the employment of the father, the homemaking duties of the mother, and the lives of her student and her siblings. Hetzel learned that her fourth-grade student had a keen interest in history. Hetzel's student took her to the backyard of her neighbor's home, showing her the old wagon, wagon wheels, and mining equipment in her neighbor's collection. Her student enthusiastically shared some of the stories from the "old man" next door who had been telling her stories about California. Hetzel also enjoyed getting to see her student's bedroom where the three little girls of the family slept. She saw the bookshelf where a dozen treasured, well-worn books were kept. She saw the embroidery of the grandmother. The following day in school, Hetzel felt like she more deeply knew her student, and she immediately introduced her student to the *Little House on the Prairie* book series, which the young girl voraciously read. At the end of the year, Hetzel gave her entire hardback series of these books to the young girl, knowing that they would be treasured and shared with younger siblings as well. The home visit was invaluable for Hetzel to more deeply understanding her student and to build rapport with her family. It provided the teacher with deep connections to the parent and student, laying a literacy foundation of shared interest in history that propelled this young Latina into hours of deep absorption in quality literature.

Finally, *community mapping projects* allow educators to explore assets and resources surrounding the school. For example, when exploring the community, a teacher may find that a local church, synagogue, or mosque offers after-school tutoring. The teacher may advise parents and students about this opportunity and work with such religious organizations to address student needs. In this way, community resources can be utilized as funds of knowledge, supporting classroom learning, and building bridges between the teacher and the students. Community mapping projects also prove to be eye openers for the teacher by illuminating the realities of home and community life of the student. When teachers realize that few well-stocked libraries and bookstores exist in many urban settings, they can become more passionate and proactive about how to bring such resources into the school community. For example, teachers may choose to write grants for classroom libraries or request donations from corporations in the area. Many community organizations run book drives to help fill the shelves of school and classroom libraries.

SUMMARY

If not carefully considered, the gap between the teacher and student widens when educators are not sensitive to their own perceptions and expectations of student performance, differences in cultural and socioeconomic status between student and teacher, and language variables between student and teacher. This section addressed both a theoretical framework, as well as practical strategies, for closing the gap between teacher and student, promoting the teacher's role as a bridge-builder in the learning context.

REFERENCES

August, D. (2002, April 25). *The importance of oral language development.* Keynote address, Los Angeles Unified School District: District 6 Administrators' Academy, Commerce, CA.

August, D., & Hakuta, K. (Eds.) (1997). *Improving schooling for language-minority children: A research agenda.* National Research Council. Washington, DC: National Academies Press.

August, D., & Pease-Alvarez, L. (1996). *Attributes of effective programs in classrooms serving English Language Learners.* Santa Cruz, CA: National Center for Research on Cultural Diversity and Second Language Learning.

Brisk, M. E. (2005). *Bilingual education: From compensatory to quality schooling* (2nd ed.). Mahwah, NJ: Lawrence Erlbaum.

Brophy, J. E. (1983). Research on the self-fulfilling prophecy and teacher expectations. *Journal of Educational Psychology, 75,* 631–661.

Carter, R. T., & Goodwin, A. L. (1994). Racial identity and education. *Review of Research in Education, 20,* 291–336.

Center for Applied Linguistics. (2006). *Project archive: National Literacy Panel on Language Minority Children and Youth.* Retrieved March 25, 2009, from http://www.cal.org.

Cisneros, S. (1984). *The house on Mango Street.* New York: Vintage Books.

Cummins, J. (1979). Cognitive/academic language proficiency, linguistic interdependence, the optimum age question and some other matters. *Working Papers on Bilingualism, 19,* 121–129.

Daniels, H. (2002). *Literature Circles: Voice and choice in the student-centered classroom,* 2nd ed. Portland, ME: Stenhouse Publishers.

Dusek, J. B., & Joseph, G. (1986). The bases of teacher expectancies: A meta-analysis. *Journal of Educational Psychology, 75,* 327–346.

Education Trust. (2003, Winter). A new core curriculum for all: Aiming high for other people's children. *Thinking K–16.*

Ferguson, R. F. (1998). Teachers' perceptions and expectations and the black–white test score gap. In C. Jencks & M. Phillips (Eds.), *The black–white test score gap* (pp. 273–317). Washington, DC: Brookings Institution.

Fine, M. (1991). *Framing dropouts: Notes on the politics of an urban public school.* Albany: State University of New York Press.

Gibbons, P. (2002). *Scaffolding language, scaffolding learning: Teaching second language learners in the mainstream classroom.* Portsmouth, NH: Heinemann.

Ginorio, A., & Huston, M. (2001). *Si, se puede! Yes, we can.* Washington, DC. American Association of University Women.

Howard, J. (1995). You can't get there from here: The need for a new logic in education reform. *Daedalus Journal of the American Academy of Arts and Sciences, 123*(2), 47–64.

Irvine, J. J. (1990). *Black students and school failure.* Westport, CT: Greenwood Press.

Lopez, N. (2003). *Hopeful girls, troubled boys: Race and gender disparity in urban education.* New York: Routledge.

Nieto, S. (1992). *Affirming diversity: The sociopolitical context of multicultural education.* New York: Longman.

U.S. Census Bureau. (2005). *U.S. Census Bureau factsheet.* Washington, DC: U.S. Government Printing Office. Retrieved November 2, 2005, from http://www.census.gov.

Wenglinsky, H. (2001). *Teacher classroom practices in student performance: How schools can make a difference.* Princeton, NJ: Educational Testing Service.

7

Cultural Differences

Cultural differences between the teacher and his or her students can create gaps of misunderstanding. Caring teachers must know their students and build bridges into their home cultures. For example, Valdés (1996) suggests that assistance to Mexican-origin families must be based on "an understanding and an appreciation and respect for the internal dynamics of these families" (p. 203). Chapter 7 prepares educators to explore these cultural differences as assets to school life both outside and inside the classroom. Teachers reframe their thinking, "discovering" that cultural differences can inform them in how to do their work better, as opposed to viewing cultural differences as potential deterrents to educational progress.

CONNECTING THE LITERACY DOMAINS IN SECOND LANGUAGE ACQUISITION

Historically, the four literacy domains—listening, speaking, reading, and writing—have been taught separately, with an emphasis on reading and writing as the "academic domains." For ELLs, however, this process of teaching each of the domains as segmented components of language is not useful (see Figure 7.1). August (2002), in a presentation to administrators in the Los Angeles Unified School District (LAUSD), notes that the domains of listening and speaking are as important as reading and writing, and they must be planned for in order to happen effectively in the classroom. Specifically, it is helpful for educators to connect speaking to writing, and listening to reading, as this connects similar processes. Speaking and

Figure 7.1 Cultural Differences

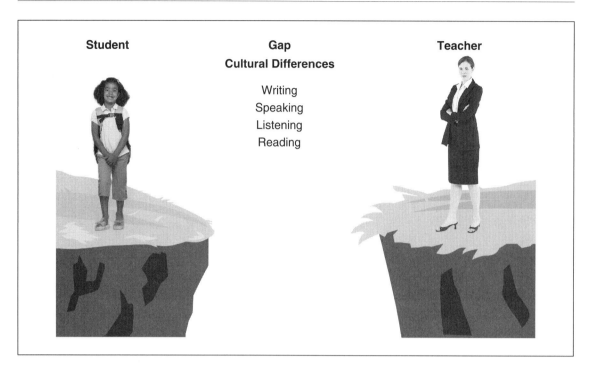

Student	Gap	Teacher
	Cultural Differences	
	Writing	
	Speaking	
	Listening	
	Reading	

writing are both about output, while listening and reading are both about input and comprehension. Similarly, when we connect listening and reading as active processes, greater comprehension can be elicited. The following section will link the domains, as well as give practical examples for how this can be done in the classroom.

Writing

Due to the fact that speaking and writing are both about output, it is helpful when educators allow ELLs to talk about their writing before they are expected to complete the writing itself. In Soto-Hinman's classroom, it was important to link speaking to the writing process with her ELLs. When ELLs are allowed to talk about what they will write about, their thinking becomes clearer, more detailed, and coherent. For students with lower levels of language proficiency, hearing another student who perhaps has more language ability will assist with the vocabulary and mental outlines needed in the writing process. Students in the first and second stages of ELD often have difficulty thinking in a second language, or using specialized language attached to the writing task. Talking out the writing task allows an ELL to practice the language, as well as to hear higher levels of language that the student might incorporate in her own writing. An ELL's thoughts and use of vocabulary might be triggered by hearing her partner interact with the language or the writing task. Speaking then becomes an oral and thinking scaffold, which leads to higher levels of language production all around.

During her first year of teaching middle school English to mostly Latino students, Soto-Hinman noticed that many of her students began their essays with "Hello, my name is . . ." Upon asking a particular student why he began his essay with this phrase, he told her matter-of-factly, "Miss, when you introduce yourself to a person, you always tell them your name first. So, in the introduction I want to make sure they know who I am." This explanation illustrated that many Latino students truly were emphasizing personal relationships over plot or sequential events. Had the instructor not taken the time to uncover this fact, she might have incorrectly assumed (which she did for some time) that her students had no foundation for stories and narrative. She would have begun her instruction presuming little to no background knowledge. Today, with insight from this student query, she carefully points out to the students the difference between spoken and written language, clarifying the differences, particularly the formality of written discourse.

In addition, it was important for Soto-Hinman's students to know the specialized language that would give them access to academic forms of writing, such as the use of transition words in particular genres of writing. For example, when writing a persuasive letter, students utilize transition words such as *first of all, secondly,* and *in conclusion,* as well as rhetorical questions and persuasive language. Specifically, a persuasive letter would anticipate and address counterarguments and provide clear evidence regarding the perspective presented. In this manner, Soto-Hinman ensured students knew what was expected of them in more academic forms of writing, but would encourage students to continue to emphasize personal relationships in their creative or journal writing. Educators must acknowledge and appreciate the skills and cultural templates that students bring to the learning process, as well as provide access to those skills with which they may be unfamiliar. Teachers should work to bridge the gap between the known and unknown, and persist in studying the cultural assets of their students, particularly as teachers identify differences or gaps between their own cultural understandings and those of their students.

Listening

Just as reading and writing are explicitly taught in school, so must academic listening. That is, teachers often do not plan or organize lessons to ensure students are actively listening. Instead, students learn to become passive listeners who do not actively engage in school, or they learn to pretend they are listening. One way to teach listening skills is to hold students accountable for the listening process. For example, during an instructional read-aloud (IRA), the teacher may give students something to listen for, such as new vocabulary words or the setting. When students hear new vocabulary read to them in the text, they may be asked to raise their hands. Similarly, students may be asked to track literary elements throughout a story—characters, setting, or conflict. Students at the lower levels of ELD may be asked to listen for one of the elements, such as character, while students at the higher levels can listen for all three elements.

In this way, ELL students must be taught listening for different purposes—for acquiring both specific and general information. The example where students listen for conflict or character scaffolds students into listening for specific information. Other examples might include providing lecture notes using the cloze procedure, where certain words have been eliminated. Throughout the lecture, students then listen specifically for places that have been left blank. This allows students to home in on important or main ideas, or key vocabulary during a lecture. ELLs must also be taught when it is appropriate to listen more holistically for the gist or overall message. Teachers model for students when it is appropriate to listen in each of these categories. Similarly, listening must be explicitly taught when addressing the *hidden curriculum,* or those procedures that are expected in school but often are not taught. The hidden curriculum in a classroom can include both the language and ritual expectations required of students that are not explicitly taught. For example, when students enter a classroom, the teacher may expect them to sit down quietly, take out their materials, and begin a warm-up activity, without ever specifically modeling or teaching those behaviors.

Approaches to listening vary by culture. For example, Hetzel's Latino students would look down when spoken to as a sign of respect. Hetzel noticed that some of her colleagues were unaware of this difference and would sternly correct their students by saying, "Look at me when I am speaking to you." This only further exasperated students who were trying to be respectful. Hetzel's Chinese American students also looked down as a sign of respect.

In correcting one Chinese student, a teacher said, "Wipe that smile off your face." However, in speaking with the parent, she later learned that the smile was a sign of embarrassment, not a sign of disrespect to the teacher. Understanding the cultural norms of your students is imperative for appropriate bridge building in the classroom. In addition, cultural norms vary within subcultures, and knowing the culture(s) of her specific students best equips the teacher to understand her students and to build bridges.

Speaking

As noted earlier in the text, speaking is crucial in acquisition of a second language. When ELLs are not given extended stretches of time to practice academic talk in the classroom, proficiency and ease with the language are stunted. Oral language scaffolds such as think-pair-share and productive group work, as described earlier in the book, become important strategies for teachers to use to elicit more talk in the classroom.

Similarly, there are cultural differences in conversation and assertiveness in the home–school partnership. For example, the Latino communities in which Hetzel worked in the San Francisco Bay Area and in Los Angeles County were filled with capable Latino parents who desired to be involved in the school. However, out of respect, the Latino families tended not to impose their desires upon the teachers. Hetzel heard a colleague say, "These Latino parents don't care what is happening at the school. They never come in to help." At this point, Hetzel asserted, "Our Latino parents do care and they care passionately. However, you need to remember that from their cultural perspective, they will let the professionals do the job. We need to visit their homes and invite them into the school community, and then we will see the partnerships form." As teachers reached out to the Latino parents, increasing numbers joined the volunteer ranks, and great resources were added to the classroom as bilingual parents were able to assist in the classroom conversation, particularly with the Spanish-speaking students.

However, in the same way, some of our Latino students will be shy about asking for help, often rooted in their deep respect for the teacher. Similarly, the teacher should bridge the gap by ensuring that all students feel comfortable asking questions and receive adequate opportunity to do so. When Hetzel taught in Thailand, she quickly learned that it is disrespectful in the Thai culture to ask the teacher questions. Understanding these cultural norms and addressing them in the classroom will help bridge the divide and provide fair opportunities for students to participate in classroom dialogue.

Reading

After exploring the assets of culture, the teacher must examine the availability of reading materials and their cultural content. Tenacious literacy instructors will bridge the gap by ensuring their students access to print and text that connect with their students' cultural backgrounds and not just with the instructors' background knowledge and experience. Gay (2000) outlines the benefits of using multicultural curriculum to teach academic content. She suggests specific ways in which to link school, home, and community, while also making school learning relevant:

> Ethnic materials should be used to teach students fundamental skills such as reading, writing, calculating, and reasoning. Students can learn reading skills using materials written by and about Blacks, Mexican Americans, Italian Americans, and Jewish Americans as well as they can from "Dick and Jane." Ethnic literature . . . can be used to teach plot, climax, metaphor, grammatical structure, and symbolism as well as anything written by Anglo Americans. . . . [Teaching] ethnic literacy, reflective self-analysis, decision making, and social activism . . . are [as] essential for living in a culturally and ethnically pluralistic society as are knowing how to read and having a salable skill. . . . Ethnic content serves the purpose of bringing academic tasks from the realm of the alien and the abstract into experiential frames of reference of ethnically different youth. (pp. 179–181)

As an educator teaching English in a 99.9% Latino community, Soto-Hinman took Gay's (2000) suggestions to heart. Each year, she began by having students read *Always Running: La Vida Loca: Gang Days in L.A.*, by Luis Rodriguez (1993). One of the scenes in the novel takes place in a city neighboring the school where Soto-Hinman taught, and the novel worked through many of the struggles her students saw every day.

In the novel, Luis, a gang member, tells his own story as he comes to a crossroad in his life where he must make a decision to choose life in a gang, which would likely lead to death, or a pathway to life by leaving the gang. Throughout the novel, students track the decisions of the author and their consequences, until his final decision to leave the gang life is made. The author not only tells his own personal story via this touching memoir, he also does so in an eloquent and convincing manner, which only someone who has gone through the struggles of *"la vida loca"* or "the crazy life" can do. Many students could relate to the difficult choices that Luis had to make throughout the novel, as well as the sacrifices and consequences involved in getting out of the gang life. In this way, Soto-Hinman used the novel to teach both literary elements—cause and effect, and sequence of events—and life lessons about the realities that many of her students encountered every day. She selected literature that engaged the students and bridged sociocultural differences between the teacher and student. Soto-Hinman did not focus on bringing in literature that exclusively reflected her heritage (she is of Costa Rican descent), but instead carefully selected texts with which the students could identify.

From *Always Running*, her students moved on to *A Raisin in the Sun*, by Lorraine Hansberry (1959/2000), which is a play about the plight of an African American family in the 1950s. The play depicts this family in a realistic light, as they struggle with issues such as poverty, discrimination, and the African American identity. Due to the fact that she taught in a predominantly Latino community, Soto-Hinman purposely presented this play as the second class reading of the year because she wanted her students to see the connection between their own struggle as Latinos and that of other people of color. This allowed her to not only teach the genre of drama, but also to introduce her students to the civil rights movement. As a culminating activity, students wrote and performed their own plays about their own family's journey and struggles in the United States. In this manner, culturally relevant teaching motivates students, and as Gay (2000) suggests, "serves the purpose of bringing academic tasks from the realm of the alien and the abstract into experiential frames of reference of ethnically different youth." As educators, we often try to superimpose our own culture or create inauthentic contexts for learning, replacing natural opportunities in our students' lives. The astute, culturally sensitive classroom practitioner links learning, connecting the students' personal contexts to mainstream culture (see Figure 7.2).

Concepts of print vary by culture, and it is critical for classroom teachers to understand some of the significant differences. For example, Arabic books are written from the "back" to the "front" by Western norms,

Figure 7.2 Cultural Context Learning Links

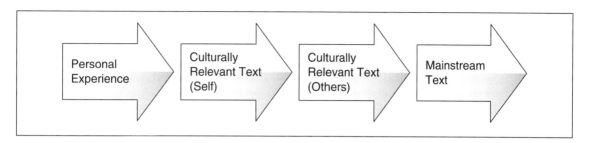

so when Hetzel taught English in Africa and received a multipage picture story written by her Arabic-speaking student that began from the "back," she praised the student for his excellent work in his L4 (fourth language) and then simply reminded him to start at the "front" for his next project. Some teachers might have asked the student to rewrite the entire book, which would have only discouraged him.

Creating a class profile of significant cultural differences in reading, writing, listening, and speaking that fits the cultures represented in the classroom can be helpful for the instructor in bridging the gap between teacher and student.

Mainstream American culture highly values parents reading to their children at home. Although this practice carries with it many benefits, it is not the only way in which children benefit from hearing language. In many other countries, the use of storytelling is a cultural norm and can have many of the same benefits. Children, especially those whose parents are not formally educated, can benefit from story elements through story-telling as well. This process also allows for a strong familial connection between child and parent that is nurtured in the same way that it might be through reading a book or story to a child. As educators, we must honor and search for other ways in which parents can interact with and support the educational system, particularly if they come from a different home culture than the teachers and are not literate in English.

PARENTAL INVOLVEMENT AND THE LITERACY DOMAINS

Cultural differences reflected in the literacy domains of reading, writing, listening, and speaking are not wrong—they are just different. Similarly, educators must challenge the notion that parents do not parent well if they rear their children in ways that do not fit American schools, American expectations, or teachers' own expectations of parenting styles. Instead, as Valdés (1996) suggests,

In this age, when there is talk about the value of diversity, both practitioners and policymakers must be willing to accept the fact that new immigrants bring with them models of living life successfully that can not only enrich our society but also provide for these new Americans in what is now a very dangerous new world. (p. 203)

As Trumbull, Rothstein-Fisch, Greenfield, and Quiroz (2001) note, communication among educators and culturally diverse families often entails assumptions based on cultural values about child rearing and schooling, and these must be understood and bridged if true partnerships are to be forged. By embracing a holistic approach that involves "the whole child, the whole curriculum, and the whole community" (Genesee, 1999, p. 15), all students can be better supported for academic success.

This holistic approach includes exploring the assets that families already bring to the educational system. That is, before the system decides that there is a deficit within the community or family, there must be a concerted effort to find assets within the community and to reconsider what such assets might look like. For example, since many families of color emphasize storytelling, the asset of oral language skills can be used as a basis for writing in the classroom. Secondly, English Language Learners may begin the writing process by first *speaking out* what they need to say in writing. Speaking before writing provides an oral language scaffold for students who may struggle with the process of writing. Often, when ELLs speak before they write, they are given more time to produce coherent and detailed responses that can then be used in their writing. In essence, this provides students with a mental outline or frame to assist them in producing more articulate writing pieces.

One strategy that can be used to move from spoken to written language in the classroom is the *think-pair-share* exercise. Before writing about a particular topic, the teacher may ask students to talk to their "elbow partner" about that topic. For example, if students are asked to predict what will happen next in a story, they can talk that through with their partner before they begin the writing process. This exercise has many benefits for ELLs in that it not only gives them time to think about their response, but also scaffolds language for them from speaking to writing. Such a process gives students adequate wait time, and allows them to negotiate meaning with their partner as well as hear more language, before they actually begin the writing process.

CULTURALLY RESPONSIVE TEACHING

Gay (2000) encourages culturally responsive teaching as a structure that provides an inclusive and accessible learning environment for students of color. Culturally responsive teaching has many advantages, including creating a bridge between teacher and student, as it promotes validation, comprehensive education, multidimensional approaches, empowerment, transformative learning, and emancipation.

Validation

Validation encompasses using cultural knowledge, prior experiences, frames of reference, and performance styles of ethnically diverse students. Since a culturally relevant lesson builds from students' heritages and experiences, a teacher might choose to introduce math approaches and contributions from students' backgrounds. For example, if students are mostly Latino, the teacher may choose to introduce Aztec math, focusing on the Aztec number system and contributions to the field. Similarly, students may learn how to solve a problem in both Aztec math terms and another number system such as the Egyptian mathematical system.

COMPREHENSIVE EDUCATION

Comprehensive education develops intellectually, socially, emotionally, and politically whole children. A comprehensive classroom builds community inside and outside of the classroom by asking parents and community members to contribute to the learning community. Gay (2000) describes the following:

> At the beginning of the school year [one teacher] gets the parents of the students to make a contractual agreement to donate two books or other forms of media to the class collection. One of these books is to be about their own ethnic group and the other about some other group that they either use with their children at home or would like their children to learn about in school. The families are given credit for their contributions by having each item stamped "Donated by _____." (p. 41)

Such donations allow parents to make financial and emotional contributions to their students' learning processes. Parents who cannot make financial contributions might be asked to suggest books from their ethnic group. For example, in one classroom, an African American parent donated a PBS video series on African American contributions to the history of the United States. A Latino parent donated books by Gary Soto, and a Chinese parent donated the book *Dragonwings* by Laurence Yep, a Chinese author.

MULTIDIMENSIONAL APPROACHES

Multidimensional approaches involve curriculum content, learning context, classroom climate, student–teacher relationships, instructional techniques, and performance assessments. Due to the fact that multidimensionality encourages thematic and interdisciplinary learning, teachers from many content areas can collaborate and plan together. Older grades might take a culturally relevant topic such as social protest and examine it from a variety of disciplines. Gay (2000) describes this approach as follows:

> The students and teachers may decide to simulate time periods when social protest was very prominent, analyzing and role playing various ethnic individuals. Within these simulations, coalition meetings can be held in which individuals from different ethnic groups express their positions on the issues of contention in various genre[s] (e.g., rhetoric, sit-ins, songs, political slogans). (p. 27)

Such an approach allows students to see how topics and themes build across the content areas, which helps them to realize connections among the disciplines. Younger grades might take topics in the context of Western expansion in the United States. With this theme, students might consider the following questions: What was the perspective of the European pioneers? The Chinese immigrants building the railroad? The Mexicans losing territory? The Native Americans whose homelands were infringed upon and whose resources were slaughtered (e.g., buffalo)?

EMPOWERMENT

Empowerment enables academic competence, personal confidence, and courage. Empowerment fosters a belief system of success and encourages social scaffolding whereby educators have planned and created an infrastructure to support high levels of academic achievement (Mehan, 1996). One such model of this type of support system is embedded in the Advancement Via Individual Determination (AVID) project, which empowers low-achieving Latino and African American students in Advanced Placement classes. The support system provided includes students and teachers doing the following:

- Explaining their problem-solving techniques to each other in small groups
- Learning the "cultural capital" of school success, including test-taking strategies, study skills, note taking, and time management
- Being mentored in academic and social skills by other students who have successfully completed school

Such a support system interwoven within AVID empowers students to break cycles of failure and inspire future generations. Programs such as AVID bridge the cultural divide that often occurs in culturally contrastive situations (teacher is of an ethnicity different from his students) where teachers must work to bridge cultural gaps and differences in expectations.

TRANSFORMATIVE LEARNING

Transformative learning recognizes the existing strengths and accomplishments of students to enhance them further. Culturally relevant pedagogy nurtures respect for all cultures and utilizes those cultural assets as resources to teaching and learning. Gay (2000) explains one such way to build on cultural assets:

> The verbal creativity that is apparent among some African Americans in informal social interactions is recognized as a story-telling gift and used to teach them writing skills. . . . The tendency of many Japanese, Chinese, and Filipino students to study together in small groups can be formalized in the classroom, providing more opportunities for them and others to participate in cooperative learning. (p. 95)

Instead of always imposing new approaches to learning, educators can benefit from seeking out what already works for students, and building upon these strengths.

EMANCIPATORY EDUCATION

Emancipatory education makes authentic knowledge about different ethnic groups accessible. Emancipation happens as cooperation, connectedness, and community are established in a classroom. Students begin to realize that they are expected to work together and that they are held accountable for each other's success, which empowers them to understand that they are in control of their own destinies. As students learn this interdependence, they also realize that self-efficacy is not enough. That is, as each begins to realize his or her own goals, there is a responsibility to assist others around them in doing the same. This multipronged approach allows for a stronger community, not merely strong individuals who only care about their own success.

Using Gay's (2000) techniques for culturally relevant pedagogy further ensures a holistic approach that educates the whole child. In addition to the academic advantages of culturally responsive instruction, culturally responsive pedagogy develops students' social consciousness and critique, cultural affirmation, competence, and exchange; community building and personal connections; individual self-worth and abilities; and an ethic of caring.

Language differences—students speaking either a second language or a dialect/variation of English—often exist between teacher and student (see Figure 7.3). Such language variations often create chasms or misunderstandings. Some teachers may mistake an English Language Learner for someone who is cognitively unable to complete more rigorous classroom tasks, and thus require less of the student. Others may view dialects or variations of English as having less value than standard forms of the language. In both instances—second languages and dialects—it is imperative that all language forms be valued and contrasted with Academic English. By contrasting or rephrasing student responses with academic forms of English, students begin to understand where and when certain forms can and should be used.

Figure 7.3 Language Variables

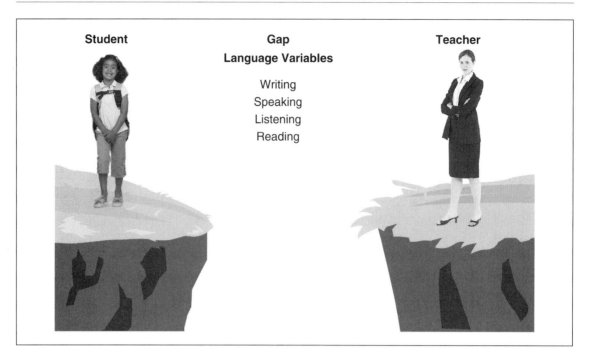

| Student | Gap
Language Variables
Writing
Speaking
Listening
Reading | Teacher |

Similarly, Valdés (1998) and Callahan (2005) warn about the harmfully low expectations implicit in "watering down" academic content for ELLs, and tracking them into strands of coursework that are below grade-level standards. Interconnected with the critical component of holding and realizing high expectations for ELLs is the need to teach them grade-level content at the same time that they acquire Academic English skills. Traditionally, ELLs have been instructed using methods that developed English skills first, before they were allowed to access more cognitively demanding core academic content. This practice has led to high numbers of ELLs attaining basic English fluency but not Academic English skills or grade-level academic proficiency in a timely manner (Scarcella, 2003; Valdés, 1998). Particularly, ELLs are often taking their entire educational careers to become fluent English proficient, in contrast to the 5–7 years that research shows is reasonable progress (Cummins, 1979). Gibbons (2002) argues strongly that academic content must not wait until language is acquired. Instead, teachers can successfully teach language *through* content.

For example, when considering content literacy in a history unit on World War I, a teacher will need to consider not only vocabulary that may be needed to access the time period itself, but also frequently used words that may impede understanding of a particular text or primary source document. Such a unit may require that words such as *trench, artillery, shelling* and *company* be introduced. Students may also need access to words such as *absurd, coincidence,* and *fortunate,* which are not directly related to the discipline or time period itself, but which may be required for comprehension nonetheless (see Figure 7.4).

Figure 7.4 Key Content Words and Frequent Interdisciplinary Words

Key Content Words	Frequent Interdisciplinary Words
• trench • artillery • shelling • company	• absurd • coincidence • fortunate

This notion of *tier-leveled words* developed by Beck, McKeown, and Kucan (2000) provides an approach in which teachers consider the instructional potential of words both related to their discipline and across a variety of contexts. In this manner, all teachers become responsible for teaching language, as well as teaching content through language.

For example, in her own classroom, Soto-Hinman explicitly taught academic discourse via the vehicle of the Socratic seminar. The *Socratic seminar* is based upon the precepts of Socrates, who believed that participants seek deeper understanding of complex ideas through rigorously thoughtful dialogue, rather than by memorizing bits of information or meeting arbitrary demands of "coverage." In order to learn the process and language of participating in an academic dialogue, her students were expected to use academic language stems, such as *"I agree and would like to add . . ."* and *"I disagree because the text seems to show . . ."* when referencing the text or referring to each other's points. The aforementioned stems are used in the transcription of a student interaction described in Figure 7.5.

The dialogue in Figure 7.5 illustrates that when a student wanted to build upon what someone else had said, she would use transitional phrases such as "I'd like to build upon my classmate's statement" or "I disagree with his point and would like to add . . ." Students also used the text to support their responses and would say, "I would like to support what my classmate has said by directing you to page ___ of the text, where it states . . ." In this manner, students explicitly learned and practiced both the process of having an academic conversation (via the vehicle of Socratic seminar) and the language expectations (vocabulary and phraseology) required of them to do so. Figure 7.6 shows some academic language stems used in Soto-Hinman's classroom during academic conversations such as a Socratic seminar.

In order to remind students to use the academic language stems, they were posted largely in class for full view by all students. When first training students to use the stems, a fishbowl exercise was utilized to model appropriate usage in an academic conversation. A *fishbowl* is an exercise where a group discussion or strategy is modeled or practiced by a small group in the middle of a classroom. Similarly, when students first began using the stems in groups, each academic stem was cut into a strip of paper and handed out to each student as a reminder to use the particular stem given in the academic conversation.

Figure 7.5   Student Interactions Using Language Stems

Student #1: Juan	Student #2: Jennifer
I think Walter in *A Raisin in the Sun* represents a dream that has been deferred for too long. Kind of like the poem that we read before we started the play.	I'd like to add to Juan's thinking about Walter because I see Walter's dream of becoming rich as destroying the entire family. He just won't recognize the needs of the rest of the family because he tries to fulfill his own needs first.
Student #3: Alex	**Student # 4: Jennifer**
I disagree with what Jennifer said a little bit. I think that Walter is doing his best to fulfill his own dreams and support his family. Walter seems to believe that by fulfilling his own dream, he will also be able to support his family.	I see what you're saying, Alex, but I'd like to add that Walter really isn't listening to the needs of his family. Walter won't recognize that the rest of the family has a collective dream of owning a home because he's too focused on himself. His selfish actions almost destroy the family.

SOURCE: Developed by Soto-Hinman 2008.

Figure 7.6   Academic Language Stems for Text Dialogue

I agree with . . . but would like to add . . .
I disagree with . . . because
I need clarification on . . .
I am confused by . . .
Can someone help me understand. . . . ?
This passage/phrase . . . reminds me of . . .
When I read . . . , I was surprised that . . .
This passage/phrase . . . strikes me because . . .
I disagree with the idea that . . . because . . .

Examples of explicit bridge-building literacy instruction would also include addressing *idioms* and *figurative language*. Idiomatic language is something that ELLs often struggle with because such language is usually culturally bound. Teachers commonly use idioms and figurative language in their daily teaching. For example, the teacher might unknowingly use the idiom, "I had butterflies in my stomach." Many students, particularly ELLs, may have never heard the idiom and can take the saying literally.

Teaching students to contrast figurative and literal language is a helpful resource in assisting students to unpack the meaning behind idioms. The *Amelia Bedelia* series of books by Peggy Parish is helpful in aiding ELLs with figurative and literal language. For example, in one text, Amelia Bedelia confuses the term *dusting,* as in cleaning, with the powder that goes on when applying makeup. In this case, students can draw a "picture" of the word with a sentence that demonstrates the student understands the difference between the two functions of the word *dusting*. This language comparative method also gives ELLs a structure or toolkit with which to unveil meaning behind future unknown words, expressions, or phrases. Teachers may also want to keep an *idiom word wall* or utilize graphic organizers to help students keep track of and learn the meaning of culturally bound, figurative words. Fred Gwynne's books, such as *The King Who Rained* (2006) and *A Chocolate Moose for Dinner* (1988), are strong texts for providing contextual discussions of American idioms. Using such bridge-building strategies to reach across the gap between the students' home language and the daily language of their teachers motivates and prepares all students for the futures they deserve.

SUMMARY

This chapter covered teaching and connecting the literacy domains—speaking to writing and listening to reading—in a culturally responsive manner. A framework for teaching in a culturally responsive context was also introduced, including beginning with students' personal experiences; adding culturally responsive texts that are about students' own cultures; adding culturally responsive texts that are about the cultures of others; and finally, adding mainstream literature. In addition, Gay's (2000) components of culturally responsive teaching were introduced as a structure to provide an inclusive and accessible learning environment for students of color. Culturally responsive teaching methods were presented as having many advantages, including creating a bridge between teacher and student, as it promotes validation, comprehensive education, multidimensional approaches, empowerment, transformative learning, and emancipation.

REFERENCES

August, D. (2002). *Presentation to Los Angeles Unified School District: District 6,* Commerce, CA.

Beck, I. L., McKeown, M. G., & Kucan, L. (2000). *Bringing words to life: Robust vocabulary instruction.* New York: Guilford.

Callahan, R. (2005). Tracking and high school English learners: Limiting opportunities to learn. *American Educational Research Journal, 42*(2), 305–328.

Cummins, J. (1979). Cognitive/academic language proficiency, linguistic interdependence, the optimum age question and some other matters. *Working Papers on Bilingualism, 19,* 121–129.

Gay, G. (2000). *Culturally responsive teaching.* New York: Teachers College Press.

Genesee, F. (Ed.). (1999). *Program alternatives for linguistically diverse students.* Santa Cruz, CA: Center for Research on Education, Diversity & Excellence (CREDE).

Gibbons, P. (2002). *Scaffolding language, scaffolding learning: Teaching Second Language Learners in the mainstream classroom.* Portsmouth, NH: Heinemann.

Gwynne, F. (1988). *A chocolate moose for dinner.* New York: Simon & Schuster.

Gwynne, F. (2006). *The king who rained.* New York: Simon & Schuster.

Hansberry, L. (2000). *A raisin in the sun.* New York: Holt, Rinehart & Winston. (Original work published 1959)

Mehan, H. (1996). *Tracking "untracking": Evaluating the effectiveness of an educational innovation.* Santa Cruz, CA: Center for Research on Education, Diversity & Excellence.

Rodriguez, L. (1993). *Always running: La vida loca: Gang days in Los Angeles.* New York: Simon & Schuster.

Scarcella, R. (2003). *Accelerating Academic English: A focus on the English learner.* Oakland: Regents of the University of California.

Soto-Hinman, I. (Ed.). (2008). *Professional Development Collaboration for Teachers of EL (PDCTEL) (6-12).* Santa Clara, CA: U.S. Department of Education. (2000).

Trumbull, E., Rothstein-Fisch, C., Greenfield, P. M., & Quiroz, B. (2001). *Bridging cultures between home and school: A guide for teachers.* Mahwah, NJ: Lawrence Erlbaum.

Valdés, G. (1996). *Con respeto: Bridging the distances between culturally diverse families and schools: An ethnographic portrait.* New York: Teachers College Press.

Valdés, G. (1998). The world outside and inside schools: Language and immigrant children. *Educational Researcher, 27,* 4–18.

8

Socioeconomic Differences

The Kerner Commission (2008), which was organized 40 years ago by President Johnson and extended by President Nixon in order "to make good on the promises of American democracy to all citizens—urban and rural, White and Black, Spanish surname, American Indian, and every minority group" (p. 1), put together a task force in 2008 to summarize progress with this mission since its inception. With some exceptions, the Kerner Commission has concluded that America has failed to focus on how to reduce poverty, inequality, racial justice, and crime. The following are some reasons why they came to this result:

- An estimated 37 million Americans live in poverty today, in the richest country in the world.
- A total of 46 million Americans are without health insurance, including 36% of those in poverty.
- The child poverty rate has increased slightly, from 15% in 1968 to 17% in 2006.
- For young children (under 5 years old), the poverty rate is almost 21% today.
- The American child poverty rate is about 4 times the average poverty rate for Western European countries.
- Poverty has deepened for those who have remained poor. The proportion of the poor below the poverty line was about 30% in 1975 and increased to 43% by 2006.
- Poor African Americans are 3 times as likely and poor Hispanics twice as likely as non-Hispanic whites to live in deep poverty, below the poverty line.

- Although the poverty rate has generally declined for African Americans since the Kerner Commission began, poverty in African American female-headed households with children under 18 was almost 44% in 2006.
- The Kerner Commission found that unemployment and underemployment were the most important causes of poverty, yet African American unemployment has continued to be twice as high as white unemployment during each of the four decades since 1968.
- The employment prospects of the nation's out-of-school 16- to 24-year-old men have declined considerably since 2000. The problem is especially acute for young African American men. Among African American high school dropouts aged 19, only 38% are employed, compared to 67% of whites (list adapted from Kerner Commission, 2008, p. 3).

Socioeconomic disparity in America thus also materializes in our school systems, where some of the greatest socioeconomic differences are made evident by the achievement gap. According to the *American School Board Journal* (Kahlenberg, 2006), social scientists have identified six primary factors that put students "at risk" for failure, all of which are common in low-income households: poverty itself, welfare dependence, absent parents, one-parent families, unwed mothers, and a parent without a high school diploma. Although many of these are factors that teachers and schools cannot directly control within a school day, educators can help mitigate them by creating bridges and scaffolds that lead *all* students to graduate from high school and have access to college. When, according to the report *Locating the Dropout Crisis* (Balfanz & Legters, 2004), nearly half of the nation's African Americans, and almost 40% of Latino students in urban districts, "attend high schools in which graduation is not the norm" (p. 5), there is something systemically wrong with the way in which we are educating our students of color, who are also often poor. According to the same report, "In 2,000 high schools, the typical freshman class shrinks by 40 percent or more by the time the students reach their senior year" (p. 5). The need to effectively educate students from low socioeconomic backgrounds is too urgent to wait until high school, as many reform efforts have suggested. Instead, districts and schools must systemically work toward closing the achievement gap to provide educational access and socioeconomic advancement to all students, building brighter futures.

Regardless of socioeconomic class, *all* parents want the best for their children. And, since children from impoverished homes may not already be equipped with implicit academic codes, it is the responsibility of teachers to make those codes explicit for them. *Explicit* means directly taught and clearly defined, without assumptions of prior knowledge. Explicit literacy instruction involves the utilization of authentic language, contextualization, and purposes. It does not mean mindless grammar drills taught out of the context of student writing or authentic literature. Instead, explicitly teaching language codes means teaching the conventions of reading and writing in a reflective manner, with real-life, culturally appropriate examples, so that students are able to use language for a range of purposes in a contextually embedded, accessible learning environment. Therefore, teachers explicitly build bridges to fill in gaps between students' home languages and the language of the dominant culture, generally typified by the teacher's language, by clearly understanding and teaching the idiosyncrasies of the dominant language as reflected in discourse patterns, interactional styles, written language codes, and resource access (see Figure 8.1).

In this chapter, teachers learn strategies to bridge socioeconomic differences so that students are able to use academic language for a range of purposes in a contextually embedded, accessible learning environment. Specifically, discourse patterns, interactional styles, written language codes, and resource access will be unpacked. Using these specific bridge-building techniques will allow teachers to fill in gaps between students' home languages and the language expectations of an often new and different dominant culture, thereby explicitly understanding and teaching the idiosyncrasies of the dominant language.

IMPLICIT AND EXPLICIT CODES

Delpit (1988), writing in the context of instructing African American students in the United States, argues that if one is not a part of the dominant culture, being told the explicit rules of that culture makes acquiring the new culture easier. That is, those implicit codes about language and

Figure 8.1 Socioeconomic Differences

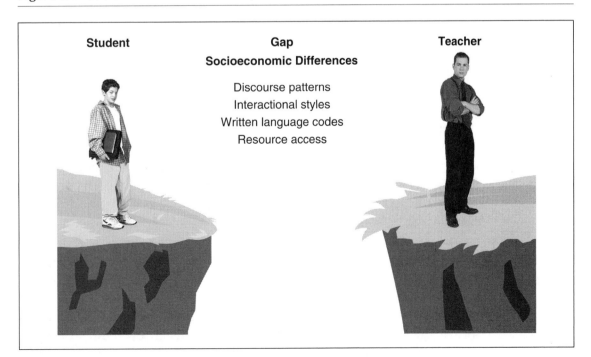

norms that have been ingrained in members of the culture must be made explicit to those outside of the culture. The work of Delpit challenges educators to truly differentiate according to *all* students' needs. She notes the following:

> Some children come to school with more accoutrements of the culture of power already in place—"cultural capital" as some critical theorists refer to it—some with less. Many liberal educators hold that the primary goal for education is for children to become autonomous, to develop fully while they are in the classroom setting without having arbitrary, outside standards forced upon them. This is a very reasonable goal for people whose children are already participants in the culture of power and who have internalized its codes. But parents who don't function within that culture often want something more. They want to ensure that the school provides their children with discourse patterns, interactional styles, and written language codes that will allow them success in the larger society. (p. 285)

Because we have the same high expectations and goals for both ELLs and SELs, we know that we must differentiate in order to meet their specific needs. For example, students who do not come to school having internalized the cultural and language codes of the dominant culture must be given time to develop those skills. Similarly, the ways in which these distinct groups develop those goals may be very different from the dominant culture, and there should be room for that within our educational systems. The following sections will address the discourse patterns, interactional styles, and written language codes that allow both ELLs and SELs entrance into the larger society of school, college, and the workplace.

DISCOURSE PATTERNS

Joos (1967) suggests that every language in the world has five registers, and that these differ for the impoverished population versus the middle class. The registers are described in Figure 8.2.

Joos (1967) found that one can drop down one register in the same conversation and still be socially accepted. However, if one were to drop down two registers or more in the same conversation, it would be regarded as socially offensive. The language registers and Joos's rule are important for educators to be aware of, and it is imperative that they be made explicit in regard to teachers' expectations of students. Students must be able to speak within the context of socially and academically appropriate registers; otherwise, they can be at risk for failing to complete high school, being denied access to college, and lack of gainful employment.

Educators should be aware of their own language register at all times so that they model the formal or academic register as often as possible.

Figure 8.2   Register Explanations

Register	Explanation
Frozen	Language that is always or nearly always the same—for example: the Lord's Prayer, wedding vow phrases, Pledge of Allegiance, etc.
Formal	The standard sentence syntax and word choice of work and school in a mainstream English environment. Is characterized by complete sentences and specific, accurate, and content-specific word choice.
Consultative	Formal register when used in conversation. Discourse pattern not quite as direct as formal register.
Casual	Language between friends and is characterized by a 400- to 800-word vocabulary. Word choice general and not specific. Conversation dependent upon nonverbal assists. Sentence syntax often incomplete.
Intimate	Language between lovers or twins.

SOURCE: Adapted from Joos, 1967.

Since many students come to school with few or infrequent models of the formal register, it is imperative that students hear formal registers modeled in school. This means that educators must be well-versed in the academic register, as well as continue to develop their own English language proficiency, especially across the content areas. Teachers must also expect and require all students to use the academic register in a respectful classroom setting. The academic register can be reinforced through continued and varied reading/language arts experiences. Teachers can model and have students specifically master the following oral language registers and learning examples, as described in Figure 8.3.

The Register Chart in Figure 8.3 is a reminder to educators that in order for students to be proficient in academic English, they must have exposure to and ample practice in a wide array of commonly used registers in mainstream English. Students also need to be able to practice these registers across the content areas. For example, although the dramatic and storytelling registers lend themselves to the subject areas of English, English language development, drama, and literature classes, the cooperative group work, classroom presentation, and student response registers can be reinforced across disciplines and across a typical school day. In order for such proficiency in academic registers to occur, teachers must be mindful of planning for such oral language situations when designing lessons.

In addition to modeling the formal or academic English register in their classrooms, educators can also contrast the registers for students. For example, some teachers become frustrated when students utilize few details and vague language in academic interactions, by favoring one-word responses or nonverbal expressions in classroom dialogue. In the

Figure 8.3 Register Examples and Learning Exercises

Register	Description/Example	Learning Exercise
Student response register	A firm tone, spoken confidently at a volume that can be heard by all other students in the room	Student debate or Socratic seminar discussion
Leadership register	The voice of roll call, the call to line up for lunch, or the call to be quiet and listen	Team captain during physical education or leadership role within the classroom
Classroom presentation register	Involves eye contact with an audience, confident bearing, pleasing and varied tone of voice, and an inviting sense of two-way communication with listeners	Student speech or formal presentation
Dramatic register	Spoken dialogue in a play, in the role of narrator or announcer; it is "larger than life," with exaggerated emotion and voice	Reader's Theater, scene re-enactment, poetry readings
Storytelling to children register	Features simplification and a sense of warmth and intimacy, no matter what the size of the crowd	Story retelling with a partner, pair-share, cross-age tutoring, or presentation to younger class
Cooperative work register	The "10-inch voice"; able to be heard within one's group but not by the next group	Literature Circles or Reciprocal Teaching

SOURCE: Adapted from Diaz-Rico, 2008.

classroom, a teacher may choose to utilize the bridge-building strategy of *teacher-guided reporting,* where the teacher elicits specific detail and language from the student, and the teacher may also offer Register Charts (Joos, 1967) to the students, contrasting the characteristics and expectations involved in each of the registers presented. Students can also practice translating a message from the casual to the formal register. That is, students can "play with language," examining how they might say something on the playground as opposed to the classroom. Note the examples in Figure 8.4.

Such a classroom exercise, as illustrated in Figure 8.4, enables students to begin exploring register, deepening their understanding of language

Figure 8.4   Register Conversations

Register	Conversations
Frozen	"Hello. How are you?" "I'm fine. How are you?" "Fine."
Formal	"Good morning, Charlotte. What was your time on your 1-mile race today?" "Good morning, Mrs. Espinoza. I cut my time by 20 seconds and ran the mile in 6 minutes and 55 seconds." "Excellent. You are doing much better with your pacing and your end sprint. I'll speak with your coach to commend him on your progress."
Consultative	"Good morning, Charlotte. How are you?" "I'm fine ma'am. And you?" "Well, thank you. Did you race today, Charlotte?" "Yes, ma'am." "How is your progress?" "It's coming along ma'am."
Casual	"Hey." "Hey." "What's up, dude?" "Nuttin' much. Whatcha doin?"

appropriateness. This formal exploration is particularly helpful to low SES students who may have come from a home where the formal English register is rarely utilized. Such a conversation and translation might also lead into a discussion about how language has changed over time. Similarly, a teacher might want to use Shakespearean language and have students translate the English of that time period into present-day English in order to further reinforce the academic register in literature.

INTERACTIONAL STYLES

Understanding language registers and interactional styles also helps to build a bridge between parents and teachers, particularly when there are significant SES differences. Often, parent–teacher interactions either on the phone or during conferences can lead to misunderstandings. If a teacher is not aware of the discourse patterns of the speaker, he or she might become frustrated. In the formal discourse pattern, the speaker or writer gets straight to the point. In contrast, in the casual-register discourse pattern, the writer or speaker goes around the issue before finally coming to the point (Joos, 1967). If, during a parent–teacher conference, the teacher has several parents to visit with, and wants to quickly review an item with the parent, but the parent wants to engage in a circular pattern of discourse, there will be frustration. If a teacher chooses to cut the conversation short in order to get to what he or she considers to be the point, the parent may view the interaction as rude, causing a misunderstanding.

Figure 8.5 illustrates a parent–teacher conference in both the formal and casual registers. If we take this example of a parent–teacher conference, it is easy to see how misunderstandings can and almost inevitably will occur with such opposite conversational styles and expectations. Many teachers might find the awareness of register differences to be enough to assist them with interactions with parents, understanding that register differences, with which they may be unfamiliar, may be common interaction styles for many of their parents. However, sometimes teachers need more specific support in communicating with parents. At Back-to-School Night or at a Parent Education Night, it might be helpful to parents to communicate a message utilizing the casual-register structure first and then retelling it in the formal register. In other cases, it might be helpful for the teacher to tell parents that she only has a couple of minutes to discuss the issue and that she is going to have to get right to the point. This is especially critical at the secondary level where one might have 200 students and 15-minute parent conferences.

Clearly, in any educational setting, some give and take is appropriate. That is, the parent or student should not always have to make all of the changes in the educational relationship. In the classroom, there will be times when participation in writing and telling stories should be and can be utilized. For example, students may be encouraged to write stories that emphasize the character and are more communal in nature. Students may also use the casual register during "sharing" or storytelling times. During formal-register times, teachers may have students retell a particular text in sequential order, or from beginning to end, with an additional emphasis

Figure 8.5 Formal-Register and Casual Register Parent Conference Dialogue

	Formal Register	**Casual Register**
Parent	"I'd like to know how my student is doing academically and with his behavior."	"How are you doing today? The weather has been quite strange, hasn't it? Are your classes quite large this year?"
Teacher	"Your child participates well, but is missing several homework assignments."	"Fine, I'm doing fine. The weather's a bit cold and my classes are a bit larger than before."
Parent	"I'll be sure to talk to him about this. What can I do to keep in better communication with you about his homework activity?"	"I thought I noticed that there were more students in this class than in my child's class last year. How is he doing, by the way?"

on the plot. Similarly, there may be times when stories can be told both in the formal- and casual-register story structure, specifically contrasting those differences for students, as well as when it is appropriate to use them. By modeling both casual and formal registers, educators send a message to students that they value all of the elements of the home culture and language. Attention to register affirms a variety of language practices, thereby bridging a gap between the student's and the teacher's language.

WRITTEN LANGUAGE CODES

While exceptions exist (e.g., the Hmong culture, which did not have a written language for many years), most cultures emphasize particular aspects of writing, and those features should be accessed and contrasted with the target writing style being taught, instead of assuming that there is no writing foundation within the students' cultures. Fillmore and Snow (2000) cite McCabe (1997) when they write about the struggle that many Second Language Learners have with the writing process:

> The emphasis in mainstream English stories is on getting the order of events correct and clear. This emphasis can seem so obviously right to an uninformed monolingual speaker of English that the narrative of the Latino child, which emphasizes personal relationships more than plot, or of the Japanese child, who may provide very terse stories rather than recounting all of the events, can be dismissed as incomprehensible. (p. 45)

As educators, many times we incorrectly assume that students come to us with little to no concept of writing, because the child's writing style differs so dramatically from our own background experiences. Rather than building upon what our students may bring to us as assets to writing from their own cultures—Latino students usually emphasize personal relationships, and Japanese students often display strength in concise writing (see Figure 8.6)—educators often ignore these assets and start at

Figure 8.6 Ethnic Group Writing Tendencies and Needs

Ethnic Group	Writing Tendencies	Writing Needs
Latino writing styles	Narrative, which emphasizes personal relationships more than plot	Point out the spoken-to-written language continuum, noting differences in spoken and written language
Japanese writing styles	Brief stories rather than recounting all of the events	Creating more detail in writing; perhaps also how to use evidence to elucidate main points

SOURCE: Adapted from McCabe, 1997, cited in Fillmore & Snow, 2000.

the beginning of the writing process. Instead, educators can build on these writing assets by contrasting writing styles from students' home cultures to those expected in academic settings.

Bridging the gap between cultural and academic writing styles will begin when the teacher first acknowledges and accepts the variety of styles present in the classroom and gradually contrasts them. For example, a teacher may begin the school year with journal writing or narrative writing styles, and then transition students into more academic and difficult forms of writing such as comparison/contrast writing. This balance affirms the assets of the home culture and scaffolds writing in such a way that it is accessible for all students.

An additional component of written codes and oral interactional styles is differing story structures. For example, the formal-register story structure is more chronological or linear in fashion. It starts at the beginning of the story and goes to the end in a sequential pattern. The most important part of the story in this sequence is the plot, which occurs in chronological order. In contrast, the casual-register story structure can begin with either the end or the most emotionally intense part of the story. The rest of the story then unfolds in vignettes (or short stories) with audience participation expected. The story ends with a summary or statement about the character, who is the most important part of the story.

Figure 8.7 can be used both for instructional planning and to explicitly contrast the differences between registers with students. For instructional planning, the chart is a useful tool when planning oral language development or writing lessons. The chart can prove to be a helpful reminder to teachers of the components of the formal register, which must be explicitly taught in order for proficiency to occur. It can also be used as an instructional tool in the classroom in order to contrast oral language and written language differences. For example, a writing sample written in the casual register (without name or identification) can be placed on the board or overhead, and the teacher can conduct a "think-aloud" regarding how to turn the sample into a formal-register text. Students can then practice translating an additional sample from the casual register into the formal register either in pairs or independently. It is important to note that teachers must emphasize that the casual register is not wrong; it is simply not often appropriate to use in an academic or professional setting, but is often used in the home environment and often in low-SES settings as well, where casual language is dominant and formal language is often absent. Therefore, students must be encouraged to learn the formal register in order to be successful both in an academic and professional setting.

RESOURCE ACCESS

In addition to discourse patterns, interactional styles, and written language codes that often vary between the low-SES ELL and his or her

Figure 8.7 Formal and Casual Register Story Structures

Formal Register: Story Structure	Casual Register: Story Structure
• Chronological/linear order • Sequential • Beginning to end • Emphasis on plot	• End of story/most emotionally intense first • Vignettes/short stories • Audience participation encouraged • Ends with a summary of character • Relational/communal aspects emphasized

SOURCE: Adapted from Joos, 1967.

teacher, issues of poverty and literacy development must also consider book access at home and the availability of adult mentors/role models.

When Hetzel surveyed her graduate students in her literacy courses, inquiring about how many books they had access to in their homes as children, the answers expressed a range of 3 to 2,000 books. Immigrant students tended to have less book access than mainstream American students who were third-, fourth-, and fifth-generation English-speaking students. This trend can also be true of SELs, or students who come from homes where there are no reading models; that is, students don't experience family members who are avid readers, so reading may not be reinforced. In one of Soto-Hinman's professional development workshops, one Caucasian participant noted that although her childhood home was rich with beautiful, leather-bound texts, she never saw an adult crack open one of those covers. Due to this fact, she did not become an avid reader herself until later on in life, as an adult. This further demonstrates that book access is critical across socioeconomic and cultural lines and that we cannot make assumptions regarding the experiences that our students have had. In addition, as educators, we have a responsibility to be positive literacy models for our students.

In addition to low-SES students having less book access in their preschool and K–12 years, critical word factors in texts have changed dramatically over time. For example, there is

Scott Foresman's reading textbook program, which has the longest record of publishing in the field. . . . From 1962 to 2000, the number of unique or different words (per text) increased from 18 to 187 for the first 10 texts in the program (Hiebert, 2005). That tenfold increase in the number of unique words to be read represents a sea of change in developmental expectations for beginning first-grade students. (Hiebert & Fisher, 2007, p. 3)

This presents a huge challenge to the ELL who has had little exposure to formal language during her early years. This increase in critical word factors in text makes it all the more important to ensure book access and adult role models for children from low-SES backgrounds.

However, low-SES children often need help with literacy-related materials as well as book access—notebooks, writing utensils, a dictionary to use at home and school, a bilingual dictionary to use at home and school, materials for reports, access to a computer station, knowledge and transportation regarding the school and community library, and so forth. Attention to these literacy- and SES-related matters will help ensure that your low-SES ELLs and SELs have equitable educational access.

SUMMARY

Although educators often cannot control what happens at home (e.g., socioeconomic factors), they certainly can impact what happens in their own classroom, including the methods they use to address linguistic differences and the amount of time they spend trying to do so. As socioeconomic and achievement gaps continue to persist in schools, it is imperative that educators seek to understand the cultural and linguistic background and needs of their students. Educator perceptions and expectations are often grounded in mental models and philosophical assumptions around students and their perceptions of their cognitive abilities, which are often based upon surface features of the language that are casual and reflect differing SES. The sociocultural and linguistic assets that students bring with them to school must be considered and incorporated into the changing face of America's schools. The more comfortable educators are with the discourse patterns, interactional styles, and written language codes that

Figure 8.8 Socioeconomic Differences

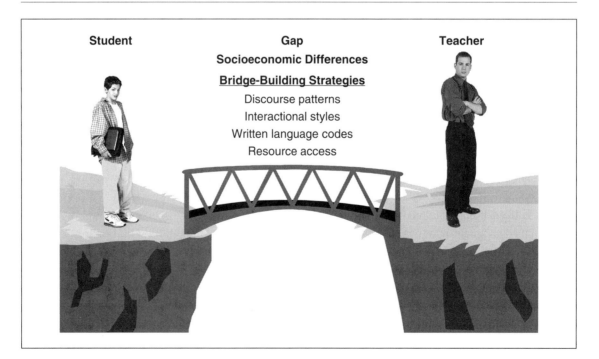

students bring with them from home, the better they will be able to both use them as assets in a classroom, and contrast them with academic expectations to further provide access to and options for their futures. Similarly, the more comfortable teachers become with the variance in language and socioeconomic status in their classrooms, the more comfortable and prepared students will be in a pluralistic society. This inclusion and "oneness" then becomes a model not only for classroom and schools, but also for changing society at large.

REFERENCES

Balfanz, R., & Legters, N. (2004). *Locating the dropout crisis.* Baltimore: Johns Hopkins University Center for Social Organization of Schools.

Delpit, L. (1988). The silenced dialogue: Power and pedagogy in educating other people's children. *Harvard Educational Review 58*(3), 280–297.

Diaz-Rico, L. (2008). *Strategies for teaching English learners.* Boston: Pearson/Allyn & Bacon.

Fillmore, L. W., & Snow, C. E. (2000). *What teachers need to know about language. Special report from ERIC Clearinghouse on Languages and Linguistics.* Washington, DC: Center for Applied Linguistics.

Hiebert, E. H. (2005). State reform policies and the reading task for first graders. *Elementary School Journal, 105,* 245–266.

Hiebert, E., & Fisher, C. W. (2007, September/October). Critical word factor in texts for beginning readers. *Journal of Educational Research, 101*(1), 3–11.

Joos, M. (1967). *The five clocks.* New York: Harcourt, Brace, & World.

Kahlenberg, R. D. (2006, April 1). Integration by income. *American School Board Journal.*

Kerner Commission. (2008). *What together we can do: A forty-year update of the National Advisory Commission on Civil Disorders—Preliminary findings.* Abilene, KS: The Eisenhower Foundation.

McCabe, A. (1997). Cultural background and storytelling: A review and implications for schooling. *Elementary School Journal, 97*(5), 453–473.

9

Language Proficiency Levels

This chapter takes into account language-based accommodations when the primary language of an ELL, or dialect of an SEL, differs from that of his or her peers. Language differences—either a second language or a dialect/variation of English—often exist between teacher and student, as mentioned in Chapter 7, but can also exist between a student and his peers. Such language differences can create gaps or misunderstandings in the classroom. A student's first language encompasses her background knowledge and experience, forming the basis for funds of knowledge that will be assets in acquiring English. In Chapter 9, teachers learn strategies that build upon L1 assets, as well as non-standard forms of English that may be spoken at home. The chapter provides suggestions for bridging the gap of grammatical, discourse/textual, sociolinguistic, and pragmatic competencies as they relate to language variability among an ELL/SEL and his or her peers (see Figure 9.1).

ACADEMIC LANGUAGE COMPETENCE

For ELLs, language competence means both learning the nuances of the English language, and academic forms of English across disciplines and content areas. Similarly, districts are under a federal mandate through No Child Left Behind and Title III to monitor (1) access to grade-level academic content instruction and (2) students' development of Academic

Figure 9.1 Language Variables

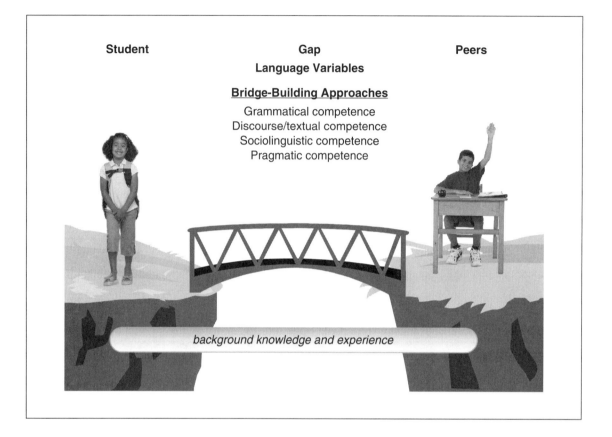

English language proficiency. Historically, educators have believed that providing ELLs with the basics of English is enough. Teaching methods that assist ELLs with only the nuances of English have caused many ELLs to remain at low levels of proficiency—if they reach proficiency at all in their educational careers. According to Goldenberg (2006), "Many [ELLs] will be limited in their English proficiency when they begin school; some will remain less than completely fluent for years" (p. 1).

Since far too many ELLs spend their entire educational careers becoming proficient in English, it is critical that educators be well-versed in the components of academic language competence. The following model by Valdés (2007), informed by the work of Canale and Swain (1980), Bachman (1990), and Littlewood (2004), details the four components of language competence: grammatical competence, discourse/textual competence, sociolinguistic competence, and pragmatic competence (see Figure 9.2). Since there are different kinds of ELLs—underschooled students, newly arrived highly educated adolescents, and long-term ELLs who have been in U.S. schools for 6 years or more—it is essential to determine where students are in terms of each of these components of language development. Those places where ELLs are underdeveloped or lack proficiency will require more emphasis and practice. It is also important to balance each of the four parts of language competence equally, being sure not to overly emphasize one over the other due to one's own comfort level.

Grammatical Competence

There are four essential components related to grammatical competence: vocabulary, syntax, morphology, and phonology. We will begin our discussion with vocabulary.

Vocabulary

With the emerging literature in best practices for reading instruction, including from the National Literacy Panel (Center for Applied Linguistics, 2006), many more educators have become savvier regarding the intricacies of grammatical competence, specifically appropriate vocabulary instruction. Still, many educators ask themselves, "How should vocabulary instruction be different for ELLs?" As introduced in Chapter 4, the Center on Instruction (Francis, Rivera, Lesaux, & Rivera, 2006) describes the importance of vocabulary instruction as follows:

> Vocabulary instruction rarely occurs despite the fact that it is the academic language of classrooms and texts that prove[s] most difficult for ELLs and in spite of the fact that the average ELL—and his classmates—need[s] between 12 and 14 exposures to a word and its meaning, across multiple contexts (different texts, classroom discussions, writing activities), in order to gain a deep understanding of a word. (p. 20)

Figure 9.2 A Holistic View of Language Competence

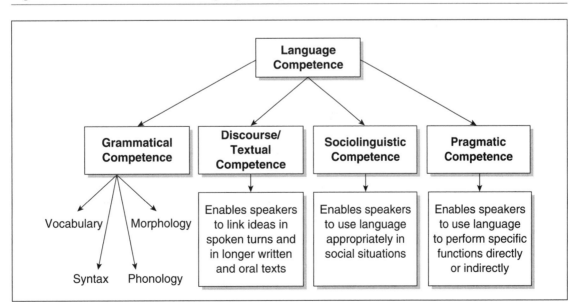

SOURCE: Adapted from Guadalupe Valdés, 2007. Used with permission.

Similarly, as Saunders and Goldenberg (1999) remind us, native English speakers usually acquire 5,000–7,000 vocabulary words prior to the start of their formal schooling (i.e., kindergarten). In contrast, ELLs come to school with a listening vocabulary in English of far fewer words, which is where the achievement gap begins for this group of students (Goldenberg, 2006). The issue for classroom teachers then becomes how to create those 12 to 14 exposures to words and their meaning across multiple contexts. Educators are often used to teaching vocabulary development inefficiently, by simply selecting 10 words at the beginning of the week and testing students on them at the end of the week. This is, in fact, one of the most inefficient ways to teach vocabulary, because a vocabulary list is the least context-embedded approach. Still other educators rely on the words in bold in their textbooks to guide them in vocabulary instruction, when the reality is that an ELL might need to know several additional English words to understand each bolded vocabulary word. For example, the bolded vocabulary word might be *conservation;* however, the ELL might also need to understand *clearcutting, erosion, rainfall, precipitation, soil, landslides, flooding, flora, fauna, vegetation,* and *survival* to truly understand the concept of *conservation* in this particular context.

Therefore, educators need to determine the English vocabulary needs of their own students—words they know and do not know (common words *and* academic words)—along with the critical vocabulary of the lesson. A simple pre-assessment of words within a unit or chapter can be helpful to determine which students may need more assistance with which words (see Figure 9.3).

Figure 9.3 Vocabulary Pre-Assessment

	I've never seen this word before.	I know a little about this word.	I understand this word.	I can teach others about this word.
Vocabulary Words				
clearcutting	X			
erosion	X			
rainfall		X		
precipitation	X			
Other Academic Words				
scientist		X		
consider	X			
debate	X			
examine		X		

SOURCE: Adapted from vocabulary assessments by Kate Kinsella, 2007.

After instruction, the teacher can go back and have the student place an "x" in the appropriate column to allow the student to self-assess again and determine growth in vocabulary development.

Often, the words selected by textbooks may not be the words with which your ELLs struggle. ELLs often will have mastered the label for a word (a surface understanding), but struggle with what th Center on Instruction (2006) calls a "deep understanding of a word"— in other words, the concept behind the word. Conceptual knowledge of words includes knowledge of the word itself as well as words that relate to it. For example, a Spanish-speaking ELL may know the label for the word *independence*, especially because it is a cognate of the Spanish word *independencia*. However, the student may not realize that the word *independence* relates to *freedom, democracy,* and *free elections,* which opens up a whole new set of related vocabulary words.

Educators often do not take the opportunity to relate vocabulary concepts with this expansion format in mind. Instead, they teach words and concepts one at a time, in isolation, which is not helpful for ELLs who come to school with far fewer English words than their native English peers. The teacher can help ELLs rapidly build their vocabulary by introducing words in an expansion format that demonstrates groups of related words and concepts (see Figure 9.4). The same is also true for SELs who may know basic words, but not their academic equivalents.

Figure 9.4 Vocabulary Expansion–Related Concepts

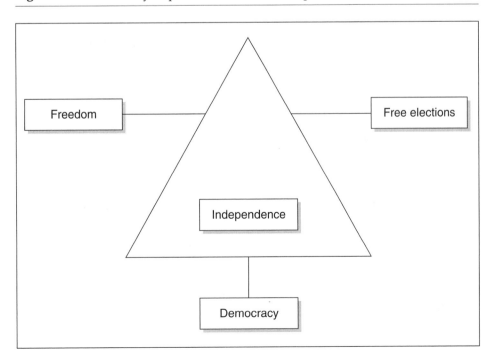

One method that builds rapid vocabulary expansion is the *4-square vocabulary* strategy outlined in Figure 9.5. This strategy involves teaching students examples of a word (synonyms), and non-examples (antonyms), before they create a sentence to define a word. Students also are taught to associate a visual or symbol with the word, which can go in the center of the graphic organizer. This strategy becomes a scaffold for vocabulary development whereby students learn to associate many characteristics shared by the target word and new words.

Figure 9.5   4-Square Vocabulary

Word *Democracy*	
Characteristics	**Examples**
Freedom	*United States*
Independence	*Commonwealth*
Free elections	*Equality*
Definition	**Non-Examples**
Democracy is a state of society characterized by formal equality of rights and privileges.	*Communism*
	Socialism
	Dictatorship

Word walls assist ELLs in gaining 12 to 14 exposures to words because they target terms that have been introduced in a specific lesson or unit. Making words visible and available in a classroom allows the words to be readily used and applied in context. In *The Word Wall: Teaching Vocabulary Through Immersion,* Green (1993) describes the importance of using a word wall in this way: "The Word Wall is built upon the spiral theory of mastery—repetition reinforces previously learned principles. Regular use throughout the school year allows you to recycle many words" (p. 6). That is, students will use and apply words when they are both taught those words deeply and reminded to use them in context.

Word walls can also be used for specific reasons, such as keeping a record of cognates—words that sound the same and have similar meanings in two languages. One teacher, who had primarily Spanish-speaking students, gathered the cognates from the reading passage and demonstrated to the students how many vocabulary words they already understood before they started reading the passage (see Figure 9.6).

Figure 9.6   Spanish–English Cognates Word Wall

Spanish Word	English Word
diccionario	dictionary
alfabético	alphabet
edición	edition
expression	expression

Having such word groupings posted in a classroom will remind ELLs of the language resource that they already bring with them to school as well as those they are acquiring while at school, opening up many new words for students to practice in English in both their speaking and their writing.

Word walls can also be used for specific purposes, such as posting descriptive words or adjectives while writing a creative story, or tracking words associated with the literary elements (character, setting, conflict, etc.) as the class reads a story together. Each time that a word is taught explicitly, it should go on the word wall, and students should be encouraged to use those words both in spoken and written language. Having the words up on the wall also reminds the teacher to reinforce and use the words often. When word walls are used broadly to reinforce language, they are useful to all students within a classroom, including SELs, who are reminded to use academic forms in spoken and written language.

Another helpful method to deepen vocabulary knowledge in context is to use a *word continuum*. For example, if the student is being exposed to the new vocabulary word *tepid*, introduce the word on a temperature continuum (see Figure 9.7).

Figure 9.7 Word Continuum

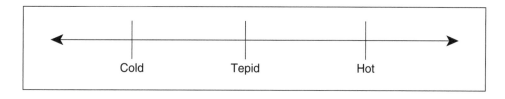

As the teacher interacted with the students (see Figure 9.8), the word continuum for water temperature grew (see Figure 9.9).

Similar to the 4-square vocabulary strategy, the word continuum shows relationships between words, and, like a word wall, the word continuum becomes a receptacle for related vocabulary that can be posted on the wall for ELLs'/SELs' easy retrieval.

Syntax

The second area under grammatical competence that needs development in order to bridge the gap between the ELL and his or her peers is that of syntax. *Syntax,* the way that words are arranged to form sentences or phrases, can be problematic for ELLs, as the rules that govern the positions of words in English may differ slightly or dramatically from those of their primary language. Unlike some languages, in English, the position of a word impacts the overall meaning. For example, changing the order of the words in the following sentences greatly impacts the overall meaning: "The teacher asked the

Figure 9.8 SEL Conversation

Teacher:	Student:
"*Tepid* is a word that refers to the temperature of water. Place your hand in this bowl of water. What does it feel like?"	"Wet."
"Is it cold or hot?"	"It's not cold. It's not hot."
"That's right. The water is *tepid.* The water temperature is between cold and hot. Say the new word, *tepid.*"	"Tepid."
"What other temperature words do you know?"	"Words like very cold, freezing."
"Very good. Let's write those words on the left side: *cold, freezing.*" "What other temperature words do you know?"	"Hot. Too much hot . . . like frying or burning . . . when the water has bubbles."
"We say that the water is *boiling.*" (The teacher writes *boiling* on the continuum.)	
"What would come between tepid and boiling?"	"The water warm."
"Yes! The water is *warm.*" (The teacher writes *warm* on the continuum.)	
"What if the water was between cold and tepid."	"I know . . . that . . . that's coola."
"Yes! We say the water is *cool.*" (The teacher writes the word *cool* on the continuum.)	
"Now, I have three bowls of water here. Who will put their hand in each one and tell the class what they feel?"	Ricardo volunteers. "This . . . this water is cold. It feel like ice." "This water . . . uh . . . it's te- tepid. It feel like normal." "This water . . . ouch! . . . I don' like this water. This water very hot!"

Figure 9.9 Word Continuum Expanded

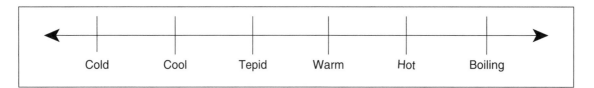

students to sit down" vs. "The students asked the teacher to sit down" vs. "Asked the teacher to down students sit." Students who have *met-alinguistic knowledge,* or the vocabulary to explain grammar, often have learned the grammar of their native language first. Again, it is important to pre-assess students in their facility with English syntax when determining what kind of instruction they may need.

One way to readily teach syntax is by using sticky notes or index cards to assist students in building syntactically correct sentences. Using a think-aloud, the teacher can demonstrate for students why she places certain words in a certain order. The teacher can then ask students for their input as she places new words in a particular order. This is also a good method for teaching students how to creatively use language, and how that impacts meaning. Teachers can use poetry to teach this concept, as it presents a rich language resource for such work. The following charts by Spinelli (cited in Kettel, 1994) represent syntactical contrasts that educators need to take into consideration when teaching ELLs who speak Chinese (Mandarin) or Spanish (see Figures 9.10 and 9.11). If a teacher has a classroom of ELLs from these backgrounds who struggle with English syntax, mini-lessons on these specific grammar concepts can be helpful.

For example, putting the sentence *No one knows correct time* on sticky notes or index cards, and then discussing how and why the definite article

Figure 9.10   English Syntax Contrast Charts

English Syntax Contrasted With Chinese (Mandarin)	**English Syntax Contrasted With Spanish**
• **Verb tense:** *I see him yesterday.* (In Chinese, the verb form is not changed to mark the time during which the action occurred—the adverb, not the verb, signals the time. Conjugating the verb form in English may prove to be difficult for the learner.) • **Subject–verb agreement:** *He see me.* (In Chinese, verbs do not change form to create subject–verb agreement.) • **Word order:** *I at home ate.* (In Chinese, prepositional phrases usually come before the verb—the rules governing adverb placement in English are difficult for many learners.) • **Plurals:** *They give me 3 dollar.* (In Chinese, like English, the marker indicates number, but the noun form does not change to indicate plural; in English, the noun form changes.) • **Articles:** *No one knows correct time.* (Chinese uses demonstrative pronouns *[this one, that one]* but not definite or indefinite articles *[a, the]*. The rules for such use in English are complex.	• **Verb conjugation:** Spanish has three groups of regular verbs, in contrast to one group in English (those that add -ed or -d), but English has more classes of irregular verbs (wildly irregular go/went/gone versus mildly irregular like send/sent, break/broke, etc.). • **Subject–verb agreement:** In Spanish, first-, second-, and third-person forms must be changed from the base form to create subject–verb agreement. It is sometimes hard to remember that in English only the third-person form is changed. • **Noun/Adjective order:** In Spanish, adjectives come sometimes before and sometimes after the noun *(un buen dia, un dia linda)*. These alterations, however, obey regular rules. • **Articles:** Spanish, like English, uses both definite and indefinite articles, but with different rules (for example, languages need the definite article: *el ingles*). Both definite and indefinite articles must match the noun to which they refer *(unos muchachos, las mujeres)*.

SOURCE: Spinelli, cited in Kettel, 1994, p. 62.

the should be added in between *knows* and *correct*, will prove helpful for a Mandarin-speaking ELL. Physically seeing the addition of the article, and contrasting the syntactical structure with a think-aloud, can prove to be a resource for students in the future. Students can also be given individual index cards or sticky notes to construct sentences in the most syntactically correct form.

Critical to bridging the syntax gap is continuous *language elaboration and modeling.* For example, consider the classroom in the Figure 9.11 dialogue between a native English-speaking teacher and his native Mandarin-speaking student.

In the Figure 9.11 dialogue, the teacher recasted the student's words, thus providing a model of appropriate syntax as well as elaboration. Notice that the teacher never corrected the student. She simply interacted in an authentic way, and the conversation moved along smoothly. The ELL, however, was picking up syntactical cues along the way from his teacher and readily incorporated new understandings of syntax in his responses. While his responses were not perfect English syntax, they continued to approximate mainstream English syntax and actually demonstrated growth in this short dialogue. Clearly, the *low affective filter* (low anxiety) and warm relationship between teacher and student assisted the student in his ability to take risks with language in the context of this conversation with his teacher.

Figure 9.11 Teacher and Mandarin-Speaking Student Dialogue

Teacher:	Mandarin-Speaking Student:
	"I go home now."
"You are going home now?"	"Yes, I going home."
"What will you take with you?"	"I take book and pencil."
"Which books will you take?"	"I take . . . I will take my book, math, and book, reading."
"You will take your math book and your reading book?"	"Yes, I take . . . I *will* take math book and reading book. And, I take . . . I *will* take my pencil."
"*Very* good Xin! I will look forward to seeing you tomorrow."	"Thank you, teacher. I . . . I *will* look forward seeing you morrow!"

Phonology and Morphology

Along with vocabulary and syntax, phonology and morphology instruction assist in bridging grammatical competence between an ELL and his or her peers. Much has been discussed around Literacy Gap #1, the gap between the student and the text, regarding the importance of phonology and morphology with ELLs. As a review, *phonology* is the study of sound units, while *morphology* is the study of units of meaning. This section will mostly reinforce the importance of teaching morphology as a way to access vocabulary with ELLs, and phonology will be simultaneously reinforced within the context of meaning. The power of morphology with ELLs is that the smaller units of meaning in words provide access to greater meaning, particularly with *bound morphemes,* or meaning units (e.g., re-, -ing) that occur in conjunction with other words. As ELLs learn the meaning of smaller units, such as prefixes, suffixes, and root words, they can create new and longer words. The predictability of meaning carried by affixes also provides students an additional resource in learning new words, in contrast to rote memorization. For example, when the student learns that the prefix *re-* means *again,* the meaning of several words immediately becomes clear (see Figure 9.12).

Figure 9.12   Prefix Chart for Vocabulary Words

Prefix	Meaning	Vocabulary Word	Definition
re-	again	redo	to do over
re-	again	reorganize	to organize again
re-	again	redraw	to draw again

Teachers can purchase or make prefix and suffix strips out of index cards and literally show students how to build words by physically putting them together in a pocket chart. Students can then build their own words using sticky notes on their desks or whiteboards. For example, one secondary ELD teacher did word-building exercises where students wrote on their individual dry erase boards (see Figure 9.13).

Once certain prefixes or suffixes are explicitly taught, students can then play word games by creating as many words as they can with those word parts. In addition, students can write creative stories using many of the target words created.

Discourse/Textual Competence

Discourse/textual competence is the second major area to bridge language competence between the ELL and his or her peers (see Figure 9.14).

Discourse/textual competence refers to students' ability to link ideas in spoken language and in longer written and oral texts. For ELLs, it is helpful to link the domains of speaking and writing because both are about output and production—one in oral language and one in written language. For example, it is helpful to allow an ELL to share with a partner about a writing topic before the students begin writing. This allows ELLs to create a mental outline of their writing before they begin to write and also allows them to clarify vocabulary and concepts with the assistance of a partner. If students are not clear, their partner can help clarify language or concepts. In this type of approach, ELLs also benefit from hearing the ideas of a partner to further clarify their own language resource. By hearing from a partner, students can expand their own ideas

Figure 9.13   Word-Building Dialogue

Teacher:	Students:
"Write the word *nation*."	(Students write *nation* on their dry erase boards.)
"What is a nation?"	"A nation is like the U.S." "A nation is a country."
"Add the suffix *-al* at the end of nation."	(Students add suffix *-al.)*
"What word do we have now?"	"National" (said in unison).
(The teacher points to the flag in the classroom.) "This is our *national* flag. The flag represents our *nation.*" "Who else can use the word *national*?"	
	"The eagle is national bird."
"Yes, the eagle is our national bird." "What else?"	"Thanksgiving is national holiday."
"Yes, Thanksgiving is a national holiday." "Very good." "*Nation* is a noun. *National* is an adjective. *National* describes another word: *national* flag, *national* bird, *national* holiday."	
"Now, add the prefix *inter-* in front of national."	(Students write *inter-* in front of national on their dry erase boards.)
"What does the word say now?"	"International" (said in unison).
"*Inter-* means *among* or *between*. For example, our school has *international* students. This means our school has students from many countries."	
"Who can use international in a sentence?"	"We have international fair at our school."
"Yes, we have an international fair here at Mulberry School. What else?"	"United Nations has international people."
"Excellent. The United Nations that we read about in our history book has members from countries all over the world. The United Nations has *international* membership."	
"Others?"	"We should think international."
"Tell me more . . . "	"We should think about all people, not just U.S."
"Yes! We should think *internationally*, considering everyone's needs. Share with your partner why you think that we should think internationally, or consider the needs of others around the world."	(Pairs of students discuss.)

Figure 9.14   Gap: Discourse/Textual Competence

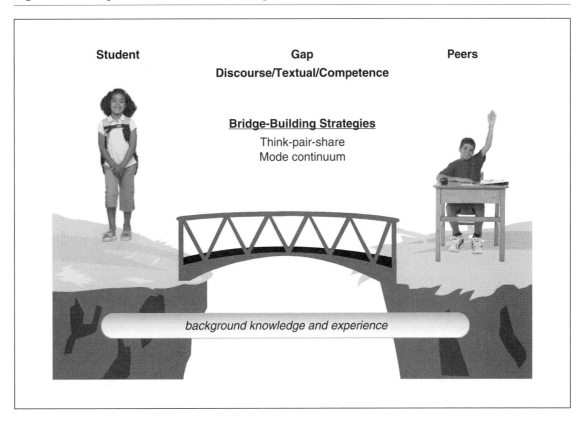

and enhance their own academic language development. For example, the students might have been asked to write about their experiences in nature camp. The students begin to talk in pairs and formulate their thoughts, as shown in Figure 9.15.

Figure 9.16 represents what Gibbons (2002) describes as the *mode continuum* from speaking to writing. On the left side of the continuum, we have social or more "spoken-like" language, which is often less cognitively demanding because of its simple grammatical structure. On the right-hand side, we have academic or more "written-like" language, which is more cognitively demanding due to its complex structure. In sharing this continuum (Figures 9.16 and 9.18) with students, it is important to remind them that we do not write the way that we speak.

For example, a teacher can contrast the same information delivered in oral context and written context (see Figure 9.17).

The teacher can share with students that no one would speak the way the written text is recorded in Figure 9.17. However, in written English, the syntax and vocabulary become quite elaborate as authors shape and reshape phrases, sentences, and longer passages, literally painting a vivid picture in the reader's mind.

Figure 9.15   Student Conversation About Nature Camp

Student #1:	Student #2:
"Do you understand?"	"We need to write bout nature camp."
"What we going to write?"	"Do you remember?"
"Yes."	"What remember?"
"Horseback riding. Swimming. Hike."	"Yes. I remember. We write about these. Okay?"
"Okay. I'll get paper."	"Remember, we write about *experiences.* Teacher say this. And must be in order."

Figure 9.16   Mode Continuum of Inquiry I

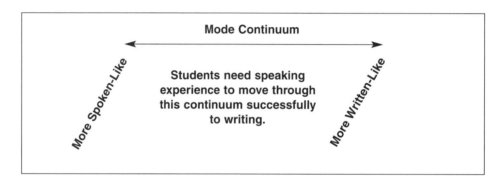

SOURCE: Adapted from Gibbons, 2002.

Figure 9.17   Oral and Written Language Contrast

Oral:	Written:
"Her dress was beautiful. I really liked it."	"Her dress, elaborately covered in sequins with an empire waist and flowing train, deeply impressed me."

Gibbons (2002) suggests an instructional scaffold for moving students from speaking to writing called the *mode continuum of inquiry.* This mode continuum lesson design includes a four-stage process, which moves students from "spoken-like" to "written-like" language.

The first step, which is the "small-group experiment," builds background knowledge around a particular concept or content area. During this stage, students are provided with a contextualized or hands-on experience, such as an experiment or simulation. The second step connects the

Figure 9.18   Mode Continuum of Inquiry II

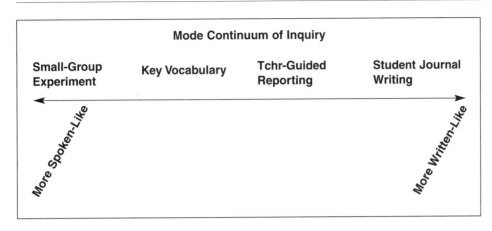

SOURCE: Adapted from Gibbons, 2002.

language or key vocabulary to the hands-on experience that students have just engaged in. For ELLs, it is essential to provide the contextualized experience before connecting the language, as it will help them to make associations and connections between the two. If an ELL has not had prior experience with a particular concept, the use of a hands-on experience builds background knowledge and language around the topic at hand. In contrast, teachers often begin with the language, and students flounder in associating the language or vocabulary with any concrete experience they have had. The fourth step in this process is *teacher-guided reporting* (TGR), which was introduced in an earlier chapter. As a review, TGR is an oral language scaffold that allows the student and teacher to jointly build what the student cannot say on his or her own. Once the student has had a contextualized experience, and the teacher has provided the academic language to associate with the experience, the student is then able to explain his or her experience because specific language scaffolds have been provided. Specifically, TGR scaffolds oral language by beginning with open-ended questions and providing encouragement, clarification, and appropriate wait time. The final step in the mode continuum of inquiry is student journal writing. This scaffolding approach to moving from oral language to written language would also be helpful for SELs who may need to build both background knowledge about a topic as well as specialized vocabulary associated with it. With both of these scaffolds in place, SELs are also more likely to be successful with the writing process.

The mode continuum of inquiry provides three levels of scaffolding—small-group experiment, key vocabulary, and teacher-guided reporting—before ELLs get to more cognitively demanding writing tasks. Since writing is the most difficult of all of the domains, and a skill that even many adults never master, it is essential that all of these scaffolds be in place before asking ELLs to write. Allowing students to interact in a contextualized experience gives them the content to write about; connecting the vocabulary to such an experience gives ELLs the language to associate the experience with; talking about the experience creates the mental framework for writing; and all of these steps allow facility with writing that may not already be there for students. Figure 9.19 is an example of the mode continuum of inquiry in a math classroom.

The geometry lesson above allows students to experience reflections and transformations in a concrete way before applying it in a math setting. Beginning with the experience before attaching the language internalizes the concept for ELLs before they are expected to use academic language in context and more abstractly in math problems. As students talk and write about their hands-on experience, both background knowledge and a language framework are established.

Another example, from an English composition class, might look like Figure 9.20.

Sociolinguistic Competence

The third area of language competence involves sociolinguistic competence (see Figure 9.21). Explicit instruction, simulations, and language stems are some of the bridge-building strategies that assist students in growing in this area of competence.

Sociolinguistic competence specifically refers to a student's ability to use language appropriately in social situations. Sociolinguistic competence builds upon the discourse/textual competence and the language continuum

Figure 9.19 California Geometry, Mode Continuum Example

California Geometry Content Standard Addressed:

22.0 Students know the effect of rigid motions on figures in the coordinate plane and space, including rotations, translations, and reflections.

Stage 1: Small-Group Experiment	Stage 2: Key Vocabulary
• Students line up in two rows facing each other. One student makes a movement with his/her body and the other must reflect that movement.	• Transformation • Reflection • Rotation • Solid figures
Stage 3: Teacher-Guided Reporting	**Stage 4: Journal Writing**
• The teacher asks students to share regarding their experiences when trying to mimic each other's movements. 　○ Open-ended question: What did you experience? What did you have to do to ensure that you got the movement correct?	• Students write a brief summary of their experiences with reflecting movements, using the key vocabulary in Stage 2.

Figure 9.20 Language Arts, Mode Continuum Example

California Language Arts Content Standard Addressed:

2.0 Writing Applications (genres and their characteristics)
2.1 Writing Narratives
c. Use concrete sensory details.

Stage 1: Small-Group Experiment Students are directed to create "Fruit Skewers." They each are to pick up a skewer and select fruit to place on their skewer from the bowls of fruit provided. They are then to enjoy eating their fruit skewer with their partner while taking note of sensory experiences.	**Stage 2: Key Vocabulary** <ul><li>Taste</li><li>Touch</li><li>Smell</li><li>See</li><li>Hear</li></ul>
Stage 3: Teacher-Guided Reporting The teacher guides the students into eliciting sensory detail descriptions of their experiences. <ul><li>What did each fruit taste like?</li><li>What did each fruit feel like?</li><li>What did each fruit smell like?</li><li>What did each fruit look like?</li><li>What did the fruit sound like when you skewered it or chewed it?</li></ul>	**Stage 4: Journal Writing** Students write a paragraph describing their experience as they skewered and ate fruit. As they write, they focus upon sensory descriptions for each type of fruit selected.

Figure 9.21 Gap: Sociolinguistic Competence

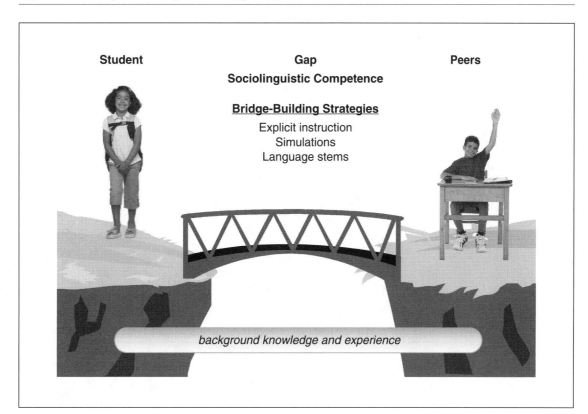

as students' language structures are contrasted and recasted according to the social context, which can include age and status as well as the purpose and conventions of the interaction or conversation. One way to do this is by providing *explicit academic language instruction,* including the contrast of social/casual language with academic language. ELLs need to know that the language used with friends or family is not the same language that should be used in a classroom or in a professional setting. They must learn the differences between casual or social language and academic language by having it explicitly modeled and practiced in a classroom setting. One way to teach this is to contrast both types of language, as displayed in Figure 9.22.

Figure 9.22   Explicit Academic Language Instruction

One way of modeling the difference between conversational and academic language is by explicitly teaching the use of academic language stems in academic conversations, such as the following:	Casual	Academic
	My idea is like _____'s idea. My idea is the same as _____'s. My idea is different from _____'s idea.	My idea is similar to _____'s idea. I agree with _____'s perspective. I also think that . . . My idea builds upon _____'s idea.

SOURCE: Adapted from Kinsella, 2007.

Teachers can post the language stems in Figure 9.22 and provide a think-aloud with students whereby they contrast the differences between the two types of language, which have been highlighted in red. The teacher can discuss with students the subtle differences between the two kinds of language usage. For example, the teacher might explain that using the word *similar* is more formal and appropriate for an academic setting compared to the word *like.* The teacher can continue to explain that using the word *like* might be appropriate when having a chat with a friend, but is not appropriate when having an academic conversation. Similarly, students need to know how and when it is appropriate to build upon one another's ideas. The last stem introduced in the visual will help remind students to use the phrase, "My idea builds or piggy-back's on _____'s idea" in order to use formal language in an academic conversation.

For further practice, teachers can simulate certain relevant or real-life situations such as a job interview or a debate, and have students select the appropriate language for that social situation. For example, the teacher might bring in a flyer for a job opening and assist students in simulating a job interview situation with the appropriate academic language expected of the student (see Figure 9.23).

Teachers should also expect and hold students accountable for appropriate academic language usage. In order to facilitate this, academic language stems should also be posted in the room or placed on sentence strips near the students' desks so that they remember to use these expressions during individual and group conversations. Having these clearly visible will provide a language resource for ELLs throughout a school day. Language used that is not appropriate to the social situation should be recasted, and then repeated correctly by students. For example, if a student responds, "I ain't brought my homework today," the teacher can recast it as, "You didn't bring your homework today? Why not?"

Figure 9.23 Teacher–Student Interview Simulation

Teacher (Interviewer):	Student (Interviewee):
"Good afternoon. It's good to meet you. Please have a seat."	"Yeah. Thanks."
"You might want to say, 'Thank you. It's good to meet you.'"	"Thank you. It's good to meet you."
"Tell me a little about yourself."	"I'm 16 years old and I like to bike ride and hang out with my friends."
"During the interview, you may want to discuss more about your interests in the job specifically and your future."	"My name is Sal and I'm 16 years old. I'd like to get some job experience in this office because I'd like to prepare myself for college and work."

Pragmatic Competence and Intercultural Pragmatics

The fourth and final area of language competence is pragmatics. *Pragmatics* is the study of communication in context, and includes three major features: (1) ability to use language for a variety of functions, (2) ability to appropriately adapt or change language according to the listener or situation, and (3) ability to follow rules for conversation and narrative (reference). Figure 9.24 includes examples of each feature.

The rest of this section will focus on the importance of *intercultural pragmatics* and how it influences concepts, feelings, and attitudes in an educational setting. Specifically, this section will discuss how to appreciate language diversity and variation in a classroom setting by utilizing an asset model. ELLs who are newcomers may come to school with accents, while ELLs who have been in the United States for longer periods of time may speak non-standard forms of English, including Chicano English, or Spanglish. Classroom teachers' tolerance for such

Figure 9.24 Pragmatic Competence

Pragmatic Competence	Examples
Functions	• Greeting, informing, demanding, promising, requesting
Adapting and Changing Language According to Situation	• Talking differently to a friend than to a principal, or in a classroom vs. the playground; adjusting language based upon the age of the person with whom you are speaking (preschooler vs. junior high students)
Following Rules for Conversations and Narrative	• Knowing how to tell a story, give a book report, or recount events of the day

SOURCE: Diaz-Rico, L. (2008).

language variations can create either a bridge or a stumbling block when meeting the academic needs of ELLs. When addressing language variations, it is essential to build upon both students' language and cultural strengths. Since sociocultural issues are closely linked to language development, it is imperative that language variations be addressed from an asset model.

For example, explain to students that the non-standard forms of English they speak are appropriate at home or with friends, but that Standard English should be used in academic and professional settings. The teacher can directly teach this by reading students a book such as *Don't Say Ain't,* by Irene Smalls. The picture book is about a young African American girl named Dana who goes to public school, but is then accepted into a private school because she does well academically. In her new context, Dana struggles to learn new language rules and expectations. By the end of the story, however, Dana discovers that the language she speaks at home can belong in specific places and situations, and that she does not have to entirely lose herself in this new context. This text can be especially validating for SELs who speak African American Vernacular English.

After having a discussion about language and language variations, the teacher can put sentences from *Don't Say Ain't* on the board, and have students rewrite them in Standard English (see Figure 9.25).

This notion of having to give up one's language in order to belong to a new culture is relevant not only for SELs, but also for ELLs. If we are not careful to view these students' primary language and/or variations of language as assets, and also demonstrate that we value them in the classroom, we are making the acquisition of language that much more difficult for our students. We are also not valuing the whole child, and that becomes transparent quickly in a classroom setting. The classroom teacher must view the home language and culture as an asset the student brings with him or her as the student enters the classroom (see Figure 9.26).

Figure 9.25 Non-Standard–Standard English Translation

Non-Standard English	Standard English
"Things ain't like dey was when I was a chile."	Things aren't like they were when I was a child.
"I ain't the bestest, but I'll teach y'all to play double Dutch."	I'm not the best, but I'll teach you all to play double Dutch.

Figure 9.26 L1 Assets, L2 New Learning

L1 Assets Springboard for L2		L2 New Learning

L1 Language
  Casual
  Academic
	⟶	L2 Language
		  Casual
		  Academic

Cultural Experiences	⟶	Cultural Experiences
Schooling	⟶	Schooling
Literary Experiences	⟶	Literacy Experiences

In addition, although some ELLs come to school without having been read to in their primary language, they often do come with a framework for narratives or storytelling. This is also the case for many SEL students. Knowing this, teachers might connect with and tap into students' prior knowledge of an oral narrative, or a particular *cuento,* which is Spanish for story, that has been told to them by their parents or family. For example, in many Latino cultures, the story of *La Llorona,* or the Weeping Woman, has been passed down. When teaching the elements of a story, in this case to Latino students, it would be helpful to begin with a culturally relevant and responsive story that students bring with them from their home culture. This, then, allows ELLs to value their home culture, demonstrate what they know, and connect new learning—literary elements—to something that is familiar to them. A conversation about a more cognitively demanding story can then ensue, and will be retained more readily by tapping into such prior knowledge of stories.

Similarly, an African American student, if asked to write a story, may be asked to first recall a story that was passed down, a hymn sung at church, or a rap heard by his or her favorite artist. Starting with something familiar about stories and the oral tradition will also allow this group of students to link oral language with the written word. In this way, knowing the assets, literacy backgrounds, and cultural understandings of your students' background experiences provides a platform from which to launch and build new language constructs, moving from the familiar to the less familiar, scaffolding new learning on top of ready assets from the home cultures of your students.

SUMMARY

This chapter described language-based accommodations when the primary language or dialect of an SEL differs from that of his or her peers. Instead of allowing such language variations to create gaps or misunderstandings between teachers and students, and students and peers in the classroom, teachers can do specific things to use such differences as a language resource, and provide additional scaffolds for language access. Specifically, in this chapter teachers learned strategies that build upon L1 and SEL assets and help bridge the gaps of grammatical, discourse/ textual, sociolinguistic, and pragmatic competencies as they relate to language variability among ELLs/SELs and their peers.

REFERENCES

Bachman, L. (1990). *Fundamental considerations in language testing.* Oxford, UK: Oxford University Press.

California State Board of Education. (2007). *Reading/language arts framework for California public schools: Kindergarten through Grade Twelve.* Sacramento, CA: Author.

Canale, M., & Swain, M. (1980). Theoretical bases of communicative approaches to second language teaching and testing. *Applied Linguistics, 1,* 1–47.

Center for Applied Linguistics. (2006). *National Literacy Panel on Language-Minority Children and Youth.* Washington, DC: US Government Printing Office. Available online at http://www.cal.org/calwebdb/nlp.

Diaz-Rico, L. (2008). *Strategies for teaching English learners.* Boston, MA: Pearson/Allyn & Bacon.

Francis, D. J., Rivera, M., Lesaux, N., & Rivera, H. (2006). *Practical guidelines for the education of English Language Learners:* Research-based recommendations for instruction and academic interventions. Retrieved April 11, 2008, from http://www.centeroninstruction.org/files/ELL1-Interventions.pdf.

Gibbons, P. (2002). *Scaffolding language, scaffolding learning: Teaching second language learners in the mainstream classroom.* Portsmouth, NH: Heinemann.

Goldenberg, C. (2006, July 26). Improving achievement for English-learners: What the research tells us. *Education Week, 25*(43), 34–36.

Green, J. (1993). *The word wall: Teaching vocabulary through immersion.* Toronto, Ont., Canada: Pippin Publishing.

Kettel, R. P. (1994). An interview with Jerry Spinelli: Thoughts on teaching writing in the classroom. *English Journal, 83*(5), 61–64.

Kinsella, K. (2007). *Academic language presentation to Madrid Middle School.* El Monte: CA.

Littlewood, W. (2004). The task-based approach: Some questions and suggestions. *ELT Journal, 58*(4), 319–326.

Saunders, W. M., & Goldenberg, C. (1999). Effects of instructional conversations and literature logs on limited- and fluent-English-proficient students' story comprehension and thematic understanding. *Elementary School Journal, 99*(4), 277–301.

Smalls, I. (2003). *Don't say ain't.* Watertown, MA: Charlesbridge.

Valdés, G. (2007, June). *Leadership, Equity & Accountability in Districts & Schools (LEADS).* Presentation at Stanford University, Palo Alto, CA.

10

Grouping Strategies

As each teacher and administrator recognizes the language variables that exist in each classroom, he or she begins to understand the wide variations among individuals and the need to create a supportive, fluid structure for language learning within the classroom, grade level, and school context. The gap between the student and his or her peers with regard to language acquisition can be bridged by creating *micro structures* within the classroom, such as homogeneous and heterogeneous groupings, coupled with open-ended, flexible, tiered assignments and broadspan teaching, and *macro structures* across grade levels and schoolwide programs that support global citizenry through language study, immersion programs, and heterogeneous and homogeneous groupings.

MICRO STRUCTURES THAT BRIDGE LANGUAGE PROFICIENCY GAPS

Micro structures that bridge language gaps among Fluent English Proficient speakers, SELs, and their ELL peers can occur at the classroom level. The most critical teaching strategies to accomplish this include (1) homogeneous and heterogeneous groupings to maximize learning; (2) broadspan teaching; and (3) the art of orchestrating open-ended, flexible tiered assignments that enable students to excel from a variety of language starting points. These strategies bridge the gap among FEPs, SELs, and ELLs by making content and language accessible to all learners, not just Fluent English and Academic English Proficient students (see Figure 10.1).

Figure 10.1 The Language Proficiency Gap

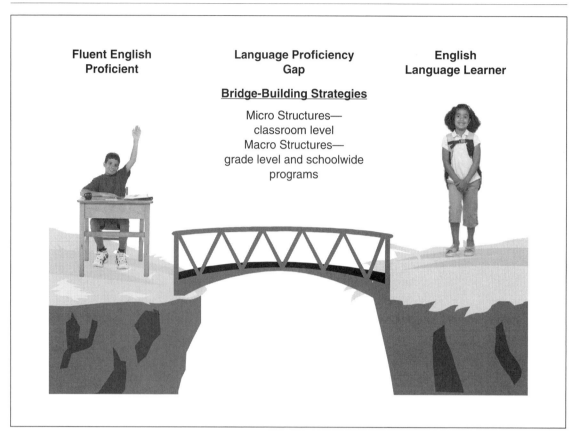

Homogeneous and Heterogeneous Groupings

One of the best ways to describe how to accommodate language variation within the classroom setting is to invite the reader into a couple of classrooms and observe master teachers at work. First, let's step into the primary classroom of Miss Castillo, a veteran teacher who has taught Spanish-speaking students for the past 12 years in California. We will describe how Miss Castillo managed a second-/third-grade combination with a 3-year age span, four different L1s, English as the language of instruction, and language proficiency levels from Beginning to Early Advanced.

Heterogeneous Grouping With Broadspan Instruction

Miss Castillo opens her school day with a heterogeneous grouping of her students. This includes *all* the students in her classroom, regardless of identified language proficiency levels. She begins the day with a heterogeneous grouping to maintain high expectations, academic rigor, and intensive language exposure for all students. Every child will eventually reach Academic English proficiency and then move on to reaching the higher expectations of the academic standards. If Miss Castillo kept all of her students grouped by their own proficiency levels throughout the entire day, they would receive less rigorous language exposure and, hence, progress more slowly through the English/academic language levels. Ensuring broad exposure to receptive language throughout the day provides opportunities for students to rapidly expand receptive vocabulary banks and gain exposure to more complex language structures prior to formally studying them and utilizing those words and structures in expressive language (see Figure 10.2).

This particular year, Miss Castillo has four different levels of English language proficiency in her classroom, along with SELs mastering Academic English. When she invites the students into her classroom at the beginning of the day, she has the children sit on the floor in a circle on individual carpet squares. She starts the class day with a number of songs and chants that are played on a CD. Miss Castillo sings along and utilizes hand motions so that every child in her class, regardless of language ability, understands the meaning of the lyrics. Children begin responding even on the first day of school, as they enjoy the music and movement and quickly begin adding English words to their repertoire as they make connections between the hand motions and the words they are hearing and singing.

After 5 to 10 minutes of music and movement, Miss Castillo moves into poetry. She reads a favorite poem from a chart, pointing to the words as she reads. The children read along as they are able, enjoying the sounds and rhyme even if they are not yet able to comprehend. Beginning students are just learning that print goes from left to right in English, while others are picking up subtle information about phoneme–grapheme relationships (e.g., *b* says /b/ in *bug*). Still other students pick up new English vocabulary (e.g., a child makes the connection between the word *spotted* and the picture of the spotted dog on the illustration on the rhyme chart). The poem is scaffolded through illustrations, rhyme, and the teacher's daily discussions of the poem. This broad exposure to receptive vocabulary (listening and reading processes) assists students at all language levels in building their vocabulary banks, thereby enriching the linguistic bank from which to draw for their expressive vocabulary (speaking and writing).

Figure 10.2   ELL Vocabulary Growth Bank

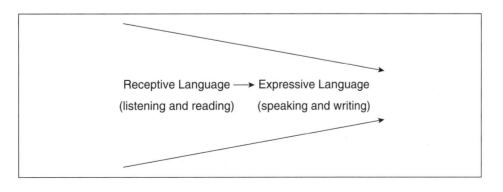

From poetry, Miss Castillo moves into routine vocabulary acquisition chants. First, she writes the date on the board. Then, she utilizes realia in the room. She points to the *calendar* on the wall as the children say the date in unison. She reviews the *days of the week,* and the children chant them as the teacher points to the words written on a chart, which is posted on the wall for the daily routine. Then, she reviews the *months of the year.* Children chant the months as the teacher points to the words on the chart. Then, she reviews *color words.* Children chant the names of the colors as the teacher points to the words that are written in the various colors. She then introduces a new number each day. Children chant the *numbers* as the teacher points to them on the calendar. The young children enjoy the routine. For Beginning students, they often just listen for the first few days and then begin participating as understanding emerges. For Early Intermediate and Intermediate students, as well as Early Advanced, they make deeper connections—associating the oral sounds and written words (phoneme–grapheme relationships), cementing meaning and *orthography* (the alphabetic spelling system). The Early Advanced students also connect subtle nuances of the English language as the teacher speaks.

This first part of Miss Castillo's day with her heterogeneous group can be called *broadspan instruction.* What is meant by the term is that the instruction reaches across a broad band of language proficiency levels—in this case, four of them—and each student is able to access language at the point at which he or she has proficiency. The teacher is careful to make each aspect of the morning routine comprehensible and context embedded so that all children can add to their English comprehension. She provides context for each word by using gestures and pointing to the words on the charts and wall. This daily routine reaches each student's language proficiency needs, and the children access meaning and build more of it daily as they utilize these routines for acquiring basic English vocabulary in a safe, supportive, nurturing environment. Miss Castillo's opening is described in Figure 10.3.

Open-Ended, Flexible Tiered Assignments

Miss Castillo's teaching continues with a heterogeneous group, but subtle changes begin to happen as she continues to use the broadspan instructional approach and then moves into open-ended, flexible tiered assignments. A special story is read to the children via an instructional read-aloud. The IRA, a technique described in Chapter 2, makes language accessible to SEL students who can focus on comprehension and higher levels of language by having a teacher read aloud to them. The story is written in big-book form so that children can see all the pictures and words as the teacher reads. The teacher reads aloud with great expression, pointing to the words and making gestures and faces to add understanding to the reading. Children listen attentively, as the picture book can be understood through the pictures as well as through the words. For example, in *Goldilocks and the Three Bears,* the children see the story in pictures as well as hear the story read aloud through words. Each child hears and comprehends at his or her point of language understanding, adding daily to his or her understanding

Figure 10.3   Opening Routines

Structure and Grouping	Literacy Processes	Activities
Opening Routines at the Rug With All Children Present Heterogeneous grouping	*Listening and Speaking*—Children listen to songs/chants and join in as they are able. All lyrics are scaffolded by hand motions. All chants are scaffolded by charts and illustrations on the wall. All poems are scaffolded by written text on the chart, illustrations, and rhyme. *Reading*—As children are able, they make connections between the spoken and written word, following the text on the wall or charts as the teacher uses a pointer to assist with tracking.	*Songs* and *Chants* to welcome in the day—(hand motions scaffold the meaning of the lyrics) *Poetry*—Favorite poems are read aloud from a chart; the teacher points to the words and children join in as they are able; illustrations and rhyme provide scaffolding. *Calendar*—Teacher points to visuals on wall as children say the date in unison. *Days of the Week*—Children chant the days of the week as the teacher points to the words. *Months of the Year*—Children chant the months of the year as the teacher points to the words. *Colors*—Children chant the names of the colors as the teacher points to the words. *Numbers*—Children chant the numbers as the teacher points to the number line on the wall.

of English. After the story is read aloud, the children play a game with a beach ball (see Figure 10.4). On each striped section of the beach ball, certain words and phrases are written that relate to story structure and generic thoughts about any story, providing language stems from which each student can build an oral sentence. Language stems include the following:

My favorite part of the story was . . .

At the beginning of the story . . .

In the middle of the story . . .

At the end of the story . . .

The setting of the story was . . .

The characters in the story were . . .

The teacher throws the beach ball. Ricardo catches it. In front of him are the words, "My favorite part of the story was . . ." Ricardo, an Early Intermediate English speaker, carefully formulates his response, "My fa-favorite part of the s-story was when d-d-de chair, it broke!" The children

Figure 10.4   Language Stems Provided in Game Context

SOURCE: Photo by June Hetzel.

and teacher laugh and smile and the teacher repeats, "My favorite part of the story was when the chair broke," recasting Ricardo's response in appropriate English grammar. She then repeats his thought again, but from the teacher's perspective, "Ricardo's favorite part of the story was when the chair broke!" Next, she assists children in meaning making as she quickly flips the big book back to find the page that illustrated the chair breaking. The teacher points to the picture and says, "Here is the chair. The chair is breaking. This is Ricardo's favorite part. Ricardo's favorite part is when the chair broke." (See Figure 10.5.)

The teacher continues to invite the children to play with the beach ball as they review story structure with sentence stems. The children love it. Most of them need assistance formulating their sentences. Half the fun is catching the ball and then having an opportunity to speak with the teacher's help. Everyone is eager to participate and there is much laughter and excitement. Those who feel timid or shy can ask a friend to help.

Next, the children walk to their desks. They are instructed to take out their pencil and writing books. Each writing page has a space for an illustration as well as lines for writing. The teacher begins instruction by demonstrating step-by-step how to draw a bear. The children follow along, drawing their own bears in the illustration space on their page. Every child in the room understands the instruction through the combination of the oral directions and Miss Castillo's step-by-step line drawing on the overhead. The children practice active listening in incremental steps as they anticipate each stroke of drawing the bear. They giggle with joy as

Figure 10.5 Transition to Open-Ended, Flexible Tiered Assignments

Structure and Grouping	Literacy Processes	Activities
Story at the Rug With All Children Present	*Listening* is strengthened as children hear a story in English with meaning reinforced through illustration, voice expression, facial expression, and gestures. *Reading* is reinforced as the teacher points to the words in the text and reads them aloud. Beginning students may just be understanding that print moves from left to right in English, whereas Early Advanced students may be fully reading the text along with the teacher.	Read Aloud With Big Book
Routine Discussion and Games With All Children Present at the Rug	*Listening and Speaking* are reinforced as the children hear and participate in questions and answers during the Story Structure game. *Reading* is reinforced as children read the language stems on the beach ball (e.g., "At the beginning of the story. . ." "My favorite part of the story was . . .)" and complete each sentence with the teacher's help as needed.	Poetry, Routine Chants Story Structure Game
Children transition to desks and receive instruction on a drawing activity in a heterogeneous group and then tiered assignments matched to language proficiency levels	*Listening and Speaking* are reinforced as children receive step-by-step instructions in drawing the bear. Children also have listening and speaking reinforced as they hear their teacher's instructions for tiered assignments, participate in Q & A, and work in pairs. *Reading and Writing* are reinforced as children utilize Picture Dictionaries, write names of animals, write sentences, and write paragraphs.	Drawing Activity for Active Listening Tiered Writing Assignment

they see their bears begin to emerge on the page. They hear their teacher say, "Draw a circle for the head," and then they see their teacher draw a circle on the overhead. They also see the teacher point to the bear's head in a large illustration of a bear. Then she points to her own head. Then she asks the children to touch their own heads. Next, the teacher says, "Draw a curved line on the left side to make the left ear of the bear." She points to the left ear of the bear in the large illustration. She also points to her own

Figure 10.6 Related Tiered Assignments

Language Proficiency Level	CA ELD Standard for K–2	Open-Ended, Tiered Assignment
Beginning ↓	"Copy words posted and commonly used in the classroom (e.g., labels, number names, days of the week)" (California Department of Education, 1999, p. 70).	Accurately label pictures of animals. The Picture Dictionary provides the "posted" words.
Early Intermediate ↓	"Write simple sentences by using key words posted and commonly used in the classroom (e.g., labels, number names, days of the week, and months)" (California Department of Education, 1999, p. 71).	Write simple sentences about animals. The Picture Dictionary provides the "posted" words.
Intermediate/Early Advanced or SELs ↓	Intermediate: "Following a model, proceed through the writing process to independently write short paragraphs of at least three lines" (California Department of Education, 1999, p. 73). Early Advanced: "Proceed through the writing process to write short paragraphs that maintain a consistent focus" (California Department of Education, 1999, p. 75).	Write short paragraphs about animals. The Picture Dictionary provides a Word Bank.

ear. Each child comprehends and follows instructions. Miss Castillo has the children touch their left ear. Next, the teacher says, "Draw a curved line on the right side of the bear's head. This will make the right ear." She points to the right ear of the bear in the illustration and also points to her ear. She asks the children to touch their own right ear. This total physical response (TPR) instruction continues until the bear is completed. This is another context-embedded art activity that utilized a broadspan instructional approach. For Beginning English speakers, they were still just comprehending one word here and there, taking in meaning from the step-by-step visual drawing sequence. They were making one-word associations—bear, head, ear, left, right. Miss Castillo's Early Intermediate, Intermediate, Early Advanced, and SEL students understood much more language, taking in full sentences and phrases and asking questions of their teacher.

Next, the teacher transitions into the open-ended, tiered writing assignment (See Figure 10.6.). She already has the children assessed at four language proficiency levels; however, she groups Intermediate and Early Advanced, along with SELs, to make a larger advanced group. Hence, her three classroom groupings include the following: (1) Beginning, (2) Early Intermediate, and (3) Intermediate/Early Advanced and SELs. She asks the "Tigers" (Beginning students) to draw pictures of other animals and label them with the animals' names. She provides a Picture Dictionary and several model papers to assist these Beginning students with this assignment. The "Leopards" (her Early Intermediate students) are expected to do the same, but they must write a full, patterned sentence about each animal (e.g., "I see a bear." "I see a fox." "I see a rabbit."). The "Polar Bears" (her Intermediate/Early Advanced and SEL students) are expected to stretch the assignment a little further. They are asked to write multiple sentences about each animal they draw (e.g., "I see a bear. It is big and brown. It is hungry and wants to catch some fish."). All students have access to the Picture Dictionaries, to the teacher's or instructional assistant's help, and to models of expected outcomes. Each student also has the opportunity to go beyond the level of his or her assignment, because the tiered assignments are related to each other in a gradual progression. It is important to keep in mind that the California ELD Standards are constructed for a transition from one level to the next, with the ultimate goal of accessing grade-level standards, which also need to be considered in planning.

The teacher capitalizes on students' interest by allowing choice in the animals they select. Interestingly, some students will, depending on their interest in a particular animal, write more about one animal than another, actually pushing themselves beyond the ELD designation. This is important because the ELD levels are not the end goal. Instead, the grade-level content standards are—and it is desirable that students even exceed minimum content standards. Children enthusiastically pursue their writing, and many hands wave in the air for assistance. Children also help one another. When they complete their assignments, they must read their words, sentences, or paragraphs to the teacher or the instructional assistant. The students then receive an animal sticker and are allowed to go to the classroom library where they can self-select books for personal enjoyment.

After students have completed their assignments, Miss Castillo transitions her students to homogeneous groupings as far as her resources allow. Keep in mind that Miss Castillo utilizes homogeneous language proficiency groupings for only small portions of the day, because keeping the children in these groupings all day would be a detriment to their language development by limiting their exposure to literature, grade-level academic standards, and other students speaking with higher proficiency levels. Beginning language proficiency students would be relegated to a more controlled vocabulary situation for a lengthier period of time. All the benefits of immersion occur during the heterogeneous sessions (e.g., exposure to higher levels of receptive vocabulary, more complex grammar, a rich literature, and grade-level academic standards) and, of course, are presented with as much context-embedded instruction and scaffolding as possible. Such a language-rich environment also assists SELs who benefit from the same instructional scaffolds as ELLs, but also need to be exposed to more complex and specialized language levels.

As the teacher transitions her students to homogeneous groupings, a part-time teacher pulls out the "Polar Bears" (in this case, a combination of Intermediate and Early Advanced students) and brings them to the room next door. Students enjoy this reading group time and read challenging material together. They also receive intensive vocabulary instruction prior to reading content-area science readers. The instructional assistant brings the "Leopards" (Early Intermediate) to a U-shaped table. There they receive intense phonics and vocabulary instruction prior to reading a controlled reader. Miss Castillo takes the "Tigers" to the second U-shaped table. There she provides intense instruction in phonemic awareness and phonics prior to the picture walk that introduces an early reader to the students. This homogeneous reading group time is interrupted by recess. After recess, the students return to their reading groups for another 20-minute segment. Then, all the students come back together for story time and another segment of writing instruction, followed by another tiered writing assignment. Consequently, the first 2 hours of class resemble fluid, flexible language groupings. We call this the "Hourglass Language Instruction Model" (see Figure 10.7) in that in any given hour, the students move back and forth from a variety of heterogeneous large groups with broadspan instruction and tiered assignments to intensive homogeneous groupings of students with similar language proficiency levels.

Figure 10.7   The "Hourglass" Language Instruction Model

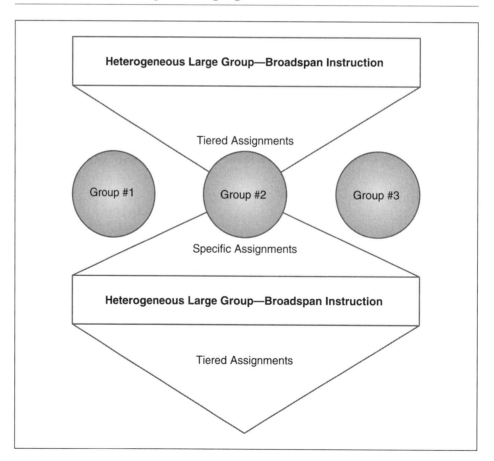

Secondary Interdisciplinary Classroom Example

Utilizing the same Hourglass Instruction Model, a team of middle school teachers sought to bridge the gap of language levels in the content areas, utilizing an interdisciplinary unit entitled "Flight and Destinations." This middle school unit provided high-interest material for Early Intermediate, Intermediate, and Early Advanced ELL students, as well as SELs. The team decided they would integrate English Language Development within three content areas: language arts, physical science, and geography. They began their block with heterogeneous, broadspan instruction that included all ELLs, regardless of proficiency level, and scaffolded instruction that was comprehensible to all learners, including SELs. The ELD standards for the unit included oral language development and writing development. Key terms for the first few days of instruction focused strongly on the physical science principles and included *flight forces, lift, weight, thrust, drag, angle of attack, Bernoulli's principle, low pressure, high pressure,* and *airfoil.*

Teacher #1 introduced the "Flight and Destinations" unit to the class and pointed to the maps of all the continents posted around the room. She then shared that they would study the history of flight and flight itself, gesturing to a flight timeline posted above the front board. She showed the book covers of several read-alouds they would share together, as well as short chapter content-area books. She then pulled out some sketches of a bird, a kite, a hot air balloon, a plane, and a rocket. She asked a student to come forward and order these "flight" posters according to where they would go on the timeline, and then the teacher taped the sketches to the timeline, providing a brief narrative for each. Next, she pulled out from her bag a toy airplane and asked an open-ended question, "How does an airplane fly?" Students provided different types of answers (e.g., "The air, it hold the plane."), but none of the students knew the technical terms. She then pulled a plastic bird out of her bag. She followed up with the open-ended question, "How does a bird fly?" This time, as hands waved, she asked students to pair-share responses first (e.g., "The bird, it has wings. It stretch the wings. The wind, it holds the birds up."). After the pair-shares, the teacher asked the students to share out with the rest of the class. Next, she asked, "What is the same about the bird and the airplane?" Students paused and thought about this. Eventually, a student notices, "D . . . de . . . dee shape the wing and shape of airplane, de wing." The classroom dialogue starts out similar to Figure 10.8 with the teacher providing language stems and reflecting back appropriate grammar.

Figure 10.8 Flight Dialogue

Teacher	Students
How does an airplane fly?	Ricky: The air, it hold the plane.
Ricky says, "The air holds the plane." Does the air make the airplane fly?	Ricky: No, the engine, it makes the plane move . . . (gestures with hand) move . . . how do you say . . . fer-r-wrd?

Figure 10.8 (Continued)

Teacher	Students
Forward. Yes, the engine helps the plane move forward. What about gravity?	Teresa: The gravity push down, but the engine strong and move the airplane.
Yes, Teresa, the engine is strong and it moves the airplane forward (teacher gestures in forward motion). What else pushes down?	Karl: The airplane! The weight of the airplane. The more the people, the more the gasoline.
Karl, yes! Very good. The weight of the airplane (teacher moves the airplane up and down) and the weight of the people (teacher points to all the students in the room) affects how much gasoline or jet fuel will be used.	

After the flight dialogue is complete and the teacher has led the students to consider the flight forces (lift, weight, thrust, drag), the teacher draws the shape of an airfoil on the board, labeling it an *airfoil,* as well as labeling *high pressure* below it and *low pressure* above it with arrows to indicate faster movement of air, and then she draws arrows vertically up from the airfoil, labeling those arrows *lift* (see Figure 10.9).

Along with the airfoil diagram, she also draws another visual vocabulary bank. She draws a simple airplane and labels the flight forces that affect it—*lift, weight, thrust,* and *drag* (see Figure 10.10).

At this point, Teacher #2 provides a short shared reading on flight as her two helpers prepare the material for the first science experiment. The shared reading includes a picture walk, interactive dialogue, repetition of vocabulary, and making connections with the timeline and board diagrams that serve as visual vocabulary banks. All of the students—Early Intermediate, Intermediate, Early Advanced, and SEL—absorb content-area vocabulary because of the scaffolding strategies utilized (e.g., realia, gestures, timeline

Figure 10.9 Bernoulli's Principle

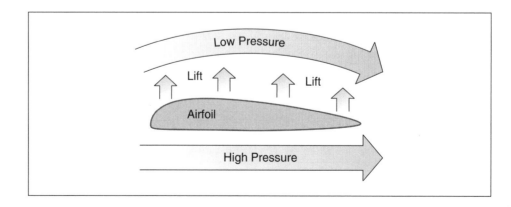

SOURCE: Hetzel & Wyma, 1995; illustrations by Diane Valko.

Figure: 10.10 Flight Forces

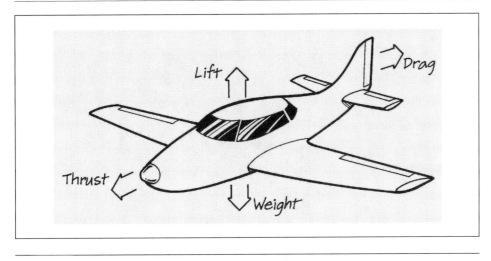

SOURCE: Hetzel & Wyma, 1995; illustrations by Diane Valko.

visuals, diagrams, vocabulary banks, etc.). In this manner, the classroom teacher makes the content accessible to all learners, thereby bridging the gaps among the ELL, SELs, and their Fluent English Proficient peers.

The lesson continues, and the teacher does a demonstration with two inflated balloons tied to strings, saying, "If I blow between the two balloons, what will happen?" Most students predict that the balloons will blow away from each other. The teacher writes this as the hypothesis on the Bernoulli's Principle Experiment Sheet, which she displays a copy of on the overhead. However, when the teacher asks for a volunteer and performs a demonstration, the students are surprised that the balloons actually move *toward* each other when the air passes between them. The experiment is repeated multiple times, and students begin to grasp that faster-moving air creates low pressure and that the higher-pressure area moves the balloon toward the low-pressure area. The teacher models filling out the experiment sheet's Results and Conclusions sections for the students.

A second experiment then ensues, and students are asked to work in pairs and make two stacks of books. They place a paper over the top of the two stacks, like a bridge. Then they are instructed to blow under the paper. Most students have hypothesized that the paper would blow away, but instead the paper sinks. The teacher asks students to dialogue with each other about what happened, and checks for understanding with the whole class before continuing with the rest of the lesson. Students fill out experiment pages in pairs, utilizing phrases, complete sentences, or paragraph responses, depending on language proficiency (see Figure 10.11).

Students then break up into three homogeneous groupings: Early Intermediate, Intermediate, and Early Advanced. They bring their experiment pages to the group and discuss in detail with their guide (teacher, instructional assistant, or volunteer). They then move into a leveled passage about flight that is at the instructional level for their language proficiency, with comprehension questions at all levels of Bloom's taxonomy. Questions also include particular emphasis on technical vocabulary development.

Figure 10.11   Balloon Experiment Illustrating Bernoulli's Principle

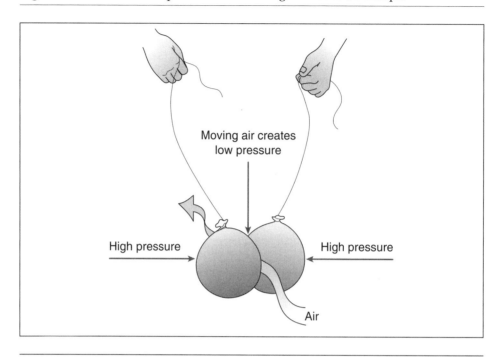

SOURCE: Hetzel & Wyma, 1995; illustrations by Diane Valko.

Moving back into the large, heterogeneous group, students enjoy a shared reading of a biography on the Wright brothers. The teacher again reviews the key vocabulary with the large group and then prepares them for a third hands-on experiment: the building of a Wing-on-a-String. Students follow written directions accompanied by visual illustrations. The teacher demonstrates first, carefully explaining the directions, step-by-step. Students then receive materials and work in pairs. Their written follow-up assignment includes paired writing of their hypothesis, results, and conclusion in the appropriate sections on their lab sheet (see Figure 10.12).

The follow-up tiered assignment is to produce a travel brochure to attract people to come see the Wright brothers' experimental flight at Kitty Hawk. The teacher models the assignment at the Early Advanced ELD level, while providing minimum expectations for all levels of ELLs in the classroom (see Figure 10.13 on page 223).

Overall, these middle school teachers maintained the same hourglass instruction language model as the primary teacher—moving in and out of heterogeneous and homogeneous groupings, providing broadspan instruction with scaffolding and realia, and making the content accessible to all learners, regardless of proficiency levels. The emphasis on vocabulary continues to build the receptive and expressive technical vocabulary banks for these young learners. The structures and grouping, literacy processes, and activities are outlined in Figure 10.14 on page 223 for reader convenience.

The "Hourglass Language Instruction Model" is but one of many ways of grouping students within a classroom that includes multiple levels of English proficiency. This grouping model is an effective way to bridge the literacy gaps by making grade-level content standards and ELD standards accessible to all learners, including ELLs and SELs.

Figure 10.12 Wing-on-a-String Experiment

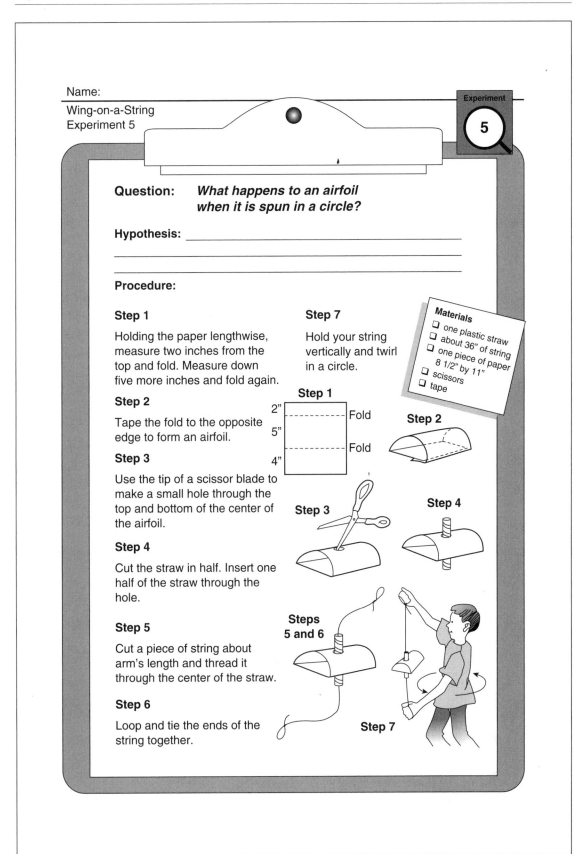

Name:

Wing-on-a-String
Experiment 5

Experiment

5

Question: *What happens to an airfoil when it is spun in a circle?*

Hypothesis: _____

_____

Procedure:

Step 1

Holding the paper lengthwise, measure two inches from the top and fold. Measure down five more inches and fold again.

Step 2

Tape the fold to the opposite edge to form an airfoil.

Step 3

Use the tip of a scissor blade to make a small hole through the top and bottom of the center of the airfoil.

Step 4

Cut the straw in half. Insert one half of the straw through the hole.

Step 5

Cut a piece of string about arm's length and thread it through the center of the straw.

Step 6

Loop and tie the ends of the string together.

Step 7

Hold your string vertically and twirl in a circle.

Materials
☐ one plastic straw
☐ about 36" of string
☐ one piece of paper 8 1/2" by 11"
☐ scissors
☐ tape

Step 1

2" ----- Fold

5"

----- Fold

4"

Step 2

Step 3

Step 4

Steps 5 and 6

Step 7

(Continued)

Figure 10.12 (Continued)

Name:

Wing-on-a-String
Experiment 5

Experiment
5

Results and Conclusions:

1. What happened to the airfoil when you spun around? ____
   _____
   _____
   _____
   _____
   _____

2. How do you explain this result? _____
   _____
   _____
   _____
   _____

3. Use your results to describe how a helicopter rises. ____
   _____
   _____
   _____
   _____

4. What other questions about airfoils or helicopters could
   you explore? _____
   _____
   _____
   _____
   _____

Science Challange: Set up an experiment to test this question:
Will a paper airfoil spun at a 45 degree angle rise?
Write your question, hypothesis, procedure, and materials list
on another sheet of paper. Then test the hypothesis and record
your conclusions.

SOURCE: Hetzel & Wyma, 1995; illustrations by Diane Valko.

Figure 10.13 Tiered Travel Brochure and ELD Standards

Early Intermediate ELD, Grades 6–8 ↓	"Write simple sentences by using key words posted and commonly used in the classroom" (California Department of Education, 1999, p. 71.)
Intermediate ELD, Grades 6–8 ↓	"Use more complex vocabulary and sentences appropriate for language arts and other content areas (e.g., math, science, history-social science)" (California Department of Education, 1999, p. 74).
Early Advanced ELD, Grades 6–8 ↓	"Develop a clear thesis and support it by using analogies, quotations, and facts appropriately" (California Department of Education, 1999, p. 75).

Figure 10.14 Structure and Grouping, Literacy Processes, and Activities Chart, Grades 6–8 Interdisciplinary Flight and Destinations Unit

Structure and Grouping	Literacy Processes	Activities
Heterogeneous group for introduction of vocabulary, map work, and shared read-aloud. Students remain at desks. Hands-on experiments conducted in *pairs.* Students walk around and utilize outdoor space as well. Lab reports written individually or in pairs. Students work back at their desks or utilized group tables.	*Listening* practiced during vocabulary introduction and *speaking* utilized in verbal application of vocabulary and paired activity *Reading* applied during shared read-aloud and *writing* utilized on lab report	Key science vocabulary introduced with illustrations and demonstrations Maps utilized to reinforce geography words Shared read-aloud Hands-on experiments utilized to reinforce science concepts Lab report requires writing a hypothesis and explaining results and conclusions

MACRO STRUCTURES THAT BRIDGE LANGUAGE PROFICIENCY GAPS

Grade-Level Teams

In addition to micro structures that bridge literacy gaps in the classroom between a student and her peers, macro structures can also be utilized. For example, one elementary school in Southern California seeks to create global citizens. Each grade level of classroom teachers works as a team. After homeroom and roll call, students switch classrooms. So, for example, at the third-grade level, newcomers with beginning English language skills go to one room for English Language Development. Another group of fluent English-speaking students goes to a second classroom for Spanish-speaking instruction. Another group of students goes to a third classroom for instruction in Mandarin and the Chinese culture. And so forth. This type of team approach occurs at all the grade levels, and students have the advantage of enjoying heterogeneous groupings with a wide range of language proficiency levels in their homeroom, while still systematically receiving instruction in English, Spanish, or Mandarin. Students have the opportunity to rotate through these classes so that they can enjoy a variety of languages and instructional approaches. They regularly move in and out of heterogeneous and homogeneous language groupings. This regular movement between heterogeneous and homogeneous groupings is critical for ELLs, because the homogeneous groups provide the benefit of intensive English Language Development instruction, matched to the students' current ELD proficiency level, while the heterogeneous groups provide opportunity for exposure to higher levels of vocabulary and grammar as well as grade-level content standards. In this particular Southern California school setting, fluent English-speaking students and SELs are also experiencing the advantage of exposure to Spanish and Mandarin language and culture instruction, enabling all students to be better prepared as global citizens.

The model described above is similar to the Foreign Language in the Elementary School (FLES) model (Heining-Boynton, 2005) combined with ELD groupings. The goals of the FLES model are to teach "language acquisition and learning about the culture of the world language studied" (p. 29). Instruction begins in the primary grades, and effective programs provide three to five 30-minute periods per week. Students learn grammar indirectly, and schools usually write their own curriculum. Content-enriched FLES programs often elect to teach a content area through the foreign language (Heining-Boynton, 2005). The beauty of this type of program is that it provides an asset model for all languages of study, affirming speakers of multiple languages and dialects, and broadening all students' linguistic resources as they study cultures, English, and other foreign languages. The FLES model can be applied in heterogeneous or homogeneous groupings, though homogeneous groupings make the most sense for these short periods (Foorman & Torgesen, 2001; Juel & Minden-Cupp, 2000; National Reading Panel, 2000, cited in Gunning, 2006). Research indicates that students do better in small groups with identified common needs. "[G]roups, however, should be flexible. Students should be moved to higher-performing groups when their progress warrants it" (Gunning, 2006, p. 177). In this manner, we keep students from being tracked into one level and provide opportunities for them to move fluidly up the proficiency levels.

Immersion Models

Three types of immersion models also exist: partial immersion, total immersion, and two-way/dual immersion (Heining-Boynton, 2005). In *partial immersion,* students are usually taught in English for 20–50% of each school day, receiving English instruction in a variety of subjects. *Total immersion* programs, such as the primary model for California since the passage of Proposition 227, requires all instruction of content areas in English, with some exceptions in language arts. *Two-way* or *dual immersion* programs are frequently offered by magnet schools. Often, an ideal 50/50 ratio of speakers (e.g., English/Spanish or English/Mandarin) occurs at the school, with half of the day being taught in English and the other half in the second target language (Heining-Boynton, 2005).

In Africa, an international school takes on a different model. At this school, they believe fully in immersion but have an end goal of trilingual students. They have 3 years of kindergarten: K3 (age 3), K4 (age 4), and K5 (age 5). If the student's first language is Arabic, then the student might be placed in an English-immersion K3 and then a French-immersion K–4. If the child's first language is English, then he or she would have at least a year of Arabic-immersion kindergarten and a year of French-immersion kindergarten. As students reach Grades 1–12, they maintain Arabic and French skills with at least 1 hour of content-area instruction in each language per day. The rest of the day, their instruction is in English. By the time the students graduate from Grade 12, they can easily attend an English-speaking university, while also speaking Arabic and French fluently. Many of the students enter the school speaking other languages as well, but still build their fluency in the three primary languages of the school. Focus is not so much on English Language Development as it is on intensive content-area instruction in a specific language. Context-embedded teaching strategies are utilized throughout the program, with emphasis on listening, speaking, reading, and writing. The English language, and the other two languages as well, are mastered through deep content-area study.

SUMMARY

The language proficiency gap can be bridged among ELLs, SELs, and their Fluent English Proficient peers through micro structures and macro structures (see Figure 10.15). The playing field is leveled as content and language become accessible to all students through broadspan teaching with tailored, tiered assignments in the context of heterogeneous groupings. In addition, homogeneous groupings assist in targeting focus areas for English Language Development. Macro structures at the grade level or schoolwide also assist in bridging the English/academic language proficiency gap by providing focused instruction in the targeted language(s) while also providing an asset model for all heritage languages. Most important, the teacher pays close attention to the students' needs and the state's English Language Development Standards, teaching to these standards and then moving beyond them to the grade-level content-area standards.

Figure 10.15 The Language Proficiency Gap

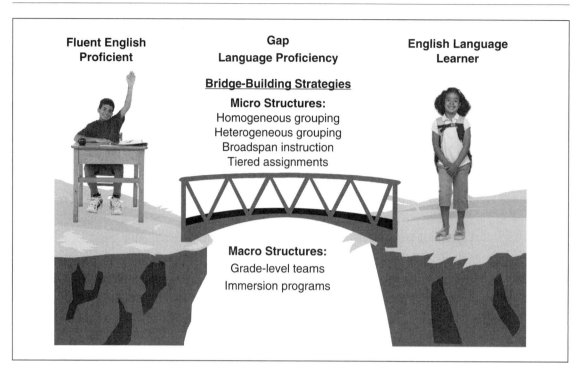

REFERENCES

California Department of Education. (1999, July). *English-language development standards for California public schools: Kindergarten through Grade Twelve.* Sacramento, CA: Author.

Center for Applied Linguistics. (2006). *National Literacy Panel on Language-Minority Children and Youth.* Washington, DC: U.S. Government Printing Office. Available online at http://www.cal.org/calwebdb/nlp.

Foorman, B. R., & Torgesen, J. (2001). Critical elements of classroom and small-group instruction promote reading success in all children. *Learning Disabilities Research and Practice, 16*(4), 204–212.

Gunning, T. G. (2006). *Closing the literacy gap.* Boston: Pearson.

Heining-Boynton, A. L. (2005, January). U.S. world language program models. *Educational Leadership, 62*(4), 29.

Hetzel, J. & Wyma, B. (1995). *Flight.* Cypress, CA: Creative Teaching Press, Inc.

Juel, C., & Minden-Cupp, C. (2000). Learning to read words: Linguistic units and instructional strategies. *Reading Research Quarterly, 35*(4), 458–492.

11

Beyond the Gap

Envisioning the Future

High expectations for all students is an essential component to successfully closing the literacy gaps (August & Hakuta, 1997; August & Pease-Alvarez, 1996; Brisk, 2005; Education Trust, 2003), and providing equitable literacy practices for all students, ELLs and SELs alike (Hollie, 2001), demonstrates these high expectations. Teachers' expectations of students are linked to their perceptions about students' abilities, their own practice, and their content knowledge (Ferguson, 1998; Hollie, 2001; Howard, 1995; Wenglinsky, 2001), and when educators are well-informed regarding the needs of the students they instruct, they can further educational progress and close the literacy gaps. Teacher understanding of student needs, data, and trend lines, as well as accurate comprehension of formative and summative assessments of students enrolled in their classes and astute understanding of literacy bridge-building practices, such as those suggested in this book, remain foundational for improving the learning process for all students.

THE LITERACY GAPS MODEL

The Literacy Gaps Model, presented in this book, has provided a theoretical framework from which to consider the literacy needs of all of your students, particularly your English Language Learners and Standard English Learners who often need specific linguistic mentorship.

Gap #1: The Gap Between the Student and the Text

By working to close the gap between the student and the text, you remove barriers that hinder decoding and comprehension progress and create bridge-building strategies that provide students access to text through scaffolded, systematic instruction, building upon students' background knowledge and experience (see Figure 11.1).

While student needs vary based upon background knowledge, experience, fluency in the primary language, and English Language Development, all students in the initial stages of reading need continued development in the area of decoding, including concepts about print, phonemic awareness, word recognition strategies such as phonics and sight words, fluency, and automaticity.

Every student, regardless of age, background experiences, or English language proficiency levels, can benefit from ongoing, systematic instruction in academic language. Students need intentional, ongoing vocabulary instruction and direct teaching about text structure. ELLs, in particular, need intentional content-area vocabulary development so that they do not lag behind their peers as they encounter increasingly complex academic language. Both ELLs and SELs need systematic instruction in syntax, learning through contrastive analysis the differences and similarities between their home languages and that of the academic institution.

In addition, passage comprehension is essential so that students, when released from the mentoring of their teachers, can independently gain meaning from text. This requires student understanding of how text is

Figure 11.1   Gap #1: The Gap Between the Student and the Text

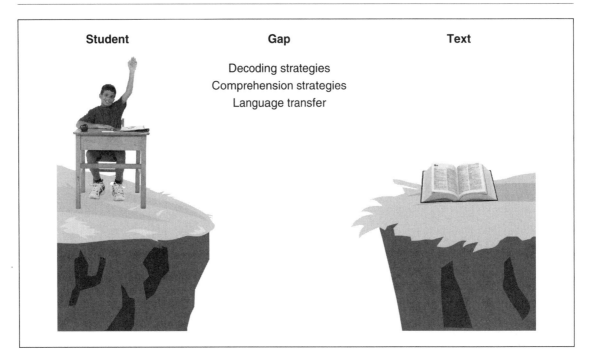

organized, how to monitor their own comprehension, and how to (re)organize text for various purposes. Moreover, all of the corequisite literacy processes to reading—listening, speaking, and writing—need to be simultaneously developed in the academic arena, so that students regularly and fully participate in academic discussions and academic writing, utilizing academic vocabulary in these contexts.

Bridging the gap between the student and the text requires a deep understanding of student background experiences and knowledge, language proficiency levels, reading levels, and utilization of appropriate formative and summative assessments. In addition, it is imperative that the classroom teacher also understand the differentiated linguistic needs of his students, including highly educated newcomers, underschooled newcomers, long-term ELLs, ELLs progressing predictably, struggling Reclassified Fluent English Proficient students, Initially Fluent English Proficient students, and Standard English Learners. The teacher must understand distinctive differences and commonalities in order to provide appropriate linguistic instruction for the varied needs of his students.

Gap #2: The Gap Between the Student and the Teacher

When considering the second gap, the gap between the student and the teacher, you must consider the differences between yourself and your students—perceptions and expectations, culture, and socioeconomic status—and again remove barriers and create access to learning through bridge-building strategies that incorporate high expectations for all learners, building upon funds of knowledge in students' own cultures (see Figure 11.2).

Regarding perceptions and expectations, teachers often have lower expectations for students with specialized linguistic needs; therefore, teachers must work to provide equitable opportunities for these students to practice and refine their academic language in the context of classroom conversation. In addition, the teacher must be wary of coddling the student by providing answers, rather than assisting the student in solving the problem himself or herself. The teacher must also provide appropriate positive attention and praise as the student makes incremental progress.

As for cultural differences between the teacher and the student, the teacher must be wary of gaps of misunderstanding. Cultural differences must be explored inside and outside the school. Teachers must build upon cultural assets as they mentor students in the reading, writing, listening, and speaking processes, acknowledging the foundations that already exist in the English Language Learners' primary language as well as in the Standard English Learners' non-Standard English system. By providing cultural context links, the teacher can start with the students' own experiences; move to texts that are culturally relevant to her students; and then move to texts that are culturally relevant to others, as well as mainstream texts. Culturally responsive teaching is an inclusive approach that attempts to build bridges between the students and their teacher as the

Figure 11.2   Gap #2: The Gap Between the Student and the Teacher

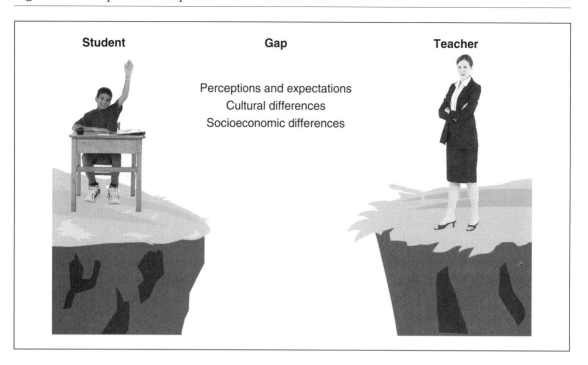

teacher sensitively validates cultural knowledge, prior experiences, frames of reference, and performance styles of her ethnically and linguistically diverse students.

Sensitive linguistic mentorship as it relates to lower socioeconomic status involves the teacher understanding that students from impoverished homes do not possess the implicit academic codes of the classroom. It is the teacher's responsibility to make these codes explicit. Systematic instruction on appropriate language register is one of the most powerful ways to bridge this socioeconomic divide.

Gap #3: The Gap Between the Student and His or Her Peers

The third gap, the gap between the student and his or her peers, requires the teacher to further unpack the complexities of differentiated learning in linguistically complex classrooms so as to meet the needs of linguistically diverse students with varied language proficiency levels (see Figure 11.3). Bridge-building strategies that were focused upon in this book include grammatical competence, discourse/textual competence, sociolinguistic competence, and pragmatic competence. In addition, micro structures such as homogeneous and heterogeneous groupings at the classroom level, as well as macrostructures such as grade-level and schoolwide programs, were suggested for approaching the differentiated needs of students requiring sensitive linguistic mentorship in linguistically complex classrooms.

The Literacy Gaps Model is a theoretical model that can be applied to every classroom, providing a research-based framework from which to conceptualize learner gaps and practical bridge-building strategies. We hope you will share *The Literacy Gaps: Bridge-Building Strategies for English Language Learners and Standard English Learners* with your colleagues, opening up discussions in your professional learning communities regarding how to improve practice and student learning in linguistically complex classrooms. The Learning Gaps Model has wide applicability across the disciplines, and one could spend a lifetime analyzing contributors to the three gaps and potential bridges to close them. It is a theoretical model that can assist you through multiple stages of your teaching career, such as novice, developing practitioner, and mentor/model/lead teacher. The Literacy Gaps Model can be used by professionals as a "tool kit" organizer in which to place new methods and strategies as they emerge from the research.

The "Literacy Gaps" Framework as a Reform Tool in Districts and Schools

The Literacy Gaps Model, as with most instructional tools, is best utilized systemically across a school, district, or teacher education program.

Figure 11.3 Gap #3: The Gap Between the Student and His or Her Peers

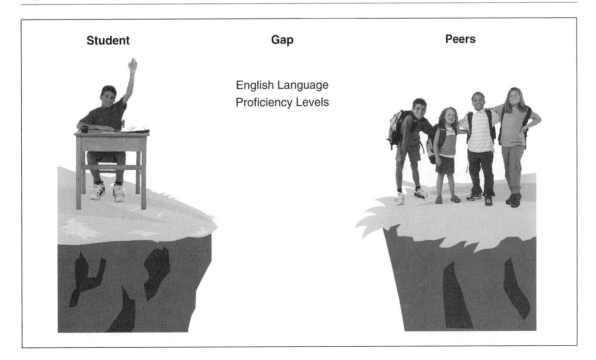

In order to truly change instruction for all of our ELLs and SELs, entire systems must be philosophically on the same page regarding high expectations and the importance of providing appropriate instructional support for students with specialized linguistic needs. What follows are recommendations for states, districts, schools, and teacher preparation programs when considering using the Literacy Gaps Model to systemically reform instructional practice.

States and Districts

From a broader policy standpoint, the Literacy Gaps Model presents a practical way to focus on the subgroups of students often left behind—ELLs and struggling students who have linguistic needs, such as SELs. By focusing in and systematically incorporating the best instructional practices for ELLs and SELs, the Literacy Gaps Model can bring all stakeholders to the table to take responsibility for these two groups of students. We must not merely shine a light on the needs of ELLs and SELs, but must also view the assets that they bring, and how we as educators might need to conceptualize entire educational systems differently in order to close the achievement gap. To that end, states and districts can do the following:

- Commit themselves to stand with one voice around the needs of ELLs and SELs by both studying their needs and systematically implementing new instructional practices.
- Provide focused professional development and bring professional learning communities (PLCs) together, embracing the foundational concepts of the literacy gaps and systemically utilizing this model as a tool for reform, helping ELLs and SELs, as well as all other students, to succeed and flourish.
- Hire and retain teachers and instructional principals/leaders who know how to meet the needs of ELLs and SELs, and make this mission central to their work.
- Rethink and rewrite traditional curriculum and standards to seamlessly take into account the needs of ELLs and SELs, so that their needs are not accounted for separately, or merely as a by-product of years of failure in the current educational system, but are central to the core curriculum.

School Sites

At the school site level, every stakeholder, and especially every teacher, must take responsibility for the instructional needs of ELLs and SELs. If there is one teacher in a school at a particular grade level who does not believe in the philosophical underpinnings of the Literacy Gaps Model and provides instruction without structured support for ELLs and SELs, and another teacher embraces the philosophical foundations of the Literacy Gaps Model and provides careful, systematic scaffolding, there is little consistency for students from year to year, or period to period. For example, any student in need of a specialized analysis for an individualized educational plan (IEP) can benefit from the student study team asking questions about gaps such as the following (also see Figure 11.4):

1. *What gaps inhibit the student from understanding the text?*

2. *What gaps do we see between the student and his or her teacher?*

3. *What gaps do we see between the student and his or her peers?*

Responses to these "gaps" questions for a particular student might include the need to utilize cognates for vocabulary building as well as vision testing for Gap #1, further literacy training related to SELs for the teacher in Gap #2, and strategies for classroom management and differentiation strategies in Gap #3. The Literacy Gaps Model provides a tool through which educators can identify, organize, and strategize regarding "next steps" in the educational process so as to provide the best possible learning scenarios for ELLs and SELs.

In addition, bridge-building questions are also important to ask:

1. *What bridge-building strategies will enhance student understanding of the text?*

2. *What bridge-building strategies will enhance the learning relationship between the student and his or her teacher?*

3. *What bridge-building strategies will enable the teacher to more readily meet the needs of a linguistically complex classroom, particularly in light of this particular student?*

Bridge-building strategies take into account the assets of the ELL or SEL. For example, the teacher could build upon the student's strength in oral storytelling as a springboard for responding to and writing stories. Or, the teacher might utilize cognates to build upon the student's knowledge of his first language (L1) and enhance his acquisition of vocabulary in his second language (L2). Or, the teacher might recruit a community volunteer to assist with a pull-out group during reading time.

Teacher Education Programs

Teacher education programs are especially poised to eliminate literacy gaps, instead of perpetuating them, by training teachers before they ever reach the classroom or encounter students. The Literacy Gaps Model is a framework that teacher training institutions can use to equip their candidates with a tool to analyze the specialized needs of any learner. The Literacy Gaps Model is an important contribution to every teacher's tool kit, providing a systematic way to analyze and meet students' linguistic needs. (Keep in mind, however, that the same three gaps exist in the math class, the history class, and so forth.) Teacher training institutions will be wise to carefully examine their scope and sequence to pay particular

Figure 11.4 Gaps Analysis Form

Name: _____ Grade: _____ Date: _____

Homeroom/Advisory Teacher: _____ Room #: _____

Gaps Question *Identify Barriers*	Observations and Assessments *Identify Student Strengths*	Bridge-Building Strategies *Identify Bridges*
What gaps inhibit the student from understanding the text?		
What gaps do we see between the student and his or her teacher?		
What gaps do we see between the student and his or her peers?		

attention to ELLs and SELs, providing the Literacy Gaps Model as one of the theoretical frameworks with which candidates might analyze and strategize to meet student needs. Teacher preparation programs can backwards map the content of the Literacy Gaps Model into the series of courses designed to prepare preservice teachers. This means that all of the faculty would need to collaborate and articulate around where the literacy gaps content might be purposefully integrated. Since this book is primarily about language acquisition and literacy, it might make the most sense to embed the content into reading and ELL training courses. However, since all educators are now expected to teach the academic language associated with their discipline, it would prove helpful to also touch upon, and reinforce, the content of the Literacy Gaps Model throughout the coursework associated with teacher preparation. In this way, preservice teachers hear one message and are both philosophically and pedagogically prepared to meet the needs of all students in their classrooms. We encourage the use of the Literacy Gaps Model in university, district, and school professional development, as well as in book studies for professional learning communities.

Envisioning the Future

Imagine a world in which every student could enjoy the optimal educational experience—where every teacher across the system desired to close the gaps in student performance, enabling every child to start where he or she is and move forward at an appropriate pace. That world is within our grasp as we collectively move toward an equitable educational system where every student has well-qualified teachers who are astute practitioners and can differentiate instruction based upon the individual needs of learners; where every teacher has basic understandings of the linguistic needs of ELLs and SELs; where every teacher joins hands with parents, colleagues, administration, and community members and says, "I'm going to do what it takes to help each child in my class succeed. Together, we will close the literacy gaps."

We know the world of teaching is not an easy one. We know you face challenges every day. We know you have children in your class who have myriad needs, and we know that you alone cannot meet every need. However, the national educational crisis demands that we all be child advocates and cooperatively move our communities in the right direction, addressing needs of disparity related to poverty, violence, crime, nutrition, and educational access. We do not regard the literacy gaps blindly. We know that the literacy gaps have a variety of systemic issues that contribute to their ongoing existence. However, we also realize that we each must take responsibility for making changes in the sphere in which we live—whether small or great. We all have influence. We have influence in our classroom and school community. Whether we have just begun our first year of teaching or are a 20-year veteran, we each can improve our practice, and we can model best practices for our colleagues. It starts with us—we *can* make a difference. We can actively participate in a professional learning community in which we study best practices in closing the literacy gaps. We can take a deep look, one more time, and say, "How can I change so that I love my students more, move them further ahead, scaffold my curriculum for better literacy understanding for my English Language Learners, for my Standard English Learners, and for *all* learners?"

We can all take a Teacher Oath, similar to the Hippocratic Oath taken by doctors, and commit ourselves to certain values:

I _____ (your name) value every child, regardless of race, gender, language, or ability level, and I will, so help me God, enable every child that crosses the threshold of my classroom to succeed. I will help every English Language Learner, every Standard English Learner, and *every* learner listen, speak, read, and write at his or her highest ability level. I will enable my students to be successful because I will give them my very best each and every day. I will be intentional about teaching. I will close the literacy gaps. I will assess and base my teaching upon the next step(s) in the learning process, founded on an effective assessment learning cycle. I will hold my head high, and I will take pride in my profession.

The Literacy Gaps: Bridge-Building Strategies for English Language Learners and Standard English Learners invites educators to create sociocultural environments in which English Language Learners and Standard English Learners thrive, gain confidence through their academic achievements, capitalize on the rich funds of knowledge that ELLs and SELs bring to society, experience equitable access to all that society offers, and ultimately gain the skills to be the leaders of tomorrow.

Thank you for taking this journey with us and sharing your valuable time as you read *The Literacy Gaps: Bridge-Building Strategies for English Language Learners and Standard English Learners,* and thank you for your commitment to the teaching profession. Most important, thank you for the love and dedication you demonstrate to every student every day as you support students in their literacy journey and work to close the gaps.

REFERENCES

August, D., & Hakuta, K. (Eds.). (1997). *Improving schooling for language-minority children: A research agenda.* Washington, DC: National Academies Press.

August, D., & Pease-Alvarez, L. (1996). *Attributes of effective programs in classrooms serving English language learners.* Santa Cruz, CA: National Center for Research on Cultural Diversity and Second Language Learning.

Brisk, M. E. (2005). *Bilingual education: From compensatory to quality schooling* (2nd ed.). Mahwah, NJ: Lawrence Erlbaum.

Education Trust. (2003). A new core curriculum for all: Aiming high for other people's children. *Thinking K–16, 7*(1), 1–33.

Ferguson, R. (1998). Teachers' perceptions and expectations and the black–white test score gap. In C. Jencks & M. Phillips (Eds.), *The black–white test score gap.* Washington, DC: Brookings Institution.

Hollie, S. (2001, September). Acknowledgement, affirmation, and accommodation: The non-standard language approach. (Language Teaching & Learning). *Academic Exchange Quarterly,* 1096–1453. Retrieved September 22, 2008, from http://www.thefreelibrary.com/_/print/PrintArticle.aspx?id=80679270.

Howard, J. (1995). You can't get there from here: The need for a new logic in education reform. *Daedalus Journal of the American Academy of Arts and Sciences, 123*(2), 47–64.

Wenglinsky, H. (2001). *Teacher classroom practices in student performance: How schools can make a difference.* Princeton, NJ: Educational Testing Service.

Glossary

Academic English as a Second Language Learners (AESLs): Students who have not mastered Academic English, which is the language of school, classrooms, and testing. Academic English encompasses vocabulary, syntax, grammar, and register of each discipline or content area. In addition, Academic English is not natural language and must be explicitly taught (Kinsella, 2007).

Academic Language Development (ALD): The teaching of the specialized language of each discipline, which is specific to each content area.

Academic Language Stems: Language starters used with ELLs or SELs in order to allow them to grasp the patterns of language (e.g., "I agree, but would like to add . . ." "Today I learned . . ." or "I heard my partner say . . .").

Academic Talk/Language: The language of the classroom, textbooks, and testing, as different from everyday conversation; it involves the study of at least three areas: vocabulary, syntax, and text structure.

Active Engagement: Participatory structures in classrooms that allow learners to actively listen and speak in order to practice language or internalize new information (e.g., think-pair-share, reciprocal teaching, etc.).

Affective Filter: The ways in which emotion, motivation, and self-esteem impact learning, especially language learning. The teacher should keep the affective filter low so as to minimize stress for the ELL while still maintaining high expectations.

Affixes: Prefixes and suffixes added to base words.

African American Vernacular English (AAVE): Dialect of English spoken by some African Americans with certain features derived from African languages, but readily recognizable as a variation of English.

Alphabetic Principle: The understanding that speech can be mapped to print; graphemic representations of phonemes.

Analysis-Level Questions: These require the reader to break down the ideas into elements; cue words include *categorize, classify, analyze, compare,* and *simplify.*

Annual Measurable Achievement Objective (AMAO): English language proficiency (ELP) AMAOs support the standards and assessments, and take into consideration the English language proficiency required to access content-area knowledge in reading/language arts and mathematics, and to perform at the proficient level in the state assessments in these content areas.

Anticipation Guide: A way to informally assess ELLs' and SELs' background knowledge and experience as well as their vocabulary, linking them to text content; students answer questions that relate to the story before they read the text, and then again after they've read the text. The Anticipation Guide assists the teacher in understanding student background knowledge prior to reading the text.

Application-Level Questions: These require the reader to take the ideas of the passage and to apply them in another context; cue words include *infer, construct, imagine, what if, associate,* or *chart.*

Assessments: Measurements, formal and informal, to determine student mastery of content or skills.

Automaticity: The ability to fluidly and naturally decode in a programmed way, where everything comes together all at once in a seemingly effortless fashion. It is the efficient, automatic processing of printed text or the ability to rapidly decode in meaningful chunks.

Background Knowledge: Experiential background—either one's own or experienced vicariously—that is foundational for understanding text.

Bet Lines: Key stopping points (text lines) where teachers ask students to dialogue about what they have just read and make predictions about the next section of the passage.

Bilingual: The quality of being fluent and proficient in two languages with the facility of a native speaker.

Bilingual Books: Books that are written in two languages to allow ELLs to see differences in symbol systems as well as to support their L2 with their L1.

Bilingual Education: A method of educating ELLs that teaches subjects both in their primary language and secondary languages.

Blends: Two adjacent sounds (e.g., *mp* in lamp, *pl* in plight, *sn* in snail).

Bloom's Taxonomy: Levels of questioning that are reflected in Benjamin Bloom's sixfold model: knowledge, comprehension, application, analysis, synthesis, and evaluation.

Book Access: Proximity of text in the students' environment (e.g., students have books they can read at school and at home).

Books on Tape: Recorded text that matches written text.

Bridge-Building Strategies: A variety of scaffolds to bridge gaps in learning, including contrastive analysis in the examination of pronunciation and the study of symbol systems; tutorial support through teaching assistants, parent volunteers, and peers; and books on tape, bilingual books, and translation assignments.

Broadspan Instruction: Teaching that reaches across a broad band of language proficiency levels.

California English Language Development Test (CELDT): Annual language assessment given to ELLs in California whose parents have indicated that another language is spoken at home, in order to determine both initial language proficiency as well as annual language progress.

Casual Register: Language spoken among friends. Word choice is general and not specific. Conversation is dependent upon nonverbal assists, and sentence syntax is often incomplete.

Chicano English: A variety of English spoken by some people of Hispanic descent in the Southwestern United States and California. It differs in systematic ways from Standard American English. Chicano English is not just English spoken by people who speak Spanish as a native language and who are still acquiring English. English-only speakers may speak Chicano English.

Closed-Ended Questions: Questions that require "yes" or "no" responses with minimal opportunity for elaboration.

Code Breaker: One of the four roles of effective readers, which most closely mirrors decoding. Code breaking is necessary but not sufficient without comprehension for a student to be considered a proficient reader.

Cognate Word Walls: Cognates are words that sound alike and have similar meanings in two target languages (e.g., *democracy* and *democracía* in English and Spanish). Cognate word walls are places easily visible in a classroom where cognates are listed and used as they are learned.

Cognitively Demanding Task: A student assignment that requires higher cognitive processing, such as solving a problem or analyzing a character.

Cognitively Undemanding Task: A student assignment that does not demand higher cognitive processing, such as following directions in a simple outdoor game or sorting pictures into categories of plants and animals.

Community Mapping Projects: Projects in which students identify the assets of a community, including human and social capital.

Compound Words: Multisyllabic words that contain two smaller words (e.g., *treehouse, lumberjack*).

Comprehension: Understanding of verbal or written language; understanding the meaning and intent of the speaker or writer.

Comprehension-Level Questions: These require the student to reflect on the intent of the passage; cue words include *explain, paraphrase, distinguish, interpret, defend,* and *summarize.*

Comprehension Monitoring: Reader strategies utilized to pay attention to the reader's own understanding, or metacognition, of a text.

Comprehension Strategies: Teaching scaffolds or reader methodologies that assist the reader in understanding text.

Concept Diagrams: Labeled illustrations that students compose to express their understanding of a particular concept.

Concepts About Print: Basic understanding about text (e.g., understanding if a text reads left to right or right to left; recognizing if a book opens from the left or right; knowing where the text and illustrations are located; being able to identify the front, back, and spine of the book; knowing where to begin reading the book; and accurately pointing to words the teacher reads aloud).

Conclusion: The last step in the scientific method, where a student confirms or rejects the hypothesis.

Connecting: An active reading strategy in which students make text-to-text, text-to-world, and text-to-life connections.

Consonants: Letters of the alphabet that are not vowels; class of speech sounds associated with closure or constriction of the breath channel.

Consultative Register: Formal register when used in conversation; discourse pattern not quite as direct as formal register.

Context Embedded: An instructional approach in which many nonverbal cues, such as experiential learning or visuals, are used.

Context Reduced: An instructional approach in which few nonverbal cues of any sort are provided as support to students.

Contrastive Analysis: A method by which linguistic differences, such as pronunciation and symbol systems, can be highlighted and compared in two target languages.

Cross-Age Tutoring: A method in which students from one grade level pair up and teach students from another grade level.

Cultural Context Learning Links: The process of linking personal experiences to culturally relevant text (self), to culturally relevant text (others), to mainstream text.

Culturally Relevant Texts: Literature and other texts that are significant to a student's cultural background or experiences.

Culturally Responsive Pedagogy: Teaching methodologies that acknowledge and honor the student's home culture, ranging from utilizing diverse texts to introducing a variety of culturally appropriate historical perspectives. A structure that provides an inclusive and accessible learning environment that validates students' cultures.

Decoding Strategies: A branch of reading instruction that includes word recognition strategies, such as concepts about print, phonemic awareness, phonics, and sight words.

Differentiation Strategies: Methods of addressing the instructional/proficiency needs of ELLs and SELs, as well as other specialized needs, in the classroom.

Diphthongs: Vowel glides that move from one vowel sound to another (e.g., *oy, oi, au, aw*).

Directionality: A concept of print that refers to understanding top/bottom and left/right movement of text on a page.

Discourse Pattern: Written or spoken communication or debate, which differs according to context.

Discourse/Textual Competence: This refers to students' ability to link ideas in spoken turns and in longer written and oral texts.

Echo Reading: A highly scaffolded activity where the teacher and student read orally in unison, with the teacher just ahead of the student. As the student "echoes along," he or she begins to feel what fluent reading is like. Sight words as well as phonetically consistent words are reinforced throughout the exercise.

Emancipatory Education: An educational approach that makes authentic knowledge about different ethnic groups accessible. This type of education happens as cooperation, connectedness, and community are established in a classroom.

Empowerment: The result of an educational belief system of success; encourages social scaffolding in which educators have planned and created an infrastructure to support high levels of academic achievement for all students.

English Immersion: A method of educating ELLs, where the goal of instruction is for the students to learn English, with sheltered or scaffolded support.

English Language Development (ELD): A course of study and curricula utilized by teachers to teach a second language; also describes students acquiring a second language.

English Language Learners (ELLs): Students whose primary language is not English and whose English language skills are not sufficient to allow them to function fully in Academic English.

Evaluation-Level Questions: These require the reader to make a judgment about the ideas in the passage; cue words include *support, explain, argue, defend, determine,* and *differentiate.*

Expectations: A teacher's thoughts about the educational potential of a student. It is critical that all teachers believe in the high performance potential of all students, particularly our SELs and ELLs.

Expressive Language/Vocabulary: Communication involving speaking and writing.

Feedback: Teacher's comments or responses related to the quality of student performance; built-in response within a learning activity that may come from the activity itself, the student, peers, or the teacher; response of an audience to a student performance.

Figurative Language: Language that goes beyond the literal meaning and often utilizes comparisons to describe things.

Fishbowl: A scaffolding exercise where a group discussion or strategy is modeled or practiced by a small number of students in the middle of a classroom.

Fluency: Accurate, rapid decoding of text that involves a student's ability to apply knowledge of phonics, sight words, and prosidy.

Fluent English Proficient (FEP): Describes a student who has gained proficiency in the basics of casual English, but is still acquiring Academic English.

Foreign Language in the Elementary School Model (FLES): The FLES model seeks to teach foreign language and world cultures in the elementary school, beginning in the primary grades. An asset model, FLES programs often teach a particular subject area through the foreign language.

Formal Register: The standard sentence syntax and word choice of work and school in a mainstream English environment; characterized by complete sentences and specific, accurate, and content-specific word choice.

Four-Square Vocabulary: A vocabulary strategy by which students are taught to identify examples and non-examples of a word, create a visual association, and finally define the word in a sentence using their own words.

Frozen Register: Language that is always or nearly always the same—for example, the Lord's Prayer, wedding vow phrases, Pledge of Allegiance, etc.

Frustrational Reading Level: When a text is so challenging to read that the child may become frustrated (e.g., less than 90% accuracy in decoding or less than 70% comprehension).

Fry's Instant Word List: A list of 1,000 high-frequency or sight words created by Edward Fry. The first 100 words on this list make up 50% of all written material.

Gap: A barrier in the student's ability to gain academic literacy (e.g., the gap between the student and the text, the gap between the student and the teacher, the gap between the student and his or her peers).

Global Citizenry: The ability to understand and interact with people of different ethnicities, languages, and nationalities.

Grammar: How a language is structured. Linguists use this term to refer to the knowledge that native speakers implicitly have about the structure of their own language (e.g., syntax; how to arrange words into sentences).

Grammatical Competence: Competence in the areas of vocabulary, syntax, morphology, and phonology.

Grapheme: Written representation of sound (e.g., letters, digraphs).

Graphic Organizer: Visual representation of ideas in diagram format.

Heterogeneous Grouping: When the teacher intentionally places students of different proficiency levels together for the purposes of learning a particular objective.

Historical Timelines: A record of key events in a given historical passage; timelines assist the learner in organizing his or her thinking related to the passage.

Home Language Survey: Questions used in school systems to first ascertain who may need to be tested as an ELL. One question asks what languages are spoken at home. If another language other than English is spoken at home, the student is usually referred for further language assessment.

Home Visits: When a teacher makes a social call to a student's home to get to know the student and his or her family.

Homogeneous Grouping: Grouping students for instruction according to common instructional needs or levels (e.g., by language proficiency levels).

Hourglass Language Instruction Model: A methodology involving moving students in and out of homogeneous and heterogeneous groups.

Hypothesis: The third step of the scientific method in which students make an educated guess.

Idioms: Sayings that are culturally bound and that carry figurative meaning.

Immersion: Immersing students in the target language.

Incongruity: A difference in the spoken language between a student's home and school worlds.

Independent Reading Level: When an ELL or SEL student can read a text on his or her own with about 95% degree of accuracy in decoding and 90%-plus comprehension.

Inferring: Combining background knowledge with information from the text to predict, conclude, make judgments, and interpret (from Figure 1.1, p. 14 of *Mosaic of Thought,* Keene & Zimmermann [2007]).

Initially Fluent English Proficient (IFEP): Describes a student who was tested for ELL proficiency status, but was determined to be fluent in casual or basic English, and therefore not require ELL services.

Initiation-Response-Feedback (IRF): Language exchange whereby closed-ended questions, which require only one-word responses, are utilized.

Instructional Read-Aloud (IRA): Method in which the teacher models a particular comprehension strategy while reading a text out loud so that the student(s) can focus on comprehension and not merely decoding.

Instructional Reading Level: Level at which an ELL or SEL student can read a text with teacher support in guided reading, but the book contains significant challenges in decoding or comprehension for independent reading.

Intercultural Pragmatics: The ability of native language speakers to understand the nuances of communication in other languages, often not explicit in the new language.

Intimate Register: Language between lovers or twins.

Knowledge-Level Questions: Factual recall questions that include key words such as *who, what, when, where, why, identify,* and *find* that clue the reader into the type of on-the-line, factual information that the teacher is seeking.

KWL Charts: A teaching strategy in which the teacher first gathers student background knowledge prior to reading a text and links students' understanding with the text content by purposely identifying before, during, and after questions. This chart has three columns, asking What do I know? What do I want to know? and What have I learned?

L1: The student's first language.

L2: The student's second language.

Language Forms: The tools used to accomplish the language tasks or functions, such as sentence components, comparative adjectives, or past-tense verbs.

Language Functions: Tasks accomplished by way of language.

Language Proficiency Level: The student's range of linguistic ability.

Language Transfer: When an individual is able to understand something in his or her L2 by relating a concept from the L1.

Linkages: Connecting of the known with the unknown.

Literacy Domains: Listening, speaking, reading, and writing.

Literacy Gap #1: The gap between the student and the text that hinders decoding and comprehension progress.

Literacy Gap #2: The gap between the student and the teacher.

Literacy Gap #3: The gap between the student and his or her peers.

Literature Circles: A reading approach whereby students read a common text and utilize an active reading strategy—such as *illustrating, questioning, connecting* or *paraphrasing*—to discuss the text.

Macro Structures: Schoolwide or grade level–wide grouping structures.

Matthew Effects Model: A model based on Keith Stanovich's work, illustrating literacy progress for all K–12, monolingual or bilingual, ELL or SEL students, showing the students stepping up into success or stepping down into failure.

Metacognitive Strategies: Teaching strategies that model thinking about one's own thinking processes while reading—for example, encouraging students to listen to the voice in their mind that speaks while they read (e.g., "What is the author trying to say? This reminds me of . . .").

Metalinguistic Knowledge: The vocabulary used to explain grammar.

Micro Structures: Grouping strategies within the classroom that assist ELLs.

Mode Continuum of Inquiry: Developed by Gibbons (2002), the continuum is a four-stage process, which moves students from spoken-like to written-like language; the stages consist of small-group experiment, key vocabulary, teacher-guided reporting, and student journal writing.

Monolingual: Describes a student who is fluent in only one language.

Morphology: The study of linguistic units of meaning.

Newcomer: A new arrival or immigrant to a country.

Non-Standard English: Language variations that are not considered Academic English (i.e., dialects); however, these variations most often have consistent grammar systems and value in particular contexts.

Observations: Part of the scientific method whereby students observe and collect data.

Open-Ended Questions: Questions that require more than one- or two-word responses from students. These questions often allow for multiple entries and can be answered in a variety of ways.

Oral Cloze: A highly scaffolded activity where the teacher reads aloud and the student follows along. When the teacher pauses, the student orally fills in the missing word.

Oral Summaries: These provide opportunities for students to verbally give a short statement about the main idea of a paragraph or passage.

Pair-Share: A paired student verbal interaction scaffold, whereby students think about a particular response individually and then share it with a partner to refine their thinking.

Pair-Square: Similar to the pair-share except the teacher asks two sets of partners to dialogue on a topic.

Paraphrasing: A reader role in which a student summarizes responses or a segment of text in his or her own words.

Perceptions: Internalized belief systems regarding students' educational potential or abilities.

Phoneme: Individual sound units. There are 44 phonemes in the English language.

Phoneme Blending: Refers to the student's ability to bring together isolated sounds into words.

Phoneme Manipulation: The student can change the order of phonemes or manipulate sounds within or between words.

Phonemic Awareness: Understanding that spoken words can be segmented into individual sound units (phonemes); this includes *word awareness, rhyme recognition, rhyme production, sound matching, sound matching production, sound isolation, phoneme blending, sound addition or subtraction, sound segmentation,* and *phoneme manipulation.*

Phonics: A method to decode words; the study of phoneme–grapheme relationships.

Phonology: The study of sounds.

Picture Dictionaries: Glossaries with words and visuals.

Primary Language: The first or main language of instruction.

Primary Language Instruction: Teaching provided in the students' L1.

Question: The first step in the scientific method, whereby students create a question that will guide their observation and data collection.

Question–Answer Relationship (QAR): A fourfold view of passage comprehension strategy that includes "Right There" and "Think and Search" as text-oriented questions, and "Author and You" and "On My Own" as reader-oriented questions.

Questioning: The ability to comprehend a text enough to pose key questions to oneself or the author.

Readability: The reading level of a text; the accessibility of a text.

Reader's Theater: A fun exercise that involves a script and multiple opportunities to read passages individually or in unison with classmates. With its wonderfully embedded repetition, this is an excellent place for ELLs to experience and develop fluency and prosidy.

Realia: Real-world objects (e.g., shells or rocks) used to make instruction comprehensible to students.

Recasting: A process by which the teacher restates, in academic terms, what a student has just said using informal or social language.

Receptive Language/Vocabulary: Involves the modes of listening and reading.

Reclassified Fluent English Proficient (RFEP): Describes a student who has acquired enough fluency with English to no longer be identified as an ELL. This student, however, is not yet fluent in Academic English and still requires scaffolding of language and learning.

Register: Specialized use of a language for a defined situation or occasion. A common example is the "baby talk" register that is used to talk with a baby or an animal.

(Re)organization of Text: Involves the student making the text his or her own by actually changing its form (e.g., rewriting a story in simpler register for younger children, taking a short story and writing a Reader's Theater script, outlining).

Research: The part of the scientific method where the individual seeks to answer his or her question through experimentation. Research results will indicate whether or not the hypothesis can be proven.

Rhyme Production: The student, when given a word (e.g., *bat*), can produce other words (e.g., *cat*) with the same rhyme scheme.

Rhyme Recognition: The student recognizes two words that rhyme (e.g., *able/table*).

Scaffolding: Temporary instructional support systems that should be taken away once students reach an appropriate level of proficiency with a particular skill or content.

Schema: Background knowledge and experience that lays the foundation for reading comprehension.

Schwa: An unstressed vowel sound similar to short *u* (e.g., the vowel sound heard in *the*).

Self-Monitoring: When a student takes charge of his or her own learning, noticing what he or she understands or does not understand in the reading process.

Shadowing: The process of unveiling/observing a day or specific period of time (e.g., an hour) in the life of an ELL in order to determine his or her level of academic engagement—in the domains of listening and speaking—and with the purpose of changing instructional practice.

Sight Words: Often called high-frequency words. Many times they are words that do not follow typical phonetic patterns (e.g., *through, thorough, thought*) and must be memorized. Dolch and Fry have identified high-frequency word lists that they recommend students learn by sight in order to increase automaticity and fluency in the reading process.

Simulations: A way to teach ELLs the difference between casual or social language and academic language by acting out certain situations, such as a job interview or a debate.

Sketch-to-Stretch: Strategy in which the reader responds to the passage intermittently through drawing pictures instead of writing words.

Sound Deletion, Addition, or Subtraction: The student can add or substitute one sound for another in words, songs, and rhymes.

Sound Isolation: The student can identify which sound is heard at the beginning, middle, or end of a word.

Sound Matching: When the student identifies which words in a group begin with the same sound.

Sound Matching Production: When the student says another word with the same initial sound as the first word.

Sound Segmentation: When the student isolates sounds in a spoken word.

Specially Designed Academic Instruction in English (SDAIE): An instructional approach whereby language and content are taught concurrently with scaffolding of language and learning.

Standard English Learners (SELs): Students who speak a variation or dialect of Standard English, such as the African American Vernacular English (AAVE), Chicano English, or Hawaiian (Pidgin) English.

Standardized Test Scores: Test score results that are meant to compare students to their peers.

Summarizing: The ability to identify important information from a text selection, and the meaning in one's own words.

Syntax: The study of rules and patterns for the formation of sentences and phrases.

Synthesis-Level Questions: These require the reader to put the elements of the passage into a whole; cue words include *revise, associate, reconstruct, write,* and *prepare.*

Synthesizing: Creating an evolution of meaning by combining understanding with knowledge from other texts/sources (from Figure 1.1, p. 14 of *Mosaic of Thought,* Keene & Zimmermann [2007])

Teacher-Guided Reporting (TGR): A verbal scaffold whereby the teacher and student together build what the student cannot say on his or her own. This process initiates more extended time-on-task in layered discussions with ELLs. TGR begins with an open-ended question, followed by teacher clarification, encouragement, and feedback, paraphrasing and recasting, and appropriate wait time.

Technical Vocabulary: Specialized vocabulary used across a discipline or content area.

Text Analyst: One of the four roles of effective readers; the student reads critically, analyzing the merits of what has been said, and determining value and accuracy of material.

Text Participant: One of the four roles of effective readers; the reader connects information in the text with background knowledge and experience.

Text Structure: The manner in which texts or passages are organized.

Text User: One of the four roles of effective readers; the student actively participates in the reading process—asking questions, making predictions, and making connections.

Text-to-Life Connections: Making a connection between a text and one's own life experiences.

Text-to-Text Connections: Making connections between two similar texts because of theme, author, or organization.

Text-to-World Connections: Making connections between a text and the world at large.

Think-Aloud Strategy: A technique where the teacher reads a passage aloud and purposefully unveils what he is thinking while reading, including questioning, making personal connections, predicting, evaluating, and clarifying.

Think-Pair-Share: An oral language scaffold where students take time to formulate their thoughts, share those thoughts with a partner in a safe social setting, and then finally share with the whole group.

Tiered Assignments: Assignments that are structured to include multiple levels of difficulty.

Tier-Level Words: These provide an approach enabling teachers to consider the instructional potential of words both related to their discipline as well as across a variety of contexts.

Total Immersion: A "sink or swim" approach where a student does not hear her L1 but receives all of her schooling in the target language (e.g., English).

Total Physical Response (TPR): An approach by which students act or reenact new vocabulary or scenes from a text.

Transfer: The process of learning something in one's first language (L1) and bringing along those concepts and skills to the second language.

Transformative Learning: This recognizes the existing strengths and accomplishments of students to enhance them further.

Translation Assignment Strategy: Students write an assignment in their native language first and then translate the assignment into English. Writing in the L1 first helps support and facilitate the L2 translation.

Two-Way Immersion: A two-way or dual-immersion language program has the students studying in their L1 half the day and in their L2 the other half of the day. There may be variations in the scheduling.

Validation: Using cultural knowledge, prior experiences, frames of references, and performance styles of ethnically diverse students to reinforce and affirm the value of each student's background.

Visualizing: A comprehension task requiring the reader to create a mental image of what he or she has read. Good readers regularly visualize the content of the passage being read.

Vocabulary: The words of a language. Differences in vocabulary are among the most noticeable contrasts between languages.

Vocabulary Knowledge Self-Assessment Chart: A class profile highlighting words that are most familiar to students (linkages) and most foreign to students (gaps).

Vowels: A class of speech sounds where the breath is not blocked; the most audible part of a syllable; the non-consonant letters.

Wait Time: The number of seconds a teacher allows a student to think before responding to a question, which should be from 5–7 seconds. English Language Learners require increased wait time in responding to a question, as they may need a few extra seconds for translating and formulating their thoughts.

Word Awareness: The student's ability to identify words in a sentence.

Word Continuum: A vocabulary strategy where the reader identifies two opposite words (e.g., *cold, hot*), a word that represents a middle concept (e.g., *tepid*), and a variety of other vocabulary words that fit along the continuum.

Word Derivations: The relation of a word to its base word (e.g., nation, national, international).

Word Recognition Strategies: Decoding methods, such as phonics instruction.

World Knowledge: A student's experiences that help the reader monitor *sources of dissonance* when reading text, as well as monitor sources of agreement between experience and text.

Writer Response Journal: A method of promoting interaction with the text in the form of predicting, clarifying, making personal connections, questioning, and evaluating.

Index